Critical Femininities

What would change about our existing world if we re-imagined and re-valued femininity? *Critical Femininities* presents a multidimensional framework for re-thinking femininity. Moving beyond seeing femininity as a patriarchal tool, this book considers the social, historical, and ideological forces that shape present-day norms surrounding femininity, particularly those that contribute to femmephobia: the systematic devaluation and regulation of all that is deemed feminine.

Each chapter offers a unique application of the Critical Femininities framework to disparate areas of inquiry, ranging from breastfeeding stigma to Incel ideology, and attempts to answer pressing questions concerning the place of femininity within gender and social theory. How can we conceptualise feminine power? In what ways can vulnerability act as a powerful mode of resistance? How can we understand femininity as powerful without succumbing to masculinist frameworks? What ideological underpinnings maintain Critical Femininities as an emergent field, despite traceable origins pre-dating second-wave feminism?

As the provocative entries within this volume will certainly generate additional questions for anyone invested in society's treatment of femininity, this book offers a launching pad for the continued growth of a field that cultivates insight from a feminine frame of reference as a means of rendering visible the taken-for-granted presence of masculinity that remains pervasive within gender theory.

The chapters in this book were originally published as a special issue of *Psychology & Sexuality*.

Rhea Ashley Hoskin, Ph.D., is an interdisciplinary feminist sociologist whose work focuses on femme theory, critical femininities, and femmephobia. Her work examines perceptions of femininity and sources of prejudice rooted in the devaluation or regulation of femininity. Rhea is the Co-Founder of LGBTQ Psychology Canada and an *AMTD Global Talent Postdoctoral Fellow* at the University of Waterloo and St. Jerome's University, Canada.

Karen L. Blair, Ph.D., is an Assistant Professor of Psychology at Trent University, Canada; the Founder of KLB Research; and the Director of the Trent University Social Relations, Attitudes and Diversity Lab. Dr. Blair's work focuses on LGBTQ Psychology, relationships and health, prejudice, femmephobia, hate crimes, and Holocaust education. She is the Co-Founder of LGBTQ Psychology Canada and has been the Chair of the Canadian Psychological Association's Sexual Orientation and Gender Identity Section since 2014.

Critical Femininities

Edited by
Rhea Ashley Hoskin and Karen L. Blair

Routledge
Taylor & Francis Group

LONDON AND NEW YORK

First published 2023
by Routledge
4 Park Square, Milton Park, Abingdon, Oxon, OX14 4RN

and by Routledge
605 Third Avenue, New York, NY 10158

Routledge is an imprint of the Taylor & Francis Group, an informa business

Introduction, Chapters 1–9 © 2023 Taylor & Francis

ISBN13: 978-1-032-35978-6 (hbk)
ISBN13: 978-1-032-35979-3 (pbk)
ISBN13: 978-1-003-32965-7 (ebk)

DOI: 10.4324/9781003329657

Typeset in Myriad Pro
by codeMantra

Publisher's Note
The publisher accepts responsibility for any inconsistencies that may have arisen during the conversion of this book from journal articles to book chapters, namely the inclusion of journal terminology.

Disclaimer
Every effort has been made to contact copyright holders for their permission to reprint material in this book. The publishers would be grateful to hear from any copyright holder who is not here acknowledged and will undertake to rectify any errors or omissions in future editions of this book.

Contents

Citation Information

The chapters in this book were originally published in the journal *Psychology & Sexuality*, volume 13, issue 1 (2022). When citing this material, please use the original page numbering for each article, as follows:

Introduction
Critical femininities: A 'new' approach to gender theory
Rhea Ashley Hoskin and Karen L. Blair
Psychology & Sexuality, volume 13, issue 1 (2022) pp. 1–8

Chapter 1
Is there anything "toxic" about femininity? The rigid femininities that keep us locked in
Hannah McCann
Psychology & Sexuality, volume 13, issue 1 (2022) pp. 9–22

Chapter 2
Feminine power: a new articulation
Bernadette Barton and Lisa Huebner
Psychology & Sexuality, volume 13, issue 1 (2022) pp. 23–32

Chapter 3
Negotiating relationships with powerfulness: using femme theory to resist masculinist pressures on feminist femininities
Jocelyne Bartram Scott
Psychology & Sexuality, volume 13, issue 1 (2022) pp. 33–42

Chapter 4
Radical vulnerability: selfies as a Femme-inine mode of resistance
Andi Schwartz
Psychology & Sexuality, volume 13, issue 1 (2022) pp. 43–56

Chapter 5
"But where are the dates?" Dating as a central site of fat femme marginalisation in queer communities
Allison Taylor
Psychology & Sexuality, volume 13, issue 1 (2022) pp. 57–68

For any permission-related enquiries please visit:
http://www.tandfonline.com/page/help/permissions

Notes on Contributors

Bernadette Barton is Professor of Sociology and Director of Gender Studies at Morehead State University, USA. She writes and lectures on contemporary issues of gender, sexuality, religion, culture, and the sex industry. She is the author of *Stripped: More Stories from Exotic Dancers* (2017), *Pray the Gay Away: The Extraordinary Lives of Bible Belt Gays* (2014), and *The Pornification of America: How Raunch Culture is Ruining Our Society* (2021).

Karen L. Blair, Ph.D., is an Assistant Professor of Psychology at Trent University, Canada; the Founder of KLB Research; and the Director of the Trent University Social Relations, Attitudes and Diversity Lab. Dr. Blair's work focuses on LGBTQ Psychology, relationships and health, prejudice, femmephobia, hate crimes, and Holocaust education. She is the Co-Founder of LGBTQ Psychology Canada and has been the Chair of the Canadian Psychological Association's Sexual Orientation and Gender Identity Section since 2014.

Antonio García-Gómez is Associate Professor of Linguistics at the University of Alcalá de Henares, Madrid, Spain, where he teaches discourse analysis and functional linguistics. His expertise lies primarily in discourse analysis and discursive psychology. Professor García-Gómez's first and most developed research interest is conflict talk. A main strand of his research has focused on the study of gender, identity, and language use in new media.

Gina Grandy is Professor and Dean at Hill and Levene Schools of Business, University of Regina, Canada. Her primary research interests are in leadership, gender, stigma, and identity.

Rhea Ashley Hoskin, Ph.D., is an interdisciplinary feminist sociologist whose work focuses on femme theory, critical femininities, and femmephobia. Her work examines perceptions of femininity and sources of prejudice rooted in the devaluation or regulation of femininity. Rhea is the Co-Founder of LGBTQ Psychology Canada and an *AMTD Global Talent Postdoctoral Fellow* at the University of Waterloo and St. Jerome's University, Canada.

Lisa Huebner is Feminist, Sociologist and Professor of Women's and Gender Studies at West Chester University of Pennsylvania, USA. She writes, teaches, and appears in media about issues related to intersectionality, care work, sexual harassment, and other forms of power-based violence. She is the author of *Catheters, Slurs, and Pick-up Lines: Professional Intimacy in Hospital Nursing* (2012).

Lauren Menzie is a PhD candidate at the Department of Sociology, University of Alberta, Canada. She has research interests and has published in the areas of quasi-criminal law and governance, online engagements with law and sexual violence, the evolution of Canadian laws governing sexual offending, and discourses around sexual consent.

Hannah McCann is Lecturer in Cultural Studies at the University of Melbourne, Australia. Her research sits within critical femininity studies and explores femme identity, beauty culture, and queer fandom. She has published in several feminist and queer theory journals including the *European Journal of Women's Studies*, *Women's Studies Quarterly*, and *Sexualities*.

Gülden Sayılan is a social psychologist from Turkey who has received her PhD degree from Middle East Technical University. She works as a research assistant at Ankara Yıldırım Beyazıt University. Her research interests include social psychology of gender, prejudice and discrimination against sexual and gender minorities, masculinity studies, and political psychology.

Jocelyne Bartram Scott is Visiting Assistant Professor of Women's and Gender Studies at Texas Tech University, USA. Her research focuses on the intersections of critical femininity studies with feminist and queer theory and critical race theory. Her current major research project addresses the role of femmephobia in homosocial community creation for marginalized populations.

Andi Schwartz has a PhD in Gender, Feminist, and Women's Studies from York University. Her research interests include femme subjectivities, critical femininities, online subcultures and counterpublics, and radical softness. She co-authored a chapter on Carly Rae Jepsen for the anthology, *The Spaces and Places of Canadian Pop Culture*, edited by Neil Shyminsky and Victoria Kannen.

Sarah Stutterheim is Assistant Professor at the Department of Work and Social Psychology, Maastricht University, Netherlands. Her research is mixed-method and focuses primarily on social stigma and its effects, particularly among vulnerable groups.

Allison Taylor is a PhD candidate at the Department of Gender, Feminist and Women's Studies, York University, Canada. Taylor's SSHRC-funded, doctoral research explores queer fat femme identities, embodiments, and negotiations of femmephobia, fatphobia, and other intersecting oppressions in Canada. Her work has been published in places such as *Fat Studies: An Interdisciplinary Journal of Body Weight and Society*, *Psychology & Sexuality*, and the *Journal of Lesbian Studies*.

Beril Türkoğlu is Assistant Professor at Ankara Medipol University, Turkey. Her research is mainly focused on the dynamics of precarious manhood and womanhood; prejudice and discrimination towards sexual and gender minorities; and gender stereotypes. She is also interested in political psychology with a specific focus on socio-political attitudes and political orientation.

Lilith A. Whiley is Senior Lecturer at Kingston Business School, UK. Her interdisciplinary research interests bring together Occupational Psychology and Human Resource Management primarily from a critical perspective.

Critical femininities: a 'new' approach to gender theory

Rhea Ashley Hoskin ⓘD and Karen L. Blair

ABSTRACT

Critical femininities examines femininity through a nuanced, multidimensional framework, moving beyond femininity as a patriarchal tool, to instead consider the historical, ideological, and intersectional underpinnings of femininity, particularly those that contribute to femmephobia. While Critical Femininities is often deemed an emergent area of scholarship, this framing is both paradoxical and, conceivably, inaccurate. Rather than being a nascent field, interdisciplinary scholars have contributed to Critical Femininities for over 60 years, whether or not they labeled their research as such. Arguably, Critical Femininities is a field whose emergence can be traced back to the second wave of feminism or even earlier. However, while Dahl (2012) notes that the question of "what is femininity" is as old as de Beauvoir's (1949) *Second Sex*, there is a continued lack of scholarly endeavours not only in terms of how the question of femininity has been addressed, but also in terms of how this question is integrated within research. In this article we theorize why Critical Femininities has remained in a continuous state of emerging without recognition for its contributions as a field. We argue that the field's stalled emergence can be explained by the tendency to view femininity as unidimensional, anti-intellectual, and infantile. Moreover, we see this stalled emergence as a product of the masculine epistemological centre that informs the very fabrics of society. In response, we aim to facilitate the continued growth of the field, and to make visible the taken-for-granted presence of masculinity that remains pervasive within gender theory and epistemological frameworks.

Introduction

"Why, when we embrace (or at least engage with) critical masculinity studies as a crucial part of our knowledge formation, do we so rarely imagine the possibility of critical femininity studies?" (Dahl, 2012, p. 57)

Critical theory integrates scholarly approaches from a variety of social scientific and humanities backgrounds, with roots tracing back to sociology, philosophy, and literary criticism. Critical theories are described as those seeking to 'liberate human beings from the circumstances that' maintain oppression (Horkheimer, 1982, p. 244). Rather than simply documenting or explaining social phenomenon, critical theory develops the tools to critique and unpack systems that maintain the status quo. A central approach to critical theory is questioning how norms, power, and ideology have become calcified in their contemporary manifestation; for only then can oppressive power structures be transformed. Consequently, a critical theory framework attends to the ideological, social, and historical underpinnings that contribute to hegemonic norms, and identifies ideology as a primary means of remedying social inequalities (Freire, 2007). Critical frameworks also operate as methodol-ogies that involve scrutinising normative ideologies that define and stigmatise particular bodies (Schalk, 2017). Often, this is achieved by identifying, describing, and analysing the 'subsumed or hidden origins of social and political culture, discourses and institutions,' which function to expose the 'contingency of ideas or circumstances often presumed to be natural or unchangeable' (Hall, 2019, n.p.). For example, previous critical frameworks have attended to intersections of race and disability, examining how racism is informed by cultural perceptions and historical constructions of race (Delgardo & Stefancic, Delgado & Stefancic, 2013), or how disability is a socially and politically produced phenomenon (Burghardt, 2011; Hall, 2019). Building on these traditions of critical theory, emerging areas have focused on femininity.

While Critical Femininities is often deemed an emergent area of scholarship, this framing is both paradoxical and, conceivably, inaccurate. Rather than being a nascent field, interdisciplinary scholars have contributed to Critical Femininities for over 60 years, whether or not they labelled their research as such. Arguably, Critical Femininities is a field whose emergence can be traced back to the second wave of feminism or even earlier. However, while Dahl (2012) notes that the question of 'what is femininity' is as old as de Beauvoir's (1949) *Second Sex*, there is a continued lack of scholarly endeavours not only in terms of how the question of femininity has been addressed, but also in terms of how this question is integrated within research. Additionally, while contemporary Critical Femininities scholars call attention to the broad strokes with which second-wave feminists painted femininity (e.g., Friedan, 1963; see Hoskin, 2017b), much of the work to emerge from this canon[1] marked a shift in the way we think about femininity and was, thus, foundational to the field of Critical Femininities. After all, what is a critical theory if not one that seeks to liberate humanity? And, in the case of second-wave feminist theory, this liberation meant attending to the ways in which femininity had been used as a tool of patriarchal oppression – one that had become synonymous with womanhood, and from which many women could not escape. For example, paradigm-shifting contributions like Betty Friedan's (1963) *The Feminine Mystique* argued that through the regulatory powers of patriarchal femininity, women were domes-ticated and kept in the home longing for 'more' (i.e., careers).

Yet, as argued by theorists like bell hooks (2015), works like Friedan's overlooked how this phenomenon was predominantly experienced by white, upper-middle class, married, heterosexual, cisgender women; thus, embedding whiteness, cissexism, and heterosexism within the construction of femininity itself. Women of colour, for example, were historically excluded from the sphere of white domesticity. Rather than being kept at home to raise the children, throughout history, women of colour have worked outside the home rearing the children of privileged white women. Thus, although Friedan's work is often touted for shaping much of second-wave feminist politics, the broad strokes with which femininity was painted is an exemplar of how the construct of femininity overlooked the complex intersectional axes that inform feminine embodiments. By framing femi-ninity as a source of oppression, without attending to how it may be informed by race, class, or sexuality, *The Feminine Mystique* exemplifies the importance of wedding Critical Femininities to intersectionality.[2] Without an intersectional perspective, the field of gender theory continues to move a singular, myopic rendition of femininity forward. Critical femininities, thus, pushes scholars to think about femininity through a nuanced, multidimensional and intersectional framework, moving beyond femininity as a patriarchal tool, and even past the more contemporary critiques of femininity via neoliberal frameworks (see Dahl & Sunden, 2018; Gill & Arthurs, 2006), to instead consider the historical, ideological, and intersectional underpinnings of femininity.

Critical Femininities also moves past the analysis of femininity as an extension or experience of womanhood. For example, while the construct of woman has been dissected as a simple, unifying category, insufficient attention has been paid to femininity as a category (Dahl, 2012). Illustrating this scholarly gap, Dahl and Sunden's 2018 review of the *European Journal of Women's Studies*, found that *woman* 'appears in titles of about 300 articles' whereas femininity 'only appears in about a dozen articles' (p. 269). Outside of femininity's role as the process through which an individual assigned female at birth is socialised into womanhood (de Beauvoir, 1949), there is a lack of scholarship devoted to gender (i.e., femininity), much of which focuses instead on women (i.e. gender/sex) or on sex (i.e., female; see Van Anders, 2015). In other words, as noted by Dahl (2012), the epistemic shift from 'sex' to gender 'has not resulted in new ways of theorizing femininity on a comprehensive level' (p. 59). Instead, femininity has been maintained as a unidimensional, discrete construct (Blair & Hoskin, 2015; Hoskin, 2017a; Hoskin et al., 2020). Within this construction, femininity tends to be stereotyped, reductive, and taken-for-granted as being synonymous with womanhood and experienced as pressure to conform to patriarchal norms (Dahl, 2012; Dahl & Sunden, 2018). Critical femininities scholarship, thus, expands beyond the reductive approaches that 'always and only [tie femininity] to [the] oppression, subordination, sexualization and objectification' of women (Dahl & Sunden, 2018, p. 270). Grounding this framework in the tradition of critical theory, Critical Femininities must instead remain committed to the lives implicated in the 'discursive institutions which undergird viable practices of exclusion' and representation (Burghardt, 2011, p. 13). Thus, as critical femininities scholars, we must ask: Whose lives are implicated by the intersectional, cultural and political norms that shape patriarchal femininity[3]? And, what is the process through which these lives are implicated?

Critical femininities: stalled in a state of emergence

How can an area remain in a continuous state of becoming and emerging, without recognition for its contributions as a field? Why, despite the epistemic shift brought forth by second-wave thinkers, and the ongoing contributions of interdisciplinary scholars, has Critical Femininities as a field of inquiry not yet received the same degree of attention or recognition as the field of Masculinities? Some, like Middleton (2019), would argue that this oversight is a result of how femininity is seen as 'socially regressive or anti-intellectual' (p. 84). Supporting Middleton's claims, others argue that the tendency to eschew femininity is a product of centring masculine epistemologies (Hoskin, 2021; Schwartz, 2018). Within western dichotomous ways-of-knowing, masculinity is coded as rational and stoic; the combination of which make up notions of objectivity (Bordo, 1993; Oliver, 1994). Conversely, femininity is coded as the antithesis of objectivity: irrational and emotional. Thus, as postulated by femme scholars, the omission of femininity from epistemological frameworks reflects the sterilisation of scholarship that functions to preserve masculinist notions of objectivity, and that not only serves to maintain masculine ascendency, but also contributes to the systemic devaluation of certain kinds of knowledge (Hoskin, 2021; Mishali, 2014; Schwartz, 2018).

Conversely, or perhaps additionally, the continued state of emergence may be a product of how femininity is infantilized (Hoskin, 2017b). Even in feminist theory, scholars like Sontag (2004) describe femininity as a 'characteristic of the weak [and] the vulnerable' (p. 244) and feminine behaviour as 'childish, immature' and 'weak' (p. 281). In a similar vein, Friedan (2004) describes femininity as preventing women from 'achieving the maturity of which they are capable' and keeping them in a 'state of sexual larvae' (p.71–72). While the ubiquitous theorisation of femininity as infantile and weak upholds femmephobia, it is also structured around normative whiteness, such that Black femininity is often perceived as anything but infantile or weak (Micheline, 2019). Moreover, it is arguable that such a characterisation of femininity may have contributed to the perception of Critical Femininities as never having fully emerged or matured into a focused area of scholarship.

Others, like Titchkosky (2000), have argued that particular assumptions and values 'lie behind the social act of conceiving' a field as new (p. 197). In terms of gender theory, these assumptions and values revolve around the insidious masculine epistemological centre that not only functions to privilege and position masculinity as gender neutral, but also informs the very fabric of society from language to ways of understanding the world and each other. Largely, and not unlike normative frameworks (e.g., normative whiteness), the inherent masculinity of gender theory remains unmarked. Given that a central tenet of critical theory is to critique and unpack that which maintains the status quo, Critical Femininities must therefore name the systems that maintain masculine ascendency. Put succinctly, the status quo within gender hegemony, under patriarchy, and in gender theory is masculinity ascendency. In this way the irony of discussing masculinity via Critical Femininities functions to dislodge and illuminate masculinity as the taken-for-granted norm. Thus, rather than signalling nascency, the newness of Critical Femininities is symbolic of challenging mainstream approaches to the study of gender.

At the same time, the importance of femininity as an intersectional axis worthy of consideration is not lost on many gender theorists. Many scholars have commented on femininity's displacement within gender hegemony[4] (Paechter, 2018; Schippers, 2007) or how masculinity always takes precedence within gender theory (Schwartz, 2018). In 2007, Schippers called for additional research that centres femininity within gender hegemony. In 2012, Dahl posed the question of 'why, when we embrace (or at least engage with) critical masculinity studies as a crucial part of our knowledge formation, do we so rarely imagine the possibility of critical femininity studies?' (p. 57). Nearly a decade later, Hoskin (2019, 2020), Schwartz (2018), Paecher (2018) and countless others continue to speak of the need for the field of Critical Femininities. This special issue is a response to gender theorists' decades long call for additional theorisations of femininity that bare the same nuance and multiplicity taken within the study of masculinity, and that considers the ideological underpinnings of femininity and feminine discourse.

Critical femininities via femme theory

Ample theoretical work has examined femininity as disempowering or as a sexist tool of the patriarchy, while far 'less attention has been paid to the queer possibilities of femininity' (McCann, 2018, p. 287). Among those who *have* turned their attention towards queer femininities, femme's 'multiple genres of femininity' (Dahl, 2012, p. 58) are often noted for their potential to rethink femininity (Brushwood Rose & Camilleri, 2002; McCann, 2018; Volcano & Dahl, 2008; Scott, 2020). Consequently, many Critical Femininities scholars have turned to Femme Theory and femme scholarship more broadly as a key framework for achieving the goals set forth in the field (Dahl, 2012; Hoskin, 2021; McCann, 2018; Schwartz, 2018). Femme Theory has been defined as a framework of analysis that centres 'femme in the examination of femininity more broadly' (Hoskin & Taylor, 2019, p. 282). Femme Theory positions femme as the nucleus for understanding femininity differently, developing new ways of defining femininity, and novel approaches to understanding gender and power (Hoskin, 2019, 2020). This is achieved by theorising the commonalities across femme identities as deviations from patriarchal norms of femininity, and using the insight generated from these 'feminine failures' to understand femininity as an intersectional axis.[5] Such a framework makes salient how femininities are simultaneously devalued and regulated (Hoskin, 2017a, 2021). In short, Femme Theory offers a two-pronged approach to the study of femininity, simultaneously examining the nuance of femininities while also considering femininity within hegemonic and binary structures (Hoskin, 2020).

Femme scholars argue that the way femininity 'is predominantly understood is only part of the story' (Hoskin, 2021, p. 12); or what feminist philosophers call a partial perspective (Haraway, 1988). In response, Femme Theory paints a more complete picture of femininity, cognisant of intersections of race (Keeling, 2007; Lewis, 2012; Story, 2017), disability (Erickson, 2007), sexuality, body size (Taylor, 2018), class (Skeggs, 1997), and ageing (Hoskin & Taylor, 2019; Walker, 2012). By expanding dominant feminine epistemologies, Femme Theory offers a way for scholars to radically shift the way we conceive of gender and the heterosexual matrix by rethinking some of the taken-for-granted assumptions made about femininity: that it signals sexual availability to men, that it is performed by cisgender heterosexual women who are assigned female at birth, that it is markedly white (Keeling, 2007; Lewis, 2012; Story, 2017; Tinsley, 2015) or that it stands as Other to masculinity's perceived neutrality (Hoskin, 2020). In this way, femme offers a 'way out' of the rules governing femininity – a lens that allows researchers to identify their own assumptions about femininity and feminine people (Hoskin, 2021, p. 4). Such a perspective offers a novel approach to understanding femininity beyond the typical construction of femininity as a unilaterally defined tool of patriarchal oppression (Scott, 2020).

Critical Femininities via Femme Theory allows for alternative readings of femininity that are both intersectional and liberating (Harris & Crocker, 1997; Taylor, 2018). In centring femme as a framework of analysis, Critical Femininities asks how the study and theorisation of gender can be reconfigured such that femininity is not perpetually maintained as the 'abject antithesis of our very intellectual existence [. . .] beyond a simple story of subordination, sexualization, objectification, and superficial narcissism' (Dahl, 2012, p. 61). For example, Femme Theory challenges the common assumption that femininity is in itself a source of disempowerment or inherently subordinate. Instead, Femme Theory grounds femme sub-jectivities as a means of highlighting how femininity is *made* subordinate through the societal tendency to see femininity as inferior. By challenging this notion, femmes and Femme Theory introduce the concept of femmephobia: the devaluation and regulation of femininity across intersecting identities, separate from sexism/misogyny (Hoskin, 2017a, 2019; 2020). Femmephobia offers a means of addressing the overarching ways that femininity is devalued and regulated, and inherently references the connec-tions between experiences, rather than speaking to anti-femininity in isolation. Femme theory allows for an analysis 'between' femininities (Dahl, 2012; Dahl & Sunden, 2018), but also provides a framework to address masculine ascendency and gender hegemony more broadly. Thus, Femme Theory's two-pronged theoretical contribution of simultaneously looking within and across the gender binary makes this framework of analysis paramount to the field of Critical Femininities.

Conclusion

Similar to the ways in which gender theorists have commented on the displacement of femininity within gender theory or gender hegemony, femme scholars have commented on the exclusion of femmes from LGBTQ+ and feminist histories (Blair & Hoskin, 2015; Blair & Hoskin, 2016) as well as how femmes have been overlooked as a rich resource for understanding gender (Harris & Crocker, 1997; Lewis, 2012). In response, femme theorists urge femmes to write themselves into these spaces. Likewise, Critical Femininities seeks to reconcile the marginalisation of 'fem(me)ininities in gender and sexuality studies;' a process that is achieved, in part, by turning femme literature and scholarship (Taylor, 2018, p. 4). The goal of this special issue is to bolster femme and critical femininities as theory so that both can be used as central analytical tools through which to understand gender hegemony. Following Lewis (2012), Hoskin (2019), Schwartz (2018), Davies (2020) and others, this issue con-tributes to the writing of femme and femininities into places where it has been overlooked. Critical Femininities is a response to these scholarly gaps that brings theoretical tools to aid in decentring masculinity within gender theory and to shift this normative paradigm. Thus, given masculinity's centrality within gender theory, Critical Femininities and the deliberate examination of femininity holds the possibility of developing new approaches to analyses of gender (Gill & Arthurs, 2006). Moreover, echoing critiques from femme scholars, critical theory itself has also been criticised for its focus on 'active' and 'masculinised' agents of change, which can function to perpetuate the naturalisation of masculinity and simultaneous denigration of femininity (i.e. femmephobia; Davies & Hoskin, 2021; Shelton, 2017). Thus, the development of Critical Femininities via femme theory not only offers novel approaches to gender theory, but also holds the potential to ameliorate many of the tensions of previous critical frameworks.

In line with other critical scholarship, it was our goal to create a special issue that will bolster the field of critical femininities as one that challenges the social, historical, and ideological systems that structure and produce norms of patriarchal femininity; particularly those that contribute to anti-femininity and femmephobia. This issue brings together articles that examine how norms surrounding femininity can be toxic (McCann, 2020), act as an impediment for dating (Taylor, 2020), and can mediate the effects of transprejudice (Türkoğlu & Sayılan, 2021). Contributors to the issue also explore ways of reimagining femininity by grappling with questions such as: How can we conceptualise feminine power (Barton & Huebner, 2020)? In what ways can vulnerability act as a powerful mode of resistance (Schwartz, 2020)? And, importantly, how can we understand femininity as powerful without succumbing to masculinist frameworks (Scott, 2021)? Finally, articles in this issue demonstrate the use Critical Femininities as a framework of analysis, specifically how it can provide a new approach to topics such as breastfeeding stigma (Whiley et al., 2020), Incel ideology (Menzie, 2020), or t(w)een sexual behaviour (García-Gómez,

2019). Taken together, these articles facilitate the continued growth of a field that cultivates insight from a feminine frame of reference as a means of rendering visible the taken-for-granted presence of masculinity that remains pervasive within gender theory.

To some, *Psychology & Sexuality* may seem like an odd choice for a special issue on Critical femininities. While the broad aims of *Psychology & Sexuality* are to advance the understanding of LGBTQ+ issues in psychology and allied disciplines, the journal has established its reputation for facilitating conversations across ostensibly dissident fields of inquiry (e.g., science and queer theory) and has become an outlet for critical and discursive scholarly works. *Psychology & Sexuality* is a progressive, radical journal that is best 'known for drawing from work traditionally seen as outside the remit of psychology'[6] as a means of informing current debates within the field. By bringing additional critical theory to psychological research, we aim to spark debates within the broader psychosocial research world surrounding the treatment of femininity, particularly in relation to LGBTQ+ issues. It is our hope that this issue inspires researchers within and outside of psychology to identify their own masculine-leaning theoretical and epistemological frameworks and begin to question how this might inform their work. Finally, we hope that the paradoxical nature of Critical Femininities becomes rectified through its recognition as a worthy scholarly endeavour.

Notes

1. It should be noted, however, that much of this work might position itself outside of, apart from, or prior to Critical Femininities while simultaneously, and paradoxically, constituting the canon itself.
2. Importantly, many of these criticisms and theoretical frameworks are born from Black feminist criticisms, thus making Black feminist theory integral to the development of Critical Femininities.
3. Patriarchal femininity refers to the norms and powers that regulate femininity (Hoskin 2017a). See McCann (2020) for an overview.
4. Gender hegemony refers to the relationship between masculinity and femininity that is characterised by complementarity and masculine ascendency (Connell, 1987).
5. Femininity as an intersectional axis can take the form of embodiment, oppression, expression, privilege, among others.
6. See *Psychology & Sexuality*'s Aims & Scope.

Disclosure statement

No potential conflict of interest was reported by the authors.

Funding

This work was supported by the Ontario Ministry of Health and Long-Term Care; AMTD Waterloo Global Talent program.

ORCID

Rhea Ashley Hoskin (iD) http://orcid.org/0000-0001-9065-980X

References

Barton, B., & Huebner, L. (2020). Feminine power: a new articulation. *Psychology & Sexuality*, 1–10. https://doi.org/10.1080/19419899.2020.1771408

Blair, K. L., & Hoskin, R. A. (2015). Experiences of femme identity: Coming out, invisibility and femmephobia. *Psychology & Sexuality*, *6*(3), 229–244. https://doi.org/10.1080/19419899.2014.921860

Blair, K. L., & Hoskin, R. A. (2016). Contemporary understandings of femme identities and related experiences of discrimination. *Psychology & Sexuality*, *7*(2), 101–115. https://doi.org/10.1080/19419899.2015.1053824

Bordo, S. (1993). *Unbearable weight: Feminism, western culture and the body*. University of California Press.

Brushwood Rose, C., & Camilleri, A. (2002). *Brazen femme: Queering femininity*. Arsenal Pulp.

Burghardt, M. (2011). The human bottom of non-human things: On critical theory and its contributions to critical disability studies. *Critical Disability Discourse/Discours critiques dans le champ du handicap (CDD/DCCH)*, *3*(art. 2), 1–16. https://cdd.journals.yorku.ca/index.php/cdd/article/view/31560/31234

Connell, R. W. (1987). *Gender and power: Society, the person and sexual politics*. Polity.

Dahl, U. (2012). Turning like a femme: Figuring critical femininity studies. *Nora - Nordic Journal of Feminist and Gender Research*, *20*(1), 57–64. https://doi.org/10.1080/08038740.2011.650708

Dahl, U., & Sunden, J. (2018). Femininity in european journal of women's studies. *European Journal of Women's Studies*, *25*(3), 269–277. https://doi.org/10.1177/1350506818774742

Davies, A., & Hoskin, R. A. (2021). Using femme theory to foster a feminine-inclusive early childhood education practice. *Equity as praxis in early childhood education and care in Ontario*. In Z. Abawi, A. Eizadirad, & R. Berman (Eds.), *Equity as praxis in early childhood education and care* (pp. 107–124). Canadian Scholars Press.

Davies, A. W. J. (2020). "Authentically" effeminate? bialystok's theorization of authenticity, gay male femmephobia, and personal identity. *Canadian Journal of Family and Youth*, *12*(1), 104–123. https://journals.library.ualberta.ca/cjfy/index.php/cjfy/article/view/29493

de Beauvoir, S. (1949). *The second sex*. Random House.

Delgado, R., & Stefancic, J. (2013). *Critical race theory: the cutting edge* (3 ed ed.). Temple University Press.

Erickson, L. (2007). Revealing femmegimp: A sex-positive reflection on sites of shame as sites of resistance for people with disabilities. *Atlantis*, *31*(2), 42–52. https://journals.msvu.ca/index.php/atlantis/article/view/679/669

Freire, P. (2007). *Pedagogy of the Oppressed*. Continnuum.

Friedan, B. (1963). *The feminine mystique*. W.W. Norton & Company.

Friedan, B. (2004). The Crisis in woman's identity. In A. Prince & S. Silva-Wayne (Eds.), *Feminisms and womanisms: A women's studies reader* (pp. 67–75). Women's Press.

García-Gómez, A. (2019). T(w)een sexting and sexual behaviour:(d) evaluating the feminine other. *Psychology & Sexuality*, 1–13. https://doi.org/10.1080/19419899.2019.1699154

Gill, R., & Arthurs, J. (2006). New Femininities? *Feminist Media Studies*, *6*(4), 443–451. https://doi.org/10.1080/14680770600989855

Hall, M. C. (2019). Critical Disability Theory. In N. Edward & Zalta (Eds.), *The stanford encyclopedia of philosophy (winter 2019 edition)* Available at: https://plato.stanford.edu/archives/win2019/entries/disability-critical/

Haraway, D. (1988). Situated knowledges: The science question in feminism and the privilege of partial perspective. *Feminist Studies*, *14*(3), 575–599. https://doi.org/doi:10.2307/3178066

Harris, L., & Crocker, E. (1997). *Femme: Feminists lesbians and bad girls*. Routledge.

hooks, bell. (2015). *Feminist theory: From margin to center*. Routledge.

Horkheimer, M. (1982). *Critical theory*. Seabury Press.

Hoskin, R. A. (2017a). Femme theory: refocusing the intersectional lens. *Atlantis: Critical Studies in Gender, Culture & Social Justice*, *38*(1), 95–109. https://journals.msvu.ca/index.php/atlantis/article/view/4771/95-109%20PDF

Hoskin, R. A. (2017b). Femme interventions and the proper feminist subject: Critical approaches to decolonizing contemporary western feminist pedagogies. *Cogent Open Access Social Sciences*, *3*(1), 1–17. https://doi.org/10.1080/23311886.2016.1276819

Hoskin, R. A. (2019). Femmephobia: The role of anti-femininity and gender policing in LGBTQ+ people's experiences of discrimination. *Sex Roles*, *81*(11–12), 686–703. https://doi.org/10.1007/s11199-019-01021-3

Hoskin, R. A. (2020). "Femininity? It's the aesthetic of subordination": Examining femmephobia, the gender binary, and experiences of oppression among sexual and gender minorities. *Archives of Sexual Behavior*, *49*(7), 2319–2339. https://doi.org/10.1007/s10508-020-01641-x

Hoskin, R. A. (2021). Can femme be theory? Exploring the epistemological and methodological possibilities of femme. *Journal of Lesbian Studies*, *25*(1), 1–17. https://doi.org/10.1080/10894160.2019.1702288

Hoskin, R. A., Holmberg, D., Jenson, K., & Blair, K. L. (2020). Holy anorexia: Views of femininity as a potential mediator in the association between religiosity and disordered eating. *Women's Studies International Forum*, *79*, 1–9. https://doi.org/10.1016/j.wsif.2020.102345

Hoskin, R. A., & Taylor, A. (2019). Femme resistance: The fem(me)inine art of failure. *Psychology & Sexuality*, *10*(4), 281–300. https://doi.org/10.1080/19419899.2019.1615538

Keeling, K. (2007). *The witch's flight: The cinematic, the black femme and the image of common sense*. Duke University Press.

Lewis, S. F. (2012). Everything I know about being femme I learned from sula or toward a black femme-inist criticism. *Trans-Scripts, 2*, 100–125. https://cpb-us-e2.wpmucdn.com/sites.uci.edu/dist/f/1861/files/2014/10/2012_02_09.pdf

McCann, H. (2018). Beyond the visible: Rethinking femininity through the femme assemblage. *European Journal of Women's Studies, 25*(3), 278–292. https://doi.org/10.1177/1350506818767479

McCann, H. (2020). Is there anything "toxic" about femininity? The rigid femininities that keep us locked in. *Psychology & Sexuality*, 1–14. https://doi.org/10.1080/19419899.2020.1785534

Menzie, L. (2020). Stacys, Beckys, and Chads: The construction of femininity and hegemonic masculinity within incel rhetoric. *Psychology & Sexuality*, 1–17. https://doi.org/10.1080/19419899.2020.1806915

Micheline, J. A. (2019). "Ritualizing my humanity.". In K. West & J. Elliott (Eds.), *Becoming dangerous: Witchy femmes, queer conjurers, and magical rebels*(pp. 253–262). Weiser Books.

Middleton, M. (2019). Feminine exhibition design. Exhibition fall, 82–91.

Mishali, Y. (2014). Feminine trouble: The removal of femininity from feminist/lesbian/queer esthetics, imagery, and conceptualization. *Women's Studies International Forum, 44*, 55–68. https://doi.org/10.1016/j.wsif.2013.09.003

Oliver, K. (1994). *Womanizing Nietzsche: Philosophy's relation to the feminine*. Routledge.

Paechter, C. (2018). Rethinking the possibilities for hegemonic femininity: Exploring a gramscian framework. *Women's Studies International Forum, 68*, 121–128. https://doi.org/10.1016/j.wsif.2018.03.005

Schalk, S. (2017). Critical disability studies as methodology. *Lateral, 6*(1), 1. https://doi.org/10.25158/L6.1.13

Schippers, M. (2007). Recovering the feminine other: Masculinity, femininity, and gender hegemony. *Theory and Society, 36*(1), 85–102. https://doi.org/10.1007/s11186-007-9022-4

Schwartz, A. (2018). Locating femme theory online. *First Monday, 23*(7). https://doi.org/10.5210/fm.v23i7.9266

Schwartz, A. (2020). Radical vulnerability: Selfies as a Femme-inine mode of resistance. *Psychology & Sexuality*, 1–14. https://doi.org/10.1080/19419899.2020.1810745

Scott, J. B. (2020). What do glitter, pointe shoes, & plastic drumsticks have in common? Using femme theory to consider the reclamation of disciplinary beauty/body practices. *The Journal of Lesbian Studies, 25*(1), 36–52.

Scott, J. B. (2021). Negotiating relationships with powerfulness: Using femme theory to resist masculinist pressures on feminist femininities. *Psychology & Sexuality*, 1–10. https://doi.org/10.1080/19419899.2021.1878470

Shelton, J. (2017). The pedagogy of the student: Reclaiming agency in receptive subject-positions. *Journal of Curriculum Theorizing, 32*(1), 91–103. https://journal.jctonline.org/index.php/jct/article/view/681

Skeggs, B. (1997). *Formations of Class and Gender: Becoming Respectable*. Sage.

Sontag, S. (2004). The double standard of aging. In A. Prince & S. Silva-Wayne (Eds.), *Feminisms and womanisms: A women's studies reader* (pp. 269–282). Women's Press.

Story, K. A. (2017). Fear of a black femme: the existential conundrum of embodying a black femme identity while being a professor of black, queer, and feminist studies. *Journal of Lesbian Studies, 21*(4), 407–419. https://doi.org/10.1080/10894160.2016.1165043

Taylor, A. (2018). Flabulously' femme: Queer fat femme women's identities and experiences. *Journal of Lesbian Studies, 22*(4), 459–481. https://doi.org/10.1080/10894160.2018.1449503

Taylor, A. (2020). "But where are the dates?" Dating as a central site of fat femme marginalisation in queer communities. *Psychology & Sexuality*, 1–12. https://doi.org/10.1080/19419899.2020.1822429

Tinsley, O. M. (2015). Femmes of color, femmes de couleur: Theorizing black queer femininity through chauvet's la danse sur le volcan. *Yale French Studies, 128*, 131–145. https://www.jstor.org/stable/24643715

Titchkosky, T. (2000). Disability studies: The old and the new. *Canadian Journal Of Sociology / Cahiers canadiens de sociologie, 25*(2), 197–224. https://doi.org/10.2307/3341823

Türkoğlu, B., & Sayılan, G. (2021). How is masculinity ideology related to transprejudice in Turkey: The mediatory effect of femmephobia. *Psychology & Sexuality*, 1–15. https://doi.org/10.1080/19419899.2020.1870541

Van Anders, S. (2015). Beyond sexual orientation: Integrating gender/sex and diverse sexualities via sexual configurations theory. *Archives of Sexual Behavior, 44*(5), 1177–1213. https://doi.org/10.1007/s10508-015-0490-8

Volcano, D. L., & Dahl, U. (2008). *Femmes of power: Exploding queer femininities*. Serpent's Tail.

Walker, L. (2012). The future of femme: Notes on ageing, femininity, and gender theory. *Sexualities, 15*(7), 795–814. https://doi.org/10.1177/1363460711417482

Whiley, L. A., Stutterheim, S., & Grandy, G. (2020). Breastfeeding, 'tainted'love, and femmephobia: Containing the 'dirty'performances of embodied femininity. *Psychology & Sexuality*, 1–14. https://doi.org/10.1080/19419899.2020.1757501

Is there anything "toxic" about femininity? The rigid femininities that keep us locked in

Hannah McCann

ABSTRACT

In recent years there has been rising popular discourse around 'toxic masculinity', and the problems of a hegemonic gender structure that facilitates male violence and misogyny. In the public debate over whether toxic masculinity is fact or fiction, 'toxic femininity' is often raised by men's rights activists and others as an anti-feminist retort, to suggest that women can be 'toxic' too. This paper provides a sketch of how the term has been used so far, in tandem with an overview of the limitations of the more extensively discussed idea of 'toxic masculinity'. This paper suggests that rather than deploying 'toxic femininity', it is more useful to consider what might be 'toxic' about some approaches to femininity. Drawing on existing theories of femininity, including emphasised, hegemonic, normative, patriarchal femininity, pariah femininities, and femmephobia, this paper offers the notion of 'rigid femininities' to explain the structures that keep us locked into a 'toxic' gender system. This paper utilises the term toxic femininity as a jumping-off point for theorising femininity broadly. In theorising femininity, this paper offers a conceptualisation of the 'toxic' attachments that reinforce the gendered power structure/ essentialized gender.

What is 'toxic femininity', and what use might this question have for thinking and theorising femininity more broadly? The term is a spectre that sits aside invocations of mainstream discussions of 'toxic masculinity'. As Kupers (2005, p. 714) defines, toxic masculinity refers to, '...the constellation of socially regressive male traits that serve to foster domination, the devaluation of women, homophobia, and wanton violence'. If toxic masculinity refers to 'socially regressive male traits' how should we understand toxic femininity? Is there anything 'toxic' about femininity? In this paper, I use toxic femininity as a jumping-off point from which to theorise attachments that reinforce the gendered power structure. First, I explore how the specific terminology of toxic femininity has been used so far, in both popular and feminist discourse. I then turn to how the 'toxic' aspects of femininity have been theorised, albeit using other terms. Drawing on these latter existing theorisations, I offer my own approach via 'rigid femininities'. Here, the concept of rigid femininities is proposed in order to specifically attend to the 'toxic' attachments that maintain a strict gender binary. This paper is not an argument that we begin using the term toxic femininity, rather, that we take seriously what may be 'toxic' about the politics of certain approaches to femininity.

Often the specific terminology of toxic femininity – when used to feminist ends – refers to the gender expectations that keep women subservient, quiet, and submissive to men's domination and aggression. However, while such definitions attempt to address the relationality between dominant forms of masculinity and subservient forms of femininity, they frequently do so along a single axis of gender. Considering the toxic politics of certain approaches to femininity via intersections of class, race, sexuality, and more complicates simple notions of gender hierarchy. As I argue here, though 'femininity' can and ought to be untethered from a conflation with womanhood, 'toxic' approaches to femininity heavily maintain and police this conflation.

Given the more extensive discussions of toxic masculinity on offer, this paper first examines existing theorisations of toxic masculinity as a way into deeper thinking about toxicity and gender. Here, I explore the limits of this term, as a guide for later interrogation of *how* we should (and should not) talk about what is 'toxic' about femininity. In particular, I draw on Waling's (2019) suggestion that in theorising gender we ought to attend to strict adherence to the gender binary, rather than attempting to offer accounts of what is 'good' versus 'bad'. I then turn to an analysis of the use of toxic femininity in both popular media and academic discourse, before focusing on existing theories of the toxic aspects of femininity, including the terminology of emphasised, hegemonic, normative, and patriarchal femininity. I explore the mechanisms by which dominant forms of femininity are maintained, outlining theories of pariah femininities and femmephobia. Expanding beyond these terms to focus more directly on the 'toxic' attachments at the 'centre' rather than 'margins' of certain forms of femininity, I offer the concept of 'rigid femininities'.

I develop a typology of five rigid femininities: Trans-Exclusionary Feminist Femininity; Entrepreneurial Feminist Femininity; The Cult of Natural Femininity; Compulsorily Heterosexual Femininity; and Neo-Colonial Femininity. My use of the term 'rigid' is a way to encapsulate Waling's (2019) suggestion that it is a strict adherence to the gender binary that we should turn our attention to. Here 'rigid femininities' is used in a way to identify a set of approaches to femininity which reinforce inflexible ideas about gender and which bolster 'the imperialist white supremacist capitalist patriarchy' (Hooks, 2013, p. 5). The focus here is not only on what is *cast out* in the policing of boundaries of femininity, but rather the politics and attachments that keep certain rigid notions of femininity in place. These hinge on beliefs that certain forms of femininity will provide success, liberation, or upward mobility, and operate at the centre of dominant forms of femininity while often masquerading as marginalised. Each of these demonstrates the possible 'toxic' logics of femininities that reinforce various dimensions of a binary gendered logic while maintaining racial, class, and other norms. Here such as logic is defined as that which collapses assigned female sex status with womanhood/femininity/heterosexual attraction to men, and casts this into opposition to male/manhood/masculinity/attraction to women.

Rather than merely critiquing certain feminine 'styles' (ways of looking feminine) or proposing 'healthier' femininities (which would, as Waling (2019) suggests, continue to prop up hard gender binary distinctions), in this article I offer a way to navigate the politics of femininity via various intersections and attachments. This analysis provides a different way to understand how there are hierarchies that act *within* and *between* femininities, as well as insight into how we might engage with the question of femininity to illuminate the 'toxicity' of particular gendered attachments.

Toxic versus hegemonic masculinity

Before turning to what might be toxic about femininity, it is first useful to unpack the idea of 'toxic masculinity'. The term first appeared in the 1990s, in reference to destructive behaviours adopted by men in trying to achieve notions of successful manhood (for example, see Karner, 1996). Preceding this, Connell (1987) had already coined the term 'hegemonic masculinity', to refer to the way that men's power is systematically institutionalised, a dominance bolstered by men themselves. As Connell (1987) suggests, 'The public face of hegemonic masculinity is not necessarily what powerful men are, but what sustains their power and what large numbers of men are motivated to support' (p. 185). Connell's aim was to outline the systematic nature of men's domination not only over women as patriarchy theory suggests, but over men too – that is, over subordinate masculinities. In this way, Connell's theorisation offered a way to understand hierarchies *between* men, not just between genders. Refining the concept in 2005 with Messerschmidt (Connell & Messerschmidt, 2005), they suggest that, 'Masculinity is not a fixed entity embedded in the body or personality traits of individuals' (p. 836). Connell and Messerschmidt clarify that masculinities (hegemonic or otherwise) ought not to be understood as an essential gender substance, but rather, as a set of practices and accomplishments. Further, Connell and Messerschmidt (2005, p. 848) contend that femininity ought to be given greater attention for the way that it is complicit in shaping masculinities, as 'gender is always relational'.

While hegemonic masculinity is still a popular rubric adopted and adapted within masculinity studies, outside of the academy, the term toxic masculinity has gained greater attention. Toxic masculinity is often used in a way that echoes the intent of hegemonic masculinity, to understand how gender norms also harm some men. Yet, the term is arguably a 'misinterpretation' of Connell's work (Waling, 2019, p. 5), insofar as it flattens any theorisation of hierarchy for understanding masculinity. Popular media abounds with examples of how toxic masculinity explains men's violence, the misogyny of male politicians, men's risk-taking behaviour and more (see, for example, Gill, 2019; Milton, 2019; Walsh, 2019). Along these lines, the American Psychological Association has recently released guidelines about working with men and boys, though the term 'traditional masculinity' is used in place of both hegemonic and toxic masculinity (Pappas, 2019).

Within the academy, toxic masculinity has been taken up in small part in health and psychology, rather than gender or cultural studies. For example, as health researchers Kirby and Kirby (2019) suggest, toxic masculinity is a useful rubric for highlighting the gender normative behaviours that some men engage in that are harmful. They argue that cultural constructions of 'blokey' identity can lead men to engage in unhealthy practices including 'overindulgence in unhealthy foods, excessive alcohol consumption and smoking' (Kirby & Kirby, 2019, p. 18). Yet the approach adopted in papers such as these reflects one of the key problems with the under-theorisation of 'toxic masculinity' in terms of its untethering from Connell's original concept. Kirby and Kirby's four cases consist of a man in his 60 s with alcoholic cirrhosis, a man in his thirties with HIV/AIDS, a man in his fifties with head and neck cancer, and a man in his fifties with colon cancer. Here 'risky' behaviours are lumped in together as equivalent, and as demonstrating the 'costs' of living up to expectations of manhood: drinking, unprotected sex, smoking, and a low fibre diet. The man with HIV/AIDS is identified as bisexual, though the sexuality remains unmarked in the other cases. In contrast to using toxic masculinity as a theoretical basis, Connell's hierarchy would allow us to see that the masculinity of the bisexual man sits unevenly in relation to the other cases. Indeed, it might be his experience of 'subordinate masculinity' that shapes his risk-taking behaviour, as he navigates a homophobic and biphobic world. This demonstrates how, as Waling (2019) suggests, theories of toxic masculinity flatten our understanding of hierarchies among masculinities.

Furthermore, bringing in an intersectional lens following Crenshaw (1989), we might understand how sexuality, race, and/or class may have shaped and informed these 'toxic' behaviours. As Launius and Hassel (2015) suggest, an intersectional approach is vital to understanding how masculinities are shaped in relation to different aspects and expectations of identity. The limits of Kirby and Kirby's approach here (as an example) and the ways these might be ameliorated via a broader structural theorisation that draws on intersectionality are crucial for approaching the question of toxic femininity, as I turn to shortly.

Some scholars have critiqued toxic masculinity for the way that it constructs a sense that there is a contrasting 'healthy' masculinity for which men should strive. For example, Waling (2019) argues that the binary of toxic versus healthy masculinity is unhelpful. Waling warns that labelling some masculinities as 'good' and others as 'bad' only serves to reinforce a binary gendered framework (Waling, 2019, p. 2). According to Waling, theorisations of masculinity as toxic often position men as victims rather than actively involved in maintaining gendered relations; offer only a vague notion of 'healthy' masculinity; fail to recognise that some traits might be helpful in some contexts and 'toxic' in others; and propose new forms of masculinity that appropriate femininity while simultaneously negating femininity. Most crucially, Waling argues that responses to toxic masculinity that champion 'healthier' masculinity often serve only to reinforce a strict gender binary that sees masculinity as distinct from femininity, that is, unable to incorporate things understood as 'feminine' into an understanding of masculinity. Though Waling's work focuses on discussions of masculinity, her insights are similarly useful for theorising 'toxic' femininity. How might we address what is 'toxic' about certain approaches to femininity, without championing 'better' forms of femininity which may inadvertently reinforce the gender binary? As I shall discuss shortly, it is precisely the politics of conceptualising 'healthier' forms of femininity that can prove insidiously toxic.

The specific use of 'toxic femininity'

While toxic masculinity has been generally used as a lay term that echoes yet distorts Connell's hegemonic masculinity, there are three ways in which toxic femininity is currently deployed within both popular and academic discourse. Considering the current uses of 'toxic femininity' is a valuable exercise to help identify both the limits of the term and to get ahead of any broader application of the term – and to use this as a jumping-off point to consider if there *is* anything 'toxic' about femininity. Understanding popular usage of 'toxic femininity' provides an impetus for why scholars must attend in more detail to the question of 'toxicity'. That is, in order to diminish more reactionary debates about toxicity and femininity, it is necessary to confront the question of toxicity rather than simply dismiss it.

Examining a sketch of the discursive field of references to 'toxic femininity', we see that the popular definitions of the term differ markedly from its use in scholarship (summarised in Table 1). First, toxic femininity is sometimes used as a pseudo-feminist (but paradoxically anti-feminist) reaction to any use of the term 'toxic masculinity', suggesting that women can be equally 'toxic' to men. For example, as columnist Daum (2018) writes, 'In a free society, everyone, regardless of gender, is free to be a manipulative, narcissistic, emotionally destructive asshole' (n.p.). Daum proposes that toxic femininity exists because 'fragility' can be 'weaponized', such as through women feigning victimhood in order to gain power over men. At the same time, Daum identifies as a feminist throughout the piece, suggesting a 'better' form of feminism as an antidote to the supposed problems engendered by feminism. Daum might, therefore, be described as an 'antifeminist post-feminist feminist' (Projansky, 2001, p. 71). Uses of toxic femininity in this vein erase and occlude gender hierarchy masquerading as a *more* egalitarian approach to discussing harm than traditional feminist accounts that understand power as patriarchal.

Secondly, toxic femininity appears within Men's Rights Activist (MRA) discourse, used to neutralise any understanding of power as gendered. That is, toxic femininity is used as

Table 1. Overview of existing use of the specific term 'toxic femininity'.

Deployment of "toxic femininity"	Popular or scholarly discourse	Aim	Benefits	Limitations
Pseudo-feminist	Popular	To take an "egalitarian" approach to examining what is wrong with femininity, not just masculinity.	n/a – see limitations.	Ultimately anti-feminist.
Anti-feminist	Popular	To suggest that men can be the "victims" of women.	n/a – see limitations.	Used for anti-feminist ends.
Feminist	Popular and scholarly	To consider how "feminine" gender roles/patriarchal ideals can be damaging for women.	Taps into a feminist concern to analyse how expectations of femininity harm women.	Single-axis approach; subject to same limits as "toxic masculinity."

a rebuttal to toxic masculinity for the purpose of anti-feminist sentiment. We see this, for example, in the work of Minick (2018), who writes about toxic femininity as 'toxic feminism' on the conservative website *Intellectual Takeout* (which features much MRA content). Echoing Daum he writes, 'Based on their sex, women fired from a job or refused promotion can claim "victimhood" status, while a man who did the same would be laughed from the room' (Minick, 2018, n.p.). Various MRA Internet threads addressing the topic similarly involve discussions of how women act in 'toxic' ways: they are bitchy, vengeful, manipulative, and so on. Unlike Daum, this commentary does not adopt a pseudo-feminist frame, though it similarly presents mainstream feminism as the problem underpinning 'inequality'.

Thirdly, and in contrast to these reactionary uses of the term, feminists have also started to take seriously the notion of toxic femininity. These perspectives deploy the terms as synonymous with adherence to normative gender roles. That is, among feminists, the term toxic femininity aligns with traditional notions of femininity and 'how to be a woman'. For example, in a piece from *The Sydney Morning Herald* in 2018, Gilmore reflects on toxic femininity in terms of the 'gender roles that damage all of us' (n.p.). She argues that toxic femininity *enables* toxic masculinity:

> Toxic femininity is sweet and placatory, it never demands or defends, it has no strength and can only submit without protest or defiance. Women become possessions, owned by the dominant male in their life, either their father or their husband. This concept is central to patriarchy … (Gilmore, 2018, n.p.)

Gilmore uses toxic femininity in relation to women who remain subservient, quiet, and submissive to men's domination and aggression. In this way, Gilmore's discussion echoes how toxic masculinity has often been used within recent popular feminist discourse as a way of identifying aspects and symptoms of a hegemonic gender structure that facilitates male violence and misogyny. Similarly, Anthony (2018) writing in *BUST*, suggests that '"Toxic femininity" (if it exists) encourages silent acceptance of violence and domination in order to survive' (n.p.). Though she concludes that this might be more accurately and simply termed 'internalised misogyny' (Anthony, 2018, n.p.).

In the limited scholarly references to the specific term 'toxic femininity', the term is used to reflect the internalisation and reification of patriarchal ideas and norms. For example, in relation to a discussion of sexual abuse, Snider (2018) refers to toxic femininity in terms of:

> … toxicity of patriarchal ideals of femininity – the expectation that a woman be selfless, that she silence her own needs and desires for the sake of others – in a manner akin to that which has occurred in terms of patriarchal masculinity. It demands we examine the unconscious grip that outdated ideals of selflessness, docility, and lack of sexual desire continue to have over women, and the harm such ideals cause on both an individual and systemic level. (pp. 769–770)

Snider suggests that we take a psychoanalytic approach to toxic femininity, which pays greater attention to the way that women interiorise patriarchal gender expectations that ultimately enable men's abuse. Snider is careful to argue that blame should not be ascribed to individual women for reproducing patriarchal ideals. Rather, we ought to analyse the ways that women are *culturally constrained* to think and act in particular ways that *facilitate* women's vulnerability in sexual encounters.

Where does this overview of the specific uses of 'toxic femininity' leave us in terms of thinking more broadly about what might be 'toxic' about femininity? If seeking to adopt a feminist perspective, the first and second uses of the term must be rejected outright, given that they both nullify recognition of gendered hierarchies of power and represent reactionary responses to popular feminism. However, the limit of the third (feminist) approach to theorising 'toxic feminin-ity' outlined above is its reliance solely on a single-axis approach (gender). If we agree that the third definition of toxic femininity has *some* merit, we must first acknowledge that many feminists have already theorised femininity in terms of submission to patriarchal norms, albeit using different terminologies. Taking the 'gender roles that damage all of us' seriously, on top of the limits of theorising toxic masculinity as already outlined, how can we best approach the question of toxicity and femininity?

From emphasised to rigid femininities

In order to progress this question of toxicity and femininity, we must turn to how femininity has been theorised by different means. Here I turn to the concepts of emphasised femininity, hegemonic femininity, normative femininity and patriarchal femininity, in order to examine their implications for thinking through this question of 'toxicity' (summarised in Table 2). I then turn to the concepts of pariah femininities and femmephobia to understand how toxic norms of femininity are policed and enforced, and why these warrant extension before proposing 'rigid femininities' in the following section.

Connell (1987) offers an account of femininity in terms of 'emphasized femininity' described as, 'compliance with ... [gender] subordination and is oriented to accommodating the interests and desires of men' (p. 187). As Connell and Messerschmidt (2005, p. 848) later clarify, 'the concept of emphasized femininity focused on compliance to patriarchy'. Schippers (2007) has extended Connell's conceptualisation of emphasised femininity, instead terming it 'hegemonic femininity'. This contrasts with Connell's sketch insofar as Schippers suggests we cannot see femininity and masculinity in isolation from one another – rather, we must understand the braided relation that exists between hegemonic forms of both masculinity and femininity in reproducing the gender order. As Budgeon (2014) notes, while Connell's framework for femininity is valuable, it needs Schippers' extension in order to adequately address changing norms of femininity. Building on this Budgeon (2014, p. 330) importantly highlights how nominally 'progressive' ideals of femininity can end up reifying rather than challenging binary understandings of gender.

Others have used the term 'normative femininity' to describe the regulatory power of a dominant form of femininity. This is often used synonymously with 'hegemonic femininity', yet with normative femininity appealing less to an overarching political structure than to the individual reproduction of norms. Normative femininity is used in reference to how women attempt to live up to feminine ideals, and often particularly in reference to expectations regarding the body. For example, uses of normative femininity have centred on how women are encouraged to maintain body hair (Toerien et al., 2005), norms of whiteness in relation to beauty (Deliovsky, 2008), and the circulation of pernicious norms even in the world of women's bodybuilding such as maintaining a smaller body size relative to men (Boyle, 2005).

Lastly, the term 'patriarchal femininity' is used as a way to describe the structure that informs idealised feminine norms (Blair & Hoskin, 2015), and is defined as 'normative feminine ideals as they cut across dimensions of sex, gender, race, ability, and class' (Hoskin, 2019, p. 687). Hoskin (2019)

Table 2. Summary of other terms used to theorise possible 'toxic' forms of femininity.

Term	Definition	Focus	Benefits	Limitations
Emphasised femininity	Femininity that complies with patriarchal structure.	Compliance with patriarchy.	Offers a way of theorising femininity in relation to an overall power structure.	Femininity theorised as always subordinate to masculinity.
Hegemonic femininity	Femininity that works in tandem with hegemonic masculinity to reinforce gender binary.	The gendered power structure/ essentialized gender binary.	Overcomes limits of emphasised femininity, understands 'hegemony' of some forms of femininity.	Focuses more on structure, less on norms (how individual actions factor in).
Normative femininity	Femininity that reinforces ideal social norms of femininity.	Social norms (especially of embodiment and expression).	Offers insight into the individual ways that social norms of femininity are reproduced.	Focuses more on norms (and individual reproduction of), less on structure.
Patriarchal femininity	Femininity that represents reproduction of social norms as dictated by patriarchal structure.	Combination of social norms and patriarchal structure.	Focus combines previous terms to account for patriarchal structure and social norms.	Requires further explanation of mechanisms by which it is reinforced.

argues that this term accounts for both normative and hegemonic femininity and provides a framework for analysing the overarching structure that regulates the norms of femininity. Blair and Hoskin (2015, p. 232) also note that this term contains a subcategory of 'essentialised femininity', which involves maintaining a strict and biologically based notion of a gender binary. As outlined in Table 2, patriarchal femininity offers a theorisation that overcomes some of the limitations of the previous terms offered.

Yet, whichever term we adopt as the basis for understanding what might be 'toxic' about femininity, a question remains about the mechanisms by which norms/structures are enforced and maintained. One answer to this question is Schippers (2007) concept of 'pariah femininities' – that is, femininities which are non-hegemonic. For example, marking certain styles of body hair and weight as 'pariah' helps maintain the boundaries of patriarchal femininity (Darwin, 2017). According to Schippers (2007), pariah femininities are those that involve the adoption of *masculine* expectations (such as being sexually active) but that are still marked as *decidedly feminine* in their fall from grace (such as being labelled 'slut'). Pariah femininities are 'cast out' by hegemonic forms. Schippers notes that in identifying what constitutes either hegemonic masculinity or femininity, we cannot simply identify 'ideals', but rather must analyse ideals in practice. We might identify ideal role expectations and traits for hegemonic femininity, such as heterosexual desire, passivity, and compliance. However, these vary across contexts depending on their relation to the expectations of masculinity in a given place – taking into account different cultural formations – as well as what is cast out as 'pariah'. Similar to 'pariah femininities', Hoskin (2017b) uses the term 'femmephobia' to describe how the boundaries of patriarchal femininity are policed and confined to traditional notions of 'proper womanhood' (Blair & Hoskin, 2015, p. 232). Hoskin (2017a) outlines:

> I argue that femmephobia is prejudice, discrimination, or antagonism directed against someone who is *perceived* to identify, embody, or express femininely and toward people and objects gendered femininely. More specifically, the individual is targeted for their perceived deviation from patriarchal femininity. (p. 101)

Hoskin (2020) has compellingly outlined how femmephobia works to maintain the gender binary by devaluing femininity and maintaining masculinity as the norm. While pariah femininities and femmephobia address part of the question of why and how boundaries of femininity are maintained, these theories both offer the greatest focus on the 'margins' (forms of femininity that are cast out) rather than the centre (summarised in Table 3).

As outlined in the beginning of this paper, the feminist use of toxic femininity essentially echoes the notion of patriarchal femininity, that is, the 'gender roles that damage all of us' (Gilmore, 2018, n. p.). Yet while patriarchal femininity describes the structure – the top-down process – it does not directly address the question of attachment, those agentic beliefs and practices that keep us bound to this structure yet can be 'toxic' and damaging. While pariah femininities and femmephobia focus on how certain forms of femininity are marginalised, it is worth attending in greater detail to the *why* and *how* of the forms that maintain this marginalisation. Here Berlant's (2011) notion of 'cruel optimism' is valuable to bring into contact with femininities scholarship. This idea refers to adopting an orientation that feels at once profoundly confirming, yet, that is simultaneously antithetical to one's flourishing (p. 1). As Berlant (2011) describes, optimism is cruel:

> … insofar as the very pleasure of being inside a relation have become sustaining regardless of the content of the relation, such that a person or a world finds itself bound to a situation of profound threat that is, at the same time, profoundly confirming. (p. 2)

Berlant (2011) also directly describes cruel optimism, our sense of being bound to 'compromised conditions', as 'toxic' (p. 24). If we understand 'toxicity' in these terms, the question of what is toxic about femininity, therefore, becomes what *attachments* do we maintain that keeps certain forms of femininity *in place*, promoting femmephobia and casting out pariah femininities?

Table 3. Explanatory mechanisms for how 'toxic' aspects of femininity are enforced.

Term	Definition	Focus	Benefits	Limitations
Pariah femininities	Femininities that are cast out by hegemonic forms, that are marked as masculine in some way yet derided as feminine.	The margins. Expressions that are marked as problematic.	Offers a description for forms of femininity that are cast out and marginalised.	Focus is on forms of femininity marked as deviant (margin rather than centre).
Femmephobia	Devaluation and regulation of femininity, specifically those forms marked as deviating from patriarchal femininity.	The margins. Expressions of femininity that are devalued.	Offers an account of the systematic ways that femininity is regulated and devalued, and how certain forms are marked as marginal.	Focus is on forms of femininity marked as deviant and devalued (margin rather than centre).
Rigid femininities	Political positions broadly aligning with the feminine that involve belief that certain forms of femininity will provide success, liberation, or upward mobility.	The centre, which sometimes masquerades as the margins. Expressions that rigidly maintain the gendered power structure/ essentialized gender binary.	Offers a way of naming the converse of pariah femininities (the centre rather than margin) and explains 'why' beliefs are held (cruel optimism).	Still requires an understanding of femmephobia/pariah femininities to explain how some forms of femininity are marginalised.

In order to address this question directly, I deploy the term 'rigid femininities' to highlight how certain approaches to femininity cling to, repeat, and solidify hard gender boundaries that work to maintain a hierarchical system of femininity. These femininities act to rigidly enforce normative expectations of femininity along various intersections with the gender binary.

Rigid femininities

Giving consideration to the rigidity of particular femininities helps us to understand what it means to 'toxically' prop up a gendered system, and to engage with a cruel optimism, which believes that certain forms of femininity will provide success, liberation, or upward mobility. Transposing Waling's (2019) commentary to femininity, we can consider the relation between femininity and the gender binary, rather than proposing 'healthier' femininities. Indeed, in Berlant's (2011) terms, many of these toxic forms *position* themselves as 'healthier' femininities, promising subversion of patriarchal femininity, while nevertheless profoundly confirming it.

However, if we are to discuss femininity in terms of potential 'toxicity', what remains is the serious question of how to avoid the pitfalls that have plagued 'toxic masculinity' thus far. Possible pitfalls include: flattening gender hierarchies; ignoring intersectionality; reinforcing a strict gender binary; and slipping into reproducing femmephobia through marking the feminine as inherently problematic (Hoskin, 2019). Often when theories of femininity are deployed, the focus sometimes lands on how individuals embody or communicate hegemonic roles, traits, styles, or feelings. A larger question is raised here about what kinds of femininities constitute or reflect the reproduction of patriarchal norms, and which do not. Some critiques of femininity become particularly problematic when considering intersectional issues of race, class, and sexuality in terms of different expressions of, and attachments to, femininity.

Rather, as I propose below, we might take an approach that accounts for expressions of femininity that are not personal so much as political: political styles, roles, traits and feelings, that might be reproduced by individuals but are the product of cultural norms beyond individuals. This theorisation focuses on the *ideologies* that are institutionalised within some approaches to femininity. Here

I consider how norms 'harden' at certain intersections, of gender, class, the body, sexuality, and race. While these may be concretised and recirculated via activist groups, commentators, individuals, and so on, the point is to step away from simply seeing certain individual embodiments as problematic, and instead to focus on the political frameworks being deployed by individuals or otherwise. Importantly the question of toxicity is addressed here without necessarily advocating for the language of 'toxic femininity'. Instead, 'rigidity' acts as the signifier to understand what is 'toxic' about maintaining unchallenged and unchanging approaches to gender. My aim is to provide an overview of how the rigid femininities approach may be applied to examine femininity with various intersections and is by no means exhaustive. To explore the cruelty of rigid femininities, five typologies are briefly offered below (with an acknowledgement that there are many more), which engage with different axes as they intersect with the gender binary: gender; class; the body; sexuality; and race.

Trans-exclusionary feminist femininity

Exclusionary 'feminism' that makes transgender identities (and frequently specifically trans women) a target for critique can be understood as one key form of rigid femininity. Specifically, this rigid femininity serves to prop up the gender binary while paradoxically adopting a 'cruel optimism' that trans-exclusionary politics will achieve gender liberation. We can understand trans-exclusionary feminism as a rigid *femininity* insofar as it involves heavily policing the boundaries of 'proper womanhood'. Even as trans-exclusionary feminists might nominally reject normative 'feminine' gender presentation, in collapsing 'female' with 'woman' they tacitly argue for a *femmephobic* approach to femininity (Hoskin, 2017a). Trans-exclusionary feminist femininity reveals strong attachments held to what femininity must be excluded (trans femininity) versus included (femininity understood as 'natural womanhood'). This attachment to a specific form of femininity within trans-exclusionary feminist politics is further evidenced by the fact that butch cisgender women are seen by many of these feminists as possessing 'male privilege' (Tate & Pearson, 2016, p. 103) and similarly butch trans women are marginalised as they are 'considered to possess "masculine energy"' (Rossiter, 2016, p. 92).

Trans-exclusionary feminism not only casts out trans femininities as pariah, it also reproduces neoliberal feminist logics of intensifying surveillance on women's bodies (Gill, 2017), such as via intense bathroom policing practices. As Hines (2019, p. 151) outlines, 'the right of trans women to use women's public toilets has been at the centre of feminist debate around transgender [identity], bringing issues of everyday gendered embodied experience and regulation to the fore'. Trans-exclusionary feminism reinforces essentialist notions of gender, be that biological essentialism – that all women must have been assigned 'female' sex at birth – or social essentialism – that only those assigned 'female' at birth know true socialised womanhood. Though trans-exclusionary feminists have long claimed that transgender women reinforce ideal forms of femininity (see Hines, 2015), such views ironically prop up a cruelly optimistic rigid notion of femininity. Trans-exclusionary feminists reinforce notions of 'how to be a woman' (that is, as cisgender), undermining the ability to subvert or dismantle the gender binary, instead helping to maintain rigid notions of gender and femininity.

Entrepreneurial feminist femininity

A second form of rigid femininity aligns with what has been discussed by others in terms of 'lean in' feminism (Kennedy, 2018), neoliberal feminism (Rottenberg, 2014), postfeminist sensibility (Gill, 2007, 2017), and right-wing feminism (Farris & Rottenberg, 2017). This form of 'feminist' femininity demonstrates a Berlantian sense of cruel optimism in that it serves to prop up nationalist imaginaries (such as the 'American dream') that maintain the existing capitalist class structure even as it purports to challenge the gendered 'glass ceiling'. Entrepreneurial feminist femininity casts out as pariah those femininities that do not align to neoliberal structures (such as those who may rely on welfare), championing a form of neoliberal feminism built on 'relentless individualism' (Gill, 2017, p. 609).

This approach to femininity is frequently analysed in terms of normative feminine self-presentation, embodied by women who 'lean in'. For example, McRobbie (2009) dubs what I am describing as entrepreneurial feminist femininity, as the 'post-feminist masquerade' which involves 'a re-ordering of femininity so that old-fashioned styles (rules about hats, bags, shoes, etc.), which signal submission to some invisible authority … are reinstated' (p. 66). However, as McCann (2018) argues, analyses like McRobbie's inadvertently centre the body, such that roles and orientations are collapsed into styles and ways of looking. Following this, we might consider how the most important aspect of entrepreneurial feminist femininity is *not* what it 'looks' like but, rather, the politics of neoliberalism championed by this approach. This form of femininity is fundamentally rigid as it fails to engage with questioning the gender binary whatsoever. Instead, entrepreneurial feminist femininity assumes the naturalness of the binary as a starting point for advocating for entrepreneurialism within the existing class and gender structure. Above all else, entrepreneurial feminist femininity reveals an attachment to the social structure as it is, merely learning how to succeed within it (whatever that may 'look' like), and ultimately maintaining the status quo.

The cult of natural femininity

Turning more directly to questions of embodiment, we can also understand claims to 'natural beauty' as a form of rigid femininity that ultimately underpins a gendered power structure/essentia-lized gender binary. While hyper-feminine styles cannot help but reveal the performativity of gender, by contrast, 'natural beauty' insidiously poses as a remedy to gender normative regimes while masking its own normative operation (McCann, 2015). Closely related to trans-exclusionary feminist femininity, this form promotes the notion that socialised femininity can be stripped bare to reveal a true gendered self-underneath. As Ferreday (2007) compellingly points out, such views see femininity '… as something that is superimposed on some mystical "authentic" self which cries out to be liberated from the artificially imposed constraints of high heels, makeup and restrictive clothing' (p. 6).

This form of femininity casts out hyper-feminine styles as pariah (such as queer femme identities), which are often highly raced and classed. It also promotes neoliberal sensibilities of 'intense surveillance of women's bodies' (Gill, 2017, p. 609), in order to achieve 'authenticity' via fitness, skin care, self-love and other activities that broadly fall under achieving 'wellness'. The cult of natural femininity reveals rigid attachments to the idea of a 'natural' gender binary, a cruel optimism that replaces one set of gendered expectations (beauty ideals) with another (natural femininity). Though this form of rigid femininity involves imagining liberation from hyper-feminine constraints, it never-theless also often involves the hyper-consumption of beauty products promising access to 'natural femininity'. Thus, while the cult of natural femininity masquerades as more authentic, reifying the very idea of 'natural' gender expression, it is also highly constructed.

Compulsorily heterosexual femininity

Next, I turn to forms of femininity that strictly reinforce compulsory heterosexuality, such that notions of 'proper womanhood' are equated with femininity that is compulsorily heterosexual. This type of rigid femininity does not refer to individual (hetero)sexual orientation but, rather, the political forms of femininity that actively promote heterosexuality as morally 'right', and mandatory in Rich's (1980) original sense. Compulsorily heterosexual femininity rigidly adheres to the hetero-sexual matrix that fundamentally underpins the gender binary (Butler, 1990). That is, compulsory heterosexual femininity reinforces the coherence between female assigned sex, womanhood, fem-ininity, and heterosexual attraction to men.

This rigid attachment to femininity as heterosexual is found in both religious and secular contexts and brought to the fore during public debates over sexuality, such as in marriage equality campaigns. Often in these campaigns, the figure of the heterosexual mother figure is deployed as moral arbiter – whether that be to denounce 'same sex' marriage or to permit it (Thomas et al., 2019). Here, even where 'same sex' marriage is granted permissibility, where the heterosexual mother figure 'endorses' it, it must be enrolled/assimilated into a fundamentally heterosexual nuclear model. In these campaigns, queer femininities remain largely invisible in favour of cisgender gay masculinities, with the spectre of the feminist lesbian (who may question the institution of marriage) decidedly cast out as pariah.

Neo-colonial femininity

Some forms of femininity, which cling to and support white supremacist colonial fantasies, operate rigidly and toxically cling to Western conceptions of the gender binary. The toxicity of this form of femininity is best understood in localised contexts, in relation to specific histories of (ongoing) colonisation. For example, considering an Australian context, we can understand how the country was 'founded' by European settlers on white supremacy, as Indigenous activist Pearson (2019) writes, this legacy continues:

> Beginning with the invasion, dispossession and regulation of Indigenous peoples, continuing with the White Australia Policy, and remaining with us today, often under the guise of 'protecting our way of life', promoting 'Australian values', 'stopping the boats', and celebrating 'Western civilisation.' (n.p.)

Neo-colonial femininity reinforces this project via a distinctly gendered lens. For example, neo-colonial femininity is expressed in the image of conservative Australian 'One Nation' politician Pauline Hanson posing as a mother washing Australian flags – an advert for keeping the current Australia Day date (known instead to Indigenous advocates as 'Invasion Day'). Similarly, we see neo-colonial femininity expressed by Australian television personality Kerri-Anne Kennerley stating hyperbolic views on men's violence in Indigenous communities, and claiming victim status after being called a racist by her co-presenter Yumi Stynes (McQuire, 2019).

This form of rigid femininity casts out anti-colonial activist femininities as pariah and reveals a strong attachment to maintaining hegemonic Western neoliberal values of individualism under a broader rubric of Nationalist identity. Further, in adopting and championing a Western ontological framework, notions of gender that do not align with a male/female binary remain invisible, and indeed are marked as dangerous. This typology, which calls attention to the alignment between certain forms of femininity and neo-colonial projects might provide a valuable place for engaging with one intersection of race and gender that goes beyond the abundance of critiques of 'white feminism' currently on offer. As Kanai (2019) suggests, simple disavowals of 'white feminism' (often adopted by white feminists) are readily absorbed into neoliberal regimes of self-regulation (the need to mark oneself as an 'intersectional feminist'). Instead, neo-colonial femininity calls on us to attend to how particular white supremacist femininities operate within a broader settler-colonial landscape.

Conclusion

Taking into account the five typologies of rigid femininity offered here, I circle back to Gilmore's (2018) invocation of toxic femininity as the 'gender roles that damage all of us' (n.p.). However, I extend this beyond 'roles', to understand the rigid and 'toxic' attachments that maintain the gendered power structure/essentialized gender binary at various intersections of gender, class, the body, sexuality, and race. Crucially to note, the typologies offered here are not exhaustive but, rather, serve as a starting point for thinking about the way that certain political approaches to femininity police the boundaries of appropriate femininity not only via casting certain forms out (pariah femininities/femmephobia), but through the *positive* yet 'toxic' attachments that they champion. Importantly, while examining rigid femininities at various intersections reveals certain 'toxic' attachments, this is less about individual forms/expressions of femininity than it is about positively reinforcing *structures* of gender. It is hoped that this theorisation of 'rigid femininities' not only helps to address the question of what might be 'toxic' about certain forms of femininity, but may also provide a fruitful approach for those seeking to rethink 'toxic masculinity'.

As I have outlined in this paper, we must take care in using the specific terminology of 'toxic femininity'. Instead, we might consider the productive ways that scholars have already theorised femininity, and extend these through considering what is 'toxic' about certain approaches to femininity at the centre. Extending these conceptualisations via Berlant's cruel optimism brings us to the question of what keeps us locked into the toxic logic of the gendered present. Unpacking various rigid femininities offers a powerful way to understand how some approaches to gender keep us locked in a toxic gendered system.

Disclosure statement

No potential conflict of interest was reported by the author.

References

Anthony, K. (2018). *Is "toxic femininity" a thing?* BUST. Retrieved October 17, 2019, from https://bust.com/feminism/195520-toxic-femininity.html

Berlant, L. (2011). *Cruel optimism.* Duke University Press.

Blair, K. L., & Hoskin, R. A. (2015). Experiences of femme identity: Coming out, invisibility and femmephobia. *Psychology & Sexuality, 6*(3), 229–244. https://doi.org/10.1080/19419899.2014.921860

Blair, K. L., & Hoskin, R. A. (2016). Contemporary understandings of femme identities and related experiences of discrimination. *Psychology & Sexuality, 7*(2), 101–115. https://doi.org/10.1080/19419899.2015.1053824

Boyle, L. (2005). Flexing the tensions of female muscularity: How female bodybuilders negotiate normative femininity in competitive bodybuilding. *Women's Studies Quarterly, 33*(1/2), 134–149. www.jstor.org/stable/40005506

Budgeon, S. (2014). The dynamics of gender hegemony: Femininities, masculinities and social change. *Sociology, 48*(2), 317–334. https://doi.org/10.1177/0038038513490358

Butler, J. (1990). *Gender trouble: Feminism and the subversion of identity.* Routledge.

Connell, R. (1987). *Gender and power: Society, the person and sexual politics.* Allen & Unwin.

Connell, R., & Messerschmidt, J. (2005). Hegemonic masculinity: Rethinking the concept. *Gender & Society, 19*(6), 829–859. https://doi.org/10.1177/0891243205278639

Crenshaw, K. (1989). Demarginalizing the intersection of race and sex: A black feminist critique of antidiscrimination doctrine, feminist theory and antiracist politics. *University of Chicago Legal Forum, 1*(8), 139–168. https://heinonline.org/HOL/LandingPage?handle=hein.journals/uchclf1989&div=10

Darwin, H. (2017). The pariah femininity hierarchy: Comparing white women's body hair and fat stigmas in the United States. *Gender, Place & Culture, 24*(1), 135–146. https://doi.org/10.1080/0966369X.2016.1276889

Daum, M. (2018). *#MeToo will not survive unless we recognize toxic femininity.* Medium. Retrieved September 7, 2019, from https://medium.com/@mdaum213/metoo-will-not-survive-unless-we-recognize-toxic-femininity-6e82704ee616

Deliovsky, K. (2008). Normative white femininity: Race, gender and the politics of beauty. *Atlantis, 33*(1), 49–59. https://journals.msvu.ca/index.php/atlantis/article/view/429

Farris, S., & Rottenberg, C. (2017). Introduction: Righting feminism. *New Formations, 91*(91), 5–15. https://doi.org/10.3898/NEWF:91.INTRODUCTION.2017

Ferreday, D. (2007). Adapting Femininities: The New Burlesque. *M/C Journal, 10*(2). http://journal.media-culture.org.au/0705/12-ferreday.php

Gill, R. (2007). Postfeminist media culture: Elements of a sensibility. *European Journal of Cultural Studies, 10*(2), 147–166. https://doi.org/10.1177/1367549407075898

Gill, R. (2017). The affective, cultural and psychic life of postfeminism: A postfeminist sensibility 10 years on. *European Journal of Cultural Studies, 20*(6), 606–626. https://doi.org/10.1177/1367549417733003

Gill, R. (2019). *Three gender norms that reinforce toxic masculinity*. Ms Magazine. Retrieved October 20, 2019, from https://msmagazine.com/2019/09/26/three-gender-norms-that-reinforce-toxic-masculinity/

Gilmore, J. (2018). *How toxic femininity is damaging us*. The Sydney Morning Herald. Retrieved September 7, 2019, from https://www.smh.com.au/lifestyle/life-and-relationships/how-toxic-femininity-is-damaging-us-20180517-p4zfvt.html

Hines, S. (2015). Feminist theories. In V. Robinson & D. Richardson (Eds.), *Introducing gender & women's studies* (pp. 23–39). Palgrave Macmillan.

Hines, S. (2019). The feminist frontier: On trans and feminism. *Journal of Gender Studies, 28*(2), 145–157. https://doi.org/10.1080/09589236.2017.1411791

Hooks, B. (2013). *Writing beyond race: Living theory and practice*. Routledge.

Hoskin, R. A. (2017a). Femme theory: Refocusing the intersectional lens. *Atlantis: Critical Studies in Gender, Culture & Social Justice, 38*(1), 95–109. https://journals.msvu.ca/index.php/atlantis/article/view/4771

Hoskin, R. A. (2017b). Femme interventions and the proper feminist subject: Critical approaches to decolonizing contemporary western feminist pedagogies. *Cogent Social Sciences, 3*(1), 1–17. https://doi.org/10.1080/23311886.2016.1276819

Hoskin, R. A. (2019). Femmephobia: The role of anti-femininity and gender policing in LGBTQ+ people's experiences of discrimination. *Sex Roles, 81*(11–12), 686–703. https://doi.org/10.1007/s11199-019-01021-3

Hoskin, R. A. (2020). "Femininity? It's the aesthetic of subordination": Examining femmephobia, the gender binary, and experiences of oppression among sexual and gender minorities. *Archives of Sexual Behavior*. https://doi.org/10.1007/s10508-020-01641-x .

Kanai, A. (2019). Between the perfect and the problematic: Everyday femininities, popular feminism, and the negotiation of intersectionality. *Cultural Studies, 34*(1), 25–48. https://doi.org/10.1080/09502386.2018.1559869 .

Karner, T. (1996). Fathers, sons, and Vietnam: Masculinity and betrayal in the life narratives of Vietnam: Veterans with post traumatic stress disorder. *American Studies, 37*(1), 63–94. www.jstor.org/stable/40642783

Kennedy, T. A. (2018). Lean in and tell me a (true) story: sheryl sandberg's revision of feminist history. In D. Letort & B. Lebdai (Eds.), *Women activists and civil rights leaders in auto/biographical literature and films* (pp. 65–88). Palgrave Macmillan.

Kirby, R., & Kirby, M. (2019). The perils of toxic masculinity: Four case studies. *Trends in Urology and Men's Health, 10*(5), 18–20. https://doi.org/10.1002/tre.712

Kupers, T. A. (2005). Toxic masculinity as a barrier to mental health treatment in prison. *Journal of Clinical Psychology, 61*(6), 713–724. https://doi.org/10.1002/jclp.20105

Launius, C., & Hassel, H. (2015). *Threshold concepts in women's and gender studies: Ways of seeing, thinking, and knowing*. Routledge.

McCann, H. (2015). Pantomime dames: queer femininity versus 'natural beauty' in *Snog, Marry, Avoid*. *Australian Feminist Studies, 30*(85), 238–251. https://doi.org/10.1080/08164649.2015.1129685

McCann, H. (2018). *Queering femininity: Sexuality, feminism and the politics of presentation*. Routledge.

McQuire, A. (2019). *Black and white witness*. Meanjin. Retrieved October 20, 2019, from https://meanjin.com.au/essays/black-and-white-witness/

McRobbie, A. (2009). *The aftermath of feminism: Gender, culture and social change*. SAGE.

Milton, J. (2019). *This man getting his haircut with an axe and a hammer is the dictionary definition of toxic masculinity*. PinkNews. Retrieved October 20, 2019, from https://www.pinknews.co.uk/2019/10/17/toxic-masculinity-man-haircut-axe-hammer-twitter-viral-video/

Minick, J. (2018). *Why feminists hate toxic femininity*. Intellectual Takeout. Retrieved October 17, 2019, from https://www.intellectualtakeout.org/article/why-feminists-hate-toxic-femininity

Pappas, S. (2019). APA issues first-ever guidelines for practice with men and boys. *CE Corner, 50*(1). Retrieved October 20, 2019, from https://www.apa.org/monitor/2019/01/ce-corner

Pearson, L. (2019). *It's not a few bad apples, it is the whole damn tree*. Indigenous X. Retrieved October 20, 2019, from https://indigenousx.com.au/its-not-a-few-bad-apples-it-is-the-whole-damn-tree/

Projansky, S. (2001). *Watching rape: Film and television in postfeminist culture*. New York University Press.

Renold, E., & Ringrose, J. (2008). Regulation and rupture: Mapping tween and teenage girls' resistance to the heterosexual matrix. *Feminist Theory, 9*(3), 313–338. https://doi.org/10.1177/1464700108095854

Rich, A. (1980). Compulsory heterosexuality and lesbian existence. *Signs: Journal of Women in Culture and Society, 5*(4), 631–660. https://doi.org/10.1086/493756

Rossiter, H. (2016). She's always a woman: Butch lesbian trans women in the lesbian community. *Journal of Lesbian Studies, 20*(1), 87–96. https://doi.org/10.1080/10894160.2015.1076236

Rottenberg, C. (2014). The rise of neoliberal feminism. *Cultural Studies*, *28*(3), 418–437. https://doi.org/10.1080/09502386.2013.857361

Schippers, M. (2007). Recovering the feminine other: Masculinity, femininity, and gender hegemony. *Theory and Society*, *36*(1), 85–102. https://doi.org/10.1007/s11186-007-9022-4

Snider, N. (2018). 'Why didn't she walk away?' Silence, complicity, and the subtle force of toxic femininity. *Contemporary Psychoanalysis*, *54*(4), 763–777. https://doi.org/10.1080/00107530.2018.1525240

Tate, C. C., & Pearson, M. (2016). Toward an inclusive model of lesbian identity development: Outlining a common and nuanced model for cis and trans women. *Journal of Lesbian Studies*, *20*(1), 97–115. https://doi.org/10.1080/10894160.2015.1076237

Thomas, A., McCann, H., & Fela, G. (2019). 'In this house we believe in fairness and kindness': Post-liberation politics in Australia's same-sex marriage postal survey. *Sexualities*, *23*(4), 475–496. https://doi.org/10.1177/1363460719830347.

Toerien, M., Wilkinson, S., & Choi, P. Y. L. (2005). Body Hair Removal: The 'Mundane' Production of Normative Femininity. *Sex Roles*, *52*(5/6), 399–406. https://doi.org/10.1007/s11199-005-2682-5

Waling, A. (2019). Problematising 'toxic' and 'healthy' masculinity for addressing gender. *Australian Feminist Studies*, *34*(101), 362–375. https://doi.org/10.1080/08164649.2019.1679021

Walsh, L. (2019). *How leaders like Boris Johnson took toxic masculinity in politics to terrifying new heights*. Independent. Retrieved October 20, 2019, from https://www.independent.co.uk/voices/boris-johnson-brexit-politics-toxic-masculinity-corbyn-eu-a9153081.html

Feminine power: a new articulation

Bernadette Barton and Lisa Huebner

ABSTRACT

Consider the messages that Western, patriarchal cultures create and disseminate about femininity: that it is weak, passive, deceitful, and manipulative. Systems of male domination devalue femininity relative to hegemonic masculinity by framing feminine attributes as opposite and in service to men and masculinity, and naturalising these characteristics to female and feminine bodies. Much gender studies scholarship critiques the constraints of feminine socialisation in patriarchy. While such feminist critiques are important and necessary, they also unwittingly uphold the second-class status of femininity, reduce the complexity of all femininities, and erase the presence and power of multiple types of femininity. In this article, the authors situate their analysis in femme theory to show how, under specific conditions, feminine ways of being are powerful on their own terms. Drawing on data from exotic dancers and bedside nurses, the authors operationalise four types of feminine power: yielding, redirection, vulnerability, and establishing connections, arguing that feminine strategies do not universally serve hegemonic masculinity, do yield success, and do increase joy.

Much gender studies scholarship critiques hegemonic femininity by exploring how feminine socialisation grooms girls and women to service men (Brownmiller, 2013; Manne, 2017) while both men and women wield feminine insults (pussy, bitch, girl, cunt, etc.) to police masculinity (Pascoe, 2011). Such work documents how femmephobia (Blair & Hoskin, 2015; Hoskin, 2017) effemimania (Serano, 2007), slut shaming/bashing (Tanenbaum, 2015), misogyny (Manne, 2017), and misogynoir (Bailey & Trudy, 2018) (and other forms of feminine-bashing) constrain the lives of Westerners. Indeed, femmephobia, what theorist Rhea Ashley Hoskin (2019) defines as 'the systematic devaluation of femininity as well as the regulation of patriarchal femininity' (p. 687) is so prevalent that many cis-women see sexual harassment and assault as a natural part of life (Huebner, 2008; Ruchti, 2012).

This is not surprising when we consider the messages that Western, patriarchal cultures create and disseminate about femininity: that it is weak, passive, deceitful, and manipulative. Systems of male domination (in the family, media, workplace, religion, etc.) socialise participants to devalue femininity relative to hegemonic masculinity (Connell, 1995) by framing feminine attributes as opposite and in service to men and masculinity, and naturalising these characteristics to female and feminine bodies. Theorist RW Connell (1987) called this 'emphasized femininity.' While we believe feminist critiques of the constraints of feminine socialisation are important and necessary, they also unwittingly uphold femininity's second-class status (Paechter, 2018; Schippers, 2007), reduce the complexity of all feminin-ities, and erase the presence and power of multiple types of femininity (Collins, 1999). For example, Black, Latina, and transnational feminist scholarship explores how women of colour use collective racial and national identities in powerful ways that demonstrate agency outside of the norm (Brodsky, 2003;

Garcia, 2012; Collins, 2000; Williamson, 2017). Additionally, queer theory and writing analysing femininity as experienced in same-sex relationships distinguishes femininity from femme (Nestle, 1992),
claiming femme as more positive than femininity because it is not hegemonic and not exclusively
governed by heteropatriarchal norms (Serano, 2007).

In this article, we situate our analysis of four distinct feminine behaviours – yielding, re-direction,
vulnerability, and establishing connections – within femme theory and praxis. The breadth of
scholarship on femme performance and ways of being make clear that femme expression can
disrupt and re-write conventional femininity (Duggan & McHugh, 1996), and thus challenge traditional sexism (Berlant, 2008). Femme theory offers critical thinkers space to imagine femininity
independent of systems of domination (Blair & Hoskin, 2015). Drawing on datasets of exotic dancers
and bedside nurses, we show how, under specific conditions, feminine ways of being are powerful *on
their own terms*.

Erasing the power of the feminine: androsexism and the condition of inarticulation

Why is femininity so relentlessly pilloried? What mechanisms so distort our perception that we erase
or dismiss effective feminine strategies we see in our daily lives? Patriarchal cultures purposefully
socialise people to prefer the *practices* associated with hegemonic masculinity (Connell, 1995), and
uphold 'masculinism' (Brittan, 1989) the *ideology* that justifies male domination (Bridges & Pascoe,
2016). As Brittan notes, masculinity practices vary over time whereas masculine ideology that overvalues men and masculinity relative to women and femininity is more stable, fixed, and resistant to
change (Barton & Mabry, 2018). Relatedly, as feminist theorist Cynthia Enloe (2017) observes,
patriarchy demonstrates the capacity to 'reinvent' itself with each new generation and cultural
shift. Its newest iteration is androsexism, 'a type of sexism biased in favor of "male" identified
persons, concepts, and practices.' Valdes, 1996, p. 162)

As sociologists Hochschild and Machung (2012) critiqued, gender equality in Western culture is
'stalled:' women are much freer to assume a mantle of masculinity than men are femininity, and
femininity itself is still despised. If over-valuing men and masculinity, and centring male while
othering female experience – what Sandra Bem (1993) defined as 'androcentrism' – is business as
usual, what has changed over the last 30 years is the possibility for women and girls to adopt
'masculine,' (Halberstam, 2019), 'andro,' or 'bro'-privilege, and temporarily become one of the guys
(Barton & Mabry, 2018). Thus, where traditional sexist practices simply excluded women from male
arenas, bro-privilege allows women short-lived access so long as they enact the values, behaviours,
and attitudes of hegemonic masculinity. Androsexism rests on the assumption that masculinity is so
vastly superior to femininity that no one should have to be female all the time, even girls and
women. While androsexism casts itself as 'progress' because it permits some girls and women to
sometimes be 'one of the guys, play video games, and sexualize bitches,' claiming the status of dude,
bro, or lad in a patriarchal hierarchy perpetuates femininity's second class status, while preserving
masculinism.

We recognise that assuming bro-privilege may offer some girls and women compromised power,
a temporary relief, and reprieve from objectification and subordination. Bro-privilege presents the
illusion of gender equality, casting masculinism as gender progress. Meanwhile powerful femininity
suffers a hermeneutical injustice (Fricker, 2007), what Barton (2012) theorises as a 'condition of
inarticulation,' a silencing that occurs when a phenomenon lacks concepts and words to describe it.
Patriarchy shrouds the positive dimensions of femininity in a cloak of silence and invisibility, casting
all the advantages of femininity as something girls and women 'naturally' do (Manne, 2017).
Furthermore, if a task (care-work), action (re-direction), personality trait (warm and affectionate), or
skill (mediation) – is something women and girls are disproportionately good at, patriarchy automatically constructs these as insignificant and trivial. In short, the very fact that a *woman* does
something, much less does so better than a man, devalues the skill within patriarchy. Such
a formulation ensures that Westerners never perceive feminine ways of power as compelling,

effective, and something to emulate. In the following sections, we challenge this oppressive paradigm by showing how exotic dancers and bedside nurses strategically use behaviours perceived as feminine to successfully manage customers, patients, family members, and co-workers.

Methods

The data presented here are from two separate ethnographic studies: one on exotic dancers and the other on bedside nurses. Each study drew significantly from intersectional feminist standpoint theories, which prioritises subjective worldviews and experiential knowledge (Collins, 2000; Smith, 1997). Barton interviewed 57 exotic dancers about their experiences, and logged 200 hours in strip bars. Interview subjects ranged in age from 18–48. Five were African-American, eight identified as mixed-race, 2 were Native-American, four were Jewish and the remainder white. All were cisgender and US citizens. Among the women interviewed, time spent working in strip bars ranged from four months to 14 years. Huebner interviewed 35 female bedside nurses and conducted 800 hours of observation over eight months in several units in one mid-sized hospital, on both day and night shifts. Interview subjects were 20–60 years old. 21 were white, five African-American, four Latina, and five Asian. 31 were US citizens, and four not from the United States. All the nurses were cisgender.

We did not originally ground our studies in femme theory nor construct our research designs to examine the efficacy of feminine ways of being. It was only after several years of conversations about femininity and feminine forms of power did we realise that infused within our data sets of nurses and exotic dancers were multiple illustrations of effective feminine strategies. Each of us then returned to her respective datasets to re-code for acts of feminine power. We looked especially for categories and terms that research participants used to describe how and when they felt powerful and took control over the circumstances of their labour and their lives.

Thus, the data explored here illustrate frequently reported patterns of interpersonal interaction absent direct questions about feminine power. For us, this increases the significance of the findings we share. To elaborate, imagine if Barton had asked exotic dancers a follow-up question to 'what do you like about your work?' such as, 'what allows you to best accomplish your goals?' and 'what strategies do you use to manage customers, co-workers and managers?' Those follow-up questions would produce a lot of data. Thus, the inductive dimension of the findings presented here suggest that individuals *ubiquitously* use these strategies. While we speculate that people commonly experience and express feminine power in homes, workplaces, schools, churches, and neighbourhoods, the data in this paper are not generalisable.

Findings: everyday acts of feminine power

Exotic dancers and bedside nurses deal with difficult people on a daily basis. Exotic dancers cope with rude and entitled customers while bedside nurses manage anger and frustration from pained, concerned, and confused patients and their family members. How our participants negotiated these stressors are, from one perspective, strategically developed conditioned responses to systemic oppression. At the same time, they also illustrate powerful feminine strategies effective both when dealing with bad behaviour fuelled by prejudice and institutional inequality, and the daily challenges of being human. Dancers and nurses controlled the terms of workplace interactions through connecting, yielding, re-directing, and honouring vulnerability.

Creating connections

We begin with an analysis of forming connections because this capacity – the ability to find a point of alignment with another person and generate feelings of warmth – supports other forms of feminine power. In other words, connection makes yielding, redirection, and vulnerability more effective dimensions of feminine power because connections enable trust. Nurses built trust with their patients physically and emotionally by paying attention to 'mundane' details, ensuring cleanliness, and gently touching them.

Nurses described intentionally focusing on 'small' details like visiting with each patient, getting to know their personalities, and 'showing up' on time when they said they would. Nurses explained that their patients could count on them to 'be right there when they called' and that this strategy 'increased trust.' Mary, who is black and 31, talked about paying attention to the 'small things first, … basic need things. "What can I do to make you feel more comfortable at the moment? Do you need a drink of water? Do you need a blanket? Would you like a wash cloth to wash your face?" It is the simplest little things.' Nurses also strategically employed gentle touch to calm and support their patients. Carey, who is black and 45, shared: 'I stayed with him and massaged the back of his hand. You can't really say he's going to be fine because you don't really know that. So I just stay there and let them [patients in general] talk about all their fears and get it all out.' Nurses explained that 'the little things,' allowed them to connect, demonstrate concern and care bestfor patients. A whole host of positive outcomes emerged with nurses' ability to connect with patients including improved health care and quicker recoveries.

How nurses built connections with patients varied significantly by race, nationality, and gender. Women of colour nurses mitigated simultaneous racism, sexism, and xenophobia from white patients in the process. For example, Mia, a Filipina nurse who is 53, explained that patients felt close to her because of the intimate care she provided to them, but also described how she knew she needed to reduce their discomfort with her:

> When I would go into a room and I would introduce myself, and then the patient, maybe a white, older lady would say, "Well, where are you from?" And I could see that she was uncomfortable. I felt it. They say some stuff that you know it is because of your race, because it is a trust issue.

While it is important that nurses connect with patients, it is essential that dancers connect with customers. Absent connection, income declines precipitously. Thus, the dancers best able to personally bond with customers made the most money. For example, Dianna, who is white and 25, quickly learned that the more she showed interest in a customer, the more he invested financially and emotionally in their relationship. This translated into bigger tips. She shared, 'The more personal you are with them, the more likely they're going to spend their money on you. They want to know that you care about them.' Like Dianna, April, who is white and 25, said that connecting with customers by talking with them earned her better money. She was so good at this; the other dancers dubbed her the 'club therapist.' April shared:

> I've been able to take some of the negative survival things it [exotic dancing] taught me and make me into a more effective person. It taught me how to talk to anybody. I put on different hats to talk with different people in different ways. Like, I could sit and talk to a doctor; and then go over and talk to a politician; and then go talk to someone who's a plumber; and then go talk to someone who's a carpenter. I became very versatile, very resilient.

Connections with customers spanned relatively deep and long-standing relationships with regulars to a few hours or even a single interaction, as Sabrina, who is white and 28, describes here:

> Busking is a term that a lot of side show performers use. It's a way of hustling people, you know, getting money out of people. But a good club dancer can look at somebody the right way and get them to tip when they're on stage. It doesn't really matter what they look like or how talented they are, if you look at somebody and make the right connection with them and you speak to something in them, then they'll typically tip you.

The dancers' abilities to connect with customers raised their incomes, and engendered positive feelings of validation, affirmation, and efficacy. Approximately 25% of dancers expressed that forming emotional connections with customers was both lucrative and satisfying.

Like nurses, dancers also used touch to establish a connection and control interactions. For example, Lacy, who is white and 36, managed customers with erotic touch during private dances. She explained:

My first move was to stand on the couch and push the man's arms to the side to keep him from touching me. I would lean in and push their head back so they didn't lick my breasts, but I just played the part. I was the control freak. I would tell them, 'You have one warning. Second time it's over, because I like to be in control.' And guys would like that.

While the rules of compulsory heterosexuality (Rich, 1980) structure strip clubs with mostly men buying the sexual attention of women, the past 15 years has seen an increase in female customers (Barton, 2017; Barton & Mabry, 2018). The rise in female customers, along with dancers regularly performing lesbian desire for male customers, adds a queer dimension in strip clubs. Barton (2001) found that some dancers discovered they were attracted to women while working in the sex industry, and thus formed new connections that improved their lives. When describing the female customers, Anna, who is biracial and 20, explained that the way she touched them enabled some to experience new desires:

I'm a very sensual dancer when I give a couch dance [to a woman]. It's all about the sensations like the slightest touch, because a lot of them might be in there being rough and grabby. It's just the slightest touch on your leg, and you're like, 'Oh, well, I didn't know that I could be affected like that from that simplistic touch.' And they get aroused by it, and they're like, 'Wow! You're a girl, and you just turned me on!' And they're surprised. I like it. I mean, I think it's fun. 'I opened you to a new- You didn't know you were like that! I just helped you change your life a little.'

As these examples demonstrate, adaptability is key to connection.

Dancers and nurses also suffer much abuse, rejection, and sometimes assault from customers and patients. Their job responsibilities require them to connect with people who are sometimes dis-respectful, disruptive, and difficult, and this can take a toll (Barton, 2017; Huebner, 2008; Ruchti, 2012). Nonetheless, our participants, especially the nurses, recognised that people in risky or scary circumstances act out when they are afraid, ashamed, and feel out of control. Participants created connections to reduce fear and shame, increase comfort, build trust, and in the case of dancers, get bigger tips. Their ability to forge connections strengthened bonds with customers and patients (and co-workers), allowing them to better meet their work goals and assert control over interactions.

Yielding

Under patriarchal rule, to be powerful is to have 'power over:' to dominate others and use force to achieve one's goals. The alpha man is 'king of the hill,' the only one standing after victoriously demonstrating his superior strength (Jensen, 2007). In contrast to this, we posit yielding as a feminine form of power. Among our participants, strategic yielding in their workplaces enhanced the likelihood of achieving a desired outcome. For example, Melinda, who is white, 23, and a dancer, demonstrated this skill with customers. In strip clubs, performers make most of their money giving private dances. This entails approaching patrons over and over throughout a shift, and inevitably hearing many 'nos.' Melinda managed customer rejections by yielding and returning:

They say no, right now they just might not have had enough beer. So I'll give them another half hour, another beer and a half or whatever, and come by and hit them up again. And eventually you wear them down if you're always friendly and you pop up and are like, "Hey, are you ready now?" And then eventually they'll be like, "Yeah, sure. Why not?" You just keep going around and around, and you'll find people who will want to buy you a drink, and you'll just sit down with them and chew the shit for twenty minutes, sell a couple drinks, and get up.

This ability to graciously accept no for an answer, not take it personally, and ask again when the time feels right illustrates emotional resilience, specifically the capacity to productively handle adversity (Seligman, 2012). Yielding also demonstrates deference and respect, and keeps the door open for other outcomes, as Melinda knew.

Similarly, nurses strategically yielded to colleagues, patients, and family members to provide the best care. When patients feel in control, they are more likely to comply with care instructions, especially those that are physically or emotionally unpleasant. At the same time, both nurses and dancers acknowledged that yielding can be taxing, especially to racist and sexist behaviours. Dancers frequently shrugged off customers' sexist comments like, 'Nice ass.' April said, 'Shoot, you never like it, but to them that is a compliment.' Nurses also glossed over demeaning sexist and racist interactions with patients. For example, Mary shared that an elderly white male patient told her that she reminded him of his mammy. She felt very upset and demeaned by this, but stifled her disgust to best help her patient. Yielding is difficult, requires strength, resilience, and it is powerful. It saves face for patients and customers, manages emotion, and gets the job done. We want to be clear that we support the work of minority members resisting oppression however each believes is best. We do not offer yielding as an alternative to resistance, but *as* a form of under-appreciated and unseen resistance.

Let us place the feminine skill of yielding side by side its over-valued companion: the masculine imperative to be tough and *unyielding*, and use violence to assert oneself. In daily lived experience, upholding hegemonic masculinity – refusing to admit wrong-doing, always having to be the alpha in the room, and reacting violently to perceived slights – is exhausting, taxing, and often ineffective. It alienates people and creates a hostile climate. Violence works because people *think* it works, not because it actually does (Kruegler & Parker, 1992). Yielding to accomplish one's goals may prove superior to violence nine out of ten times, yet violence plays a starring role in patriarchy while the power of yielding suffers the condition of inarticulation. This is partly because patriarchy codes yielding as feminine and therefore inherently trivial, and partly because yielding is most effective when the person one is trying to affect does not know it.

Re-direction

Exotic dancers and bedside nurses, like many women, experience sexual harassment on the job (Barton, 2017; Huebner, 2008; Ruchti, 2012). Sexual harassment is partly a consequence of a culture that devalues normative feminine traits and overvalues masculine ones, while placing female bodies in sexual service to men. Westerners grow up seeing those who are masculine objectify and violate feminine people. At the same time, we expect survivors to claim a status of weakness (victim) instead of strength to seek justice, and perpetrators to show remorse for the same behaviour into which they are socialised and for which they are often rewarded. These gender dynamics make it difficult to adequately address and alleviate sexual harassment because, when an instance of harassment occurs, perpetrators too easily violate and survivors automatically shut down, freeze up, ignore the interaction, and move on about their day (Manne, 2017). These power dynamics are often invisible and uncommented-on in the case of mundane, daily sexual harassment (Huebner, 2008; Ruchti, 2012). This makes identifying sexual harassment in daily life thorny, and systematic recourse difficult to enforce. Women learn early on that we may be dismissed, or worse, blamed when we name an instance of harassment or assault. Redirection is thus a powerful tool interview subjects used to interrupt and deflect sexual harassment.

When customers and patients were sexually inappropriate, asked for too much, or pushed personal boundaries in other ways, our participants engaged in verbal and physical redirections to control situations, and transform harassing communications with humour and frankness. Redirection is *not* denial or avoidance of harassment. It is an effective strategy that interrupts a problematic behaviour and focuses attention elsewhere to encourage productive and positive interactions. For example, when Barton asked Sabrina how she handles the volume of customers asking for sexual favours beyond a private dance, she shared her strategies:

> A lot of times, guys would ask me for my number, and I'd just say, "I'm number one. One. That's my number – one." I had little lines like that that I would just kind of skirt around things with. Some I heard some from other dancers, and some I figured out on my own, kind of off the cuff. I tend to be pretty sarcastic at times, so that helped me in some cases. I had to figure out how to skirt questions of "Will you do more?" without losing a sale. So in those cases, "Will you do this extra thing?" "Oh, I can't do that, but we can have a lot of fun doing other stuff!" Just little things like that, and then changing the subject to something else. Or, "I can do something even better than that!" "Oh, I tease. It's so much better. You'll have memories." Selling something without selling something.

Sabrina actively reframed exploitative and potentially exploitative interactions with customers through redirection. She used unapologetic frankness to set boundaries and humour to soften her delivery. Sabrina, like most dancers, spent time and energy developing face-saving, tip-enhancing, proactive and productive strategies to manage harassing requests. She reduced and de-escalated patriarchal entitlement. She knew it is ineffective to argue with pushy customers. Instead, she sought to control the interaction by reframing expectations.

Nurses also used verbal and physical redirection to mitigate harassment. When Huebner asked Evelyn, who is white and 42, if she ever experienced inappropriate sexual behaviours from patients, Evelyn said yes. She gave an example of how she redirected one particular patient:

> He had a permanent erection, and it was painful for him to have the covers over him, and so he'd throw his covers off and just be lying there naked with his big erection, [laughs]. It was like, "Oh my god." [Laughs]. So, I told him, "You know what; I know it's painful for you, but maybe you could put your knees up and put your sheet over your knees when we walk in the room." And he was ok with me for a while after that, but I heard, trickling down from shift to shift that he was still doing it. And I think he got a kick out of it, really. He was just showing off his manhood. I'd pick the sheet up and put it over him. And I'd say, "I'm covering you up because it's uncomfortable for me to have everything displayed." You know [laughs] just tried a real nice way. So, I mean, what are you going to do? I'd go in each day and I'd go in and tell him, "Good morning Mr. So and So, remember our little rule with the sheet." [Laughs]

Like Sabrina, Evelyn used frankness and humour to change the meaning of the interaction with her patient from sexual harassment to something better in alignment with hospital norms. Evelyn explained to the patient that his actions were making nurses uncomfortable, and suggested a way to manage the pain. Like Sabrina, she softened her redirection with joking to lessen displays anger or entitlement. In this way, Evelyn improved work conditions for herself and other nurses, and the care experience for the patient. This illustrates the power of redirection.

Analysing this data we do not intend to romanticise redirection, nor minimise the harassment customers and patients inflicted on participants. A lot of the time redirection works to change oppressive dynamics, but sometimes it does not. Our examples here draw on techniques women used to deflect harassment connected to institutional inequality because dancers and nurses deal with a lot of bigoted attitudes and behaviours. The problem is the racist and sexist behaviours, not the tool women use to cope. Redirection is also effective in life situations not so explicitly under-girded by sexism and racism. It is useful when one wants to avoid a question, defuse a conflict, or highlight a solution. Our point here is that redirection is a feminine form of power that is largely unseen, and underappreciated, because women tend to do it.

Vulnerability

Participants actively engaged in emotion management to mitigate feelings of vulnerability in customers and patients. In doing so, they felt greater purpose and believed they increased customer satisfaction (dancers) and hope in patients (nurses). This kind of work in the paid labour market is a dimension of what sociologist Arlie Hochschild (1983) describes as emotional labour. We have discussed the taxing impact of emotional labour in strip bars and hospitals elsewhere (Barton, 2017; Ruchti, 2012). Here, rather than focusing on the exploitative elements of emotional labour, we explore how honouring vulnerability is a feminine power.

To be vulnerable is to share one's real self – including weaknesses, flaws, failures and low feelings – and to be present with someone else's real self. Patriarchal constructions of masculinity squarely place vulnerability in the terrain of the feminine, constructing it as 'weakness.' Despite this patri-archal socialisation, when questioned, both women and men perceive the capacity to be vulnerable as *courageous* (Brown, 2015). People also *experience* vulnerability as courageous, rather than as weakness. It feels daring and empowering to be honest and open with oneself and with other people. To explain these feelings, we draw on the work of femme scholars to show how vulnerability is an intentional bodily relation that humans create in the world (Dahl, 2017). Being vulnerable allows power to shift because doing so opens one's exterior, creating a fissure in which intense emotion and connection might emerge (Dahl, 2017). Absent vulnerability, human interactions lack the depth and richness that make life meaningful (Brown, 2015).

How our participants addressed customers' and patients' discomfort and shame demonstrated strength, resilience, and leadership. Managing vulnerability requires a combination of compassion, strategic thinking, and control. When customers and patients expressed vulnerability, our participants changed the nature of the experience to help patients and customers feel safe and comfortable. For example, Anna, a dancer, described how she eased feelings of trepidation in female customers:

> A lot of girls come in here and they're obviously uncomfortable with the atmosphere and what's going on around them, but you come over and you're like, "Hi, I'm Anna! It's nice to meet you. Do you want a dance?" "No, no. No, thank you." "Well, sweetheart, smile! Have a good time! We're not gonna hurt you; we're not gonna bite you. If there's anything that you need, let me know and I'll get it for you." And that's when they're like, "Okay! This isn't so bad. These girls are humans. They're actually nice," because a lot of the customers come in here with that mean attitude or that terrified attitude, because they think that we are the bitches.

First, Anna expressed compassion and empathy for the women. She validated their experience of discomfort being in the 'atmosphere' of a strip club. She anticipated what they were likely feeling and then solved potential problems in advance by welcoming them. In this case and in many others, our participants strategically *talked more* to put people at ease. Like Anna, many initiated conversations, conveyed enthusiasm, and sometimes shared personal details about themselves with customers, patients, friends, and family members.

At other times, strategically talking less is most effective. Because people demonstrate (and sometimes try to hide) their vulnerability in many different ways, participants knew they needed to be thoughtful about how they responded to someone feeling dependent or weak, emotional, or in pain. Mary, a nurse, illustrated this:

> You are sharing something with the patients that nobody else gets to see. You're caring for them when they are in excruciating pain. I think that is most intimate because people do not want others to see them at their lowest point. And it's so funny, that's why even when you care for people if you see them out often you will not really talk. Because you see them at a time that no one wants to acknowledge that you saw. I took care of an employee here. He appreciated the care, talked, wrote a nice note. But afterwards he would not acknowledge me at all. And I would think does he just not see me? But it is because I took care of him at his lowest point.

Participants employed strategic silences even when greatly provoked. Trixie, a nurse who is white and 29, explained why she chooses to avoid reacting to patients who lash out in frustration and anger:

> You don't yell at them back. And you have to understand that this person hasn't eaten for hours and hours and hours. He was told his surgery was going to be at this time [and now it is delayed]. So I think, put myself in his shoes; but still it's hard because it's hard not to take it personally.

It is difficult to put aside one's feelings in the face of negativity from others, even when this is part of your job. Further, because patriarchal gender norms socialise people to *expect* women to act with compassion rather than anger when caretaking men, there is little discussion of the strength it takes to do so. Learning and practicing the skill of 'not taking it personally' while allowing people to be vulnerable illustrates emotional resilience. A facility with vulnerability is a feminine power.

Conclusion

Androsexist social norms bolster the patriarchal lie that masculine ways of power are superior to feminine ones. In this manuscript, we draw on data with exotic dancers and bedside nurse to illuminate four feminine forms of power suffering a condition of inarticulation: connection, yielding, redirection, and vulnerability. While we discussed these in separate sections in this manuscript, they can and do frequently overlap, i.e. vulnerability begets connection, and yielding can be the start of redirection. Here, we seek to enlarge the cultural understanding of powerful femininity in broad strokes, and invite other scholars to explore and analyse additional examples. These four forms of power are not new, rare, nor strategies that only some women employ. With a little reflection, we expect that most reading this could generate concrete examples of many different kinds of people using one or more forms of the feminine power we just discussed in other workplaces, homes, churches, neighbourhoods, meetings, and so on. Recognising feminine ways of being as *powerful* rather than *natural* is personally transformative, deprograms patriarchal conditioning, destabilises systems of domination, advances social justice goals, and diminishes femmephobia.

Acknowledgments

The authors thank Anna Blanton, Liz Crockett, Rhea Ashley Hoskin, anonymous reviewers at *Psychology and Sexuality*, and our interview participants. We also appreciate and recognize one another for many years of conversation on powerful femininity.

Disclosure statement

No potential conflict of interest was reported by the authors.

References

Bailey, M., & Trudy. (2018). On misogynoir: Citation, erasure, and plagiarism. *Feminist Media Studies, 18*(4), 762–768. https://doi.org/10.1080/14680777.2018.1447395
Barton, B. (2001). Queer desire in the sex industry. *Sexuality & Culture, 5*(4), 3–27. https://doi.org/10.1007/s12119-001-1000-9
Barton, B. (2012). *Pray the gay away: The extraordinary lives of bible belt gays*. NYU Press.
Barton, B. (2017). *Stripped: More stories from exotic dancers*. NYU Press.
Barton, B., & Mabry, H. (2018). Andro-privilege, raunch culture, and stripping. *Sexualities, 21*(4), 605–620. https://doi.org/10.1177/1363460717737771
Bem, S. L. (1993). *The lenses of gender: Transforming the debate on sexual inequality*. Yale University Press.
Berlant, L. (2008). *The female complaint: The unfinished business of sentimentality in American culture*. Duke University Press.
Blair, K. L., & Hoskin, R. A. (2015). Experiences of femme identity: Coming out, invisibility and femmephobia. *Psychology & Sexuality, 6*(3), 229–244. https://doi.org/10.1080/19419899.2014.921860
Bridges, T., & Pascoe, C. J. (2016). Masculinity, inequality, and the 2016 presidential election. *Footnotes, 44*(8), 7.
Brittan, A. (1989). *Masculinity and power*. Basil Blackwell.
Brodsky, A. E. (2003). *With all our strength: The revolutionary association of the women of Afghanistan*. Routledge Press.
Brown, B. (2015). *Daring greatly: How the courage to be vulnerable transforms the way we live, love, parent, and lead*. Penguin.
Brownmiller, S. (2013). *Femininity*. Open Road Media.
Collins, P. H. (1999). Moving beyond gender: Intersectionality and scientific knowledge. In M. M. Ferree, J. Lorber, B. B. Hess (Eds.), *Re-visioning Gender*(pp. 261–284). Sage Publications.
Collins, P. H. (2000). *Black feminist thought: Knowledge, consciousness, and the politics of empowerment* (2nd Ed.). Routlege.
Connell, R. W. (1987). *Gender and power: Society, the person and sexual politics*. Polity.

Connell, R. W. (1995). *Masculinities*. University of California Press.

Dahl, U. (2017). Femmebodiment: Notes on queer feminine shapes of vulnerability. *Feminist Theory, 18*(1), 35–53. https://doi.org/10.1177/1464700116683902

Duggan, L., & McHugh, K. (1996). A Fem(me)inist manifesto. *Women & Performance: A Journal of Feminist Theory, 8*(2), 153–159. https://doi.org/10.1080/07407709608571236

Enloe, C. (2017). *The big push: Exposing and challenging the persistence of patriarchy*. University of California Press.

Fricker, M. (2007). *Epistemic injustice: Power and the ethics of knowing*. Oxford University Press.

Garcia, L. (2012). *Respect yourself, protect yourself: Latina girls and sexual identity*. New York University Press.

Halberstam, J. (2019). *Female masculinity*. Duke University Press.

Hochschild, A. R. (1983). *The managed heart: Commercialization of human feeling*. University of California Press.

Hochschild, A. R., & Machung, A. (2012). *The second shift: Working families and the revolution at home*. Penguin.

Hoskin, R. A. (2017). Femme interventions and the proper feminist subject: Critical approaches to decolonizing contemporary Western feminist pedagogies. *Cogent Open Access Social Sciences, 3*(1), 1–17.

Hoskin, R. A. (2019). Femmephobia: The role of anti-femininity and gender policing in LGBTQ+ people's experiences of discrimination. *Sex Roles, 81*(11–12), 686–703. https://doi.org/10.1007/s11199-019-01021-3

Huebner, L. C. (2008). It is part of the job: The impact of work culture on how waitresses and nurses perceive sexual harassment. *Sociological Viewpoints, 24*(1),75–90.

Jensen, R. (2007). *Getting off: Pornography and the end of masculinity*. South End Press.

Kruegler, C., & Parker, P. (1992). Identifying alternatives to political violence: An educational imperative. In J. J. Fahey & R. Armstrong (Eds.), *A peace reader: Essential readings on war, justice, non-violence and world order* (pp. 267–278). Mahwah, NJ: Paulist Press.

Manne, K. (2017). *Down girl: The logic of misogyny*. Oxford University Press.

Nestle, J. (ed). (1992). *The persistent desire: A femme-butch reader*. Alyson Books.

Paechter, C. (2018). Rethinking the possibilities for hegemonic femininity: Exploring a gramscian framework. *Women's Studies International Forum, 68*, 121–128. Pergamon. https://doi.org/10.1016/j.wsif.2018.03.005

Pascoe, C. J. (2011). *Dude, you're a fag: Masculinity and sexuality in high school*. University of California Press.

Rich, A. (1980). Compulsory heterosexuality and lesbian existence. *Signs: Journal Of Women And Culture in Society, 5*(4), 631–660.

Ruchti, L. C. (2012). *Catheters, slurs, and pick-up lines: Professional intimacy in hospital nursing*. Temple University Press.

Schippers, M. (2007). Recovering the feminine other: Masculinity, femininity, and gender hegemony. *Theory and Society, 36*(1), 85–102. https://doi.org/10.1007/s11186-007-9022-4

Seligman, M. E. (2012). *Flourish: A visionary new understanding of happiness and well-being*. Simon and Schuster.

Serano, J. (2007). *Whipping girl: A transsexual woman on sexism and the scapegoating of femininity*. Seal Press.

Smith, D. (1997). Comment on Hekman's "Truth and method: Feminist standpoint theory revisited.". *Signs, 22*(2), 392–398. https://doi.org/10.1086/495164

Tanenbaum, L. (2015). *I am not a slut: Slut-shaming in the age of the internet*. Harper Perennial.

Valdes, F. (1996). Unpacking hetero-patriarchy: Tracing the conflation of sex, gender & (and) sexual orientation to its origins.". *Yale Journal of Law & the Humanities, 8*(1), 161–211.

Williamson, T. L. (2017). *Scandalize my name: Black feminist practice and the making of black social life*. Fordham University Press.

Negotiating relationships with powerfulness: using femme theory to resist masculinist pressures on feminist femininities

Jocelyne Bartram Scott

ABSTRACT

Finding power within femininity, typically through masculinised dimensions of femininity, has long been a mechanism through which to recuperate feminised identities, experiences, and aesthetics within feminism. However, privileging powerfulness to the exclusion of dimensions of powerlessness, such as vulnerability, pathologizes femininity and maintains masculinism within feminism. Using queer femme autoethnography alongside intersectional feminist, femme, queer, and critical race theories, I demonstrate this tension surrounding how feminist feminine-of-centre folx negotiate masculinist pressures related to powerfulness and powerlessness in order to be considered properly feminist. I argue that continuing to prioritise powerfulness exclusively within feminism leaves little space for valuing femininized experiences, affects, and qualities, which are concomitant components of femininity. Ultimately, I conclude that the one-dimensional assertion that femininity is powerful, and only acceptable or potentially feminist when powerful, serves as a re-instantiation of a masculinist recuperation framework within feminism's relationship to femininity. I assert that moving forward critical femininity studies should advocate for moving towards an acceptance framework regarding feminism and femininity in order to move beyond individualistic debates surrounding acceptable feminist femininities.

Introduction

Femininity has long had a contentious relationship to Western feminism due to femininity's perceived inseparability from patriarchal oppressions (Hoskin, 2019a, 2019b; McCann, 2018, 2020).[1] Certainly, there have also been feminist critiques of various masculinities and their reliance upon the naturalised inferiority of femininity as well as their role in upholding interlocking oppressions (Hoskin, 2017, 2020; McCann, 2018, 2020; Pascoe, 2011). However, a key point of departure in the theoretical treatment of femininity and masculinity by Western feminist scholars has been the recuperation of these categories regarding their potentiality for feminism.

Feminism, building upon hooks (2015), is defined in this article as ' . . . a movement to end sexism, sexist exploitation, and oppression' (p. 1). It presumes an attention to intersectionality, which echoes current feminist expectations (Berger & Radeloff, 2015; Hemmings, 2011; hooks, 2015; Tong & Botts, 2017). Feminism is treated as simultaneously theoretical and embodied, which is informed by the real-life experience of being a feminist wherein these boundaries between feminist theory, identity, community, and practice are intractably blurred. It also builds upon a core animating question for feminist theory of whether it is accountable to real experiences (Hemmings, 2011; hooks, 2015; Tong & Botts, 2017).

While hegemonic masculinity is derided as a component of patriarchal oppression within feminist scholarship, articulations of feminist masculinities abound (Gardiner, 2002; Halberstam, 1998; hooks, 2015; McCann, 2018, 2020). Feminist masculinities scholarship on the whole is not preoccupied with the individual aesthetic or behavioural choices of masculine-of-centre folx as disqualifications from feminism (McCann, 2018). Rather, feminist masculinity arguably starts from acceptance. Indeed, 'female masculinity,' for example, may be given automatic feminist legitimacy (Halberstam, 1998; McCann, 2018; Schwartz, 2018).

However, with a few notable exceptions, equally rigorous investigations of the possibilities for feminist femininities that move beyond the level of the individual are largely absent (see Dahl, 2012, 2015; Hoskin, 2017, 2020; McCann, 2018, 2020). The theoretical conversation has too-often become stymied in debates over 'choice feminism' and the 'paradox' of practicing femininity as a feminist on an individual level (e.g., specific aesthetic and behavioural choices; Hemmings, 2011; McCann, 2018, 2020; Serano, 2007; Tong & Botts, 2017).[2] Maligned as simultaneously powerless, dupes of the patriarchy, (Dahl, 2012, 2015; Hoskin, 2017; Schippers, 2007), and also active agents of their own oppression (Dahl, 2015; Hoskin, 2017; McCann, 2018; Piepzna-Samarashina, 2015), it becomes clear that too often femininity itself is identified as the problem, rather than the oppressive expectations of patriarchal femininity. As a result, feminine-of centre feminists who choose the 'aesthetic of subordination' (Hoskin, 2020, p. 8) are rejecting that which is valuable: masculinity.

It is this interplay between feminist scholarship and the experiences of living as a feminine-of-centre feminist that forms the basis of this piece. Building on femme and femininities scholars such as McCann (2018, 2020) and Serano (2007), I use femininity as a category of non-masculine gender expressions and identities as well as a set of non-masculine and culturally derided qualities, behaviours, and characteristics. Feminine-of-centre is used as an umbrella term to designate the heterogeneity of individuals who engage with femininity.[3]

I use patriarchal femininity and normative femininity to signal related, but different dimensions of femininity, embodiment, and oppressive expectations. Patriarchal femininity refers to ' ... normative feminine ideals as they cut across dimensions of sex, gender, race, ability, and class. The term patriarchal femininity encompasses concepts such as normative or hegemonic femininity, but specifically refers to the regulatory power and gender policing used to maintain normative feminin-ity' (Hoskin, 2019b, p. 3). Patriarchal femininity weaponises normative femininity into a set of unachievable standards that uphold racist, classist, sexist, colonialist, sizeist, heterosexist, and ableist oppressions. Patriarchal femininity refers to *both* these oppressive expectations *and* the societal coercion and policing in place that maintains this pressure to conform.

Normative femininity, however, refers to perceived femininity (Hoskin, 2020). Specifically, norma-tive femininity signals a femininity which is interpreted as socially appropriate. It is a femininity that is considered gender conforming and is assumed to exist upon cisgender women's bodies (Hoskin, 2019b). I make this distinction to draw attention to the power of patriarchal femininity in its impossibility (Hoskin & Taylor, 2019; Scott, 2019).

Additionally, this distinction illustrates the slippage between perception and experience regard-ing femininity and failed femininity. Certainly, particular femininities are considered 'closer' to achieving the standards of patriarchal femininity, and as a result experience less everyday policing for their femininity, through perceived adherence to those Eurocentric, classed, ableist, cissexist, heterosexist, and sizeist standards (Hoskin, 2019b; McCann, 2020). However, by routinely disavowing normative femininity as separate from fem(me)inist femininities or by collapsing normative feminin-ity and patriarchal femininity (see McCann, 2018; Piepzna-Samarashina, 2015; Schwartz, 2018; Scott, 2019), much fem(me)inist scholarship continues to render femininity the problem.

By recuperating only particular feminine-of-centre identities and piecemeal feminine experiences through failures to achieve patriarchal femininity (see Hoskin, 2019a, 2019b; McCann, 2018, 2020; Stelly, 2009), such scholarly trends demonstrate the messiness between feminism as scholarship and living as a feminist. The core principles of feminism aforementioned do not theoretically require a particular relationship to femininity. Yet, fem(me)inist scholars consistently articulate a discomfort between femininity and feminism (Albrecht-Samarasinha, 2014; Gay, 2014; McCann, 2018, 2020; Story, 2017). Additionally, I have encountered the real-world use of this recuperation of femininity from feminists in a variety of North American regions, generations, and social positions. Such consistency indicates that this is neither a purely theoretical tension nor is it confined to a particular generation of feminine-of-centre feminists, regardless of the varied theoretical approaches to femininity within different forms of feminism (Ahmed, 2017; Dahl, 2016; McCann, 2018).[4]

The disavowal and subsequent recuperation of particular identities and experiences as feminist, which I label the recuperation framework, is a key approach used throughout this article. Using the recuperation framework, I argue from a feminist standpoint that femininity is presumed negative but that particular aspects of it can be recuperated as feminist by performing and experiencing femininity correctly according to feminist expectations. Through this framework, femininity is disavowed from feminism and then *recuperated* through an ostensible masculinisation. In doing so, the use of the recuperation framework demonstrates a masculinist value system within feminism wherein femininity *deserves* to be subordinate to masculinity, rendering and maintaining masculinity as neutral.[5] The recuperation framework can be understood as a 'sweaty concept' (Ahmed, 2017) that has been developed to represent, ' . . . a description of a body that is not at home in the world' (p. 13). In this case, it is feminine-of-centre bodies and, by extension, femininity more broadly, that is not at home within feminism.

Femininity is powerful: the current paper

In this paper I address the recuperation of femininity within feminism by approaching femininity as powerful (Barton & Huebner, 2020; Dahl, 2011; Hoskin, 2020; Lazar, 2006; McCann, 2018; Piepzna-Samarashina, 2015; Scott, 2019). Although the constellation of powerful femininity is vast, and at times contradictory, there are emergent themes of agency, action, control, strength, hardness, authority, loudness, and anger (Hoskin, 2019a; Lazar, 2006; Piepzna-Samarashina, 2015; Schwartz, 2018). This prioritisation of powerfulness in order to justify femininity is what I aim to examine for its adherence to masculinism and support of the recuperation framework. It is the concept of powerfulness, and as a result power more broadly, that is masculinised and therefore recuperable with respect to femininity, regardless of what form that feminine power takes. I am not contesting that femininity is powerful, and that power and powerfulness take a variety of forms including non-dominating forms of power (Barton & Huebner, 2020). Rather, I address whether femininity must be powerful in order for it to be considered feminist and if, through the erasure of powerlessness, feminism is continuing to reject femininity.

Powerlessness is as an umbrella term for all of the femininities (i.e., experiences, identities, and deployments) that fall out of, or are rejected by concepts of powerfulness. Feminised characteristics such as receptivity, emotionality, passivity, quietness, vulnerability, weakness, and softness have often been the features that feminine-of-centre folx articulate as creating feelings of feminist fraudulence or needing to be recast as powerful in order to be recuperated (Dahl, 2012, 2016; Hoskin, 2017, 2020; McCann, 2018; Piepzna-Samarashina, 2015; Schwartz, 2018; Scott, 2019).

My argument regarding feminine powerfulness is twofold. First, I argue that as a result of the recuperation framework feminist feminine-of-centre folx are regulated through masculinist pressures to prioritise cultivating femininity through powerfulness in order to be considered properly feminist. Second, I argue that continuing to prioritise powerfulness as a mechanism for legitimating femininity leaves little space for valuing femininized experiences, affects, and qualities related to powerlessness. Extending the work of Ahmed (2006), Dahl (2016), and Piepzna-Samarashina (2015), I assert that this is particularly problematic because powerlessness is inseparable from powerfulness within femininity. Crucially, although I focus here on the interplay between powerfulness and powerlessness within experiences of femininity, powerlessness is not solely confined to femininity. Part of the masculinisation of power, and the masculinism of the recuperation framework, relies upon rejecting powerlessness, despite its inescapability. Articulations of 'feminist' versus 'toxic' masculinities, for example, also draw attention to this interplay (Hooks, 2015; McCann, 2018; McCann, 2020).

As a result, I argue that moving forward the field of critical femininity studies (Dahl, 2012; Hoskin, 2020; McCann, 2018, 2020) should work towards an acceptance framework. Implementing the acceptance framework would require disassociating gender identity and embodiment from feminist legitimacy. For example, rather than legitimising feminine feminist identities through recuperation an acceptance framework treats femininity as a part of feminism without qualification. This would ultimately challenge the current trends aforementioned wherein the disavowal of femininity is seen as more legitimately feminist and there is an expectation of recuperation on the part of feminine-of-centre feminists in order to 'prove' one's commitment to feminism.

Materials, methods, and theoretical frameworks

This paper brings together a variety of materials and methods. I combine textual analysis alongside autoethnography to examine contemporary experiences of femininity with respect to negotiating powerfulness and powerlessness. Through this approach, this piece upholds feminist philosophies that the personal is political and the political is personal by using ' ... selfhood, subjectivity, and personal experience ("auto") to describe, interpret, and represent ("graphy") beliefs, practices, and identities of a group or culture ("ethno")' (Adams & Herrmann, 2020, p. 2). This tactic is in line with much existing femme and femininities scholarship (Dahl, 2011; Hoskin & Taylor, 2019), as well as longstanding traditions within feminist theorising that utilise 'scavenger' (Halberstam, 1998), inter-disciplinary (Berger & Radeloff, 2015), and self-reflexive (Hemmings, 2011) methodologies.

The two frameworks that are operationalised within this piece rely upon 'sweaty concepts' (Ahmed, 2017) that are drawn from the body and treat the ' ... descriptive work of bodily experience as conceptual work' (p. 13). Specifically, the recuperation framework derives from the repetition of a 'bodily experience that is trying' (pg. 13), feminine-of-centre feminist embodiment. In line with this methodology, descriptive 'sweaty moments' are included throughout the piece and serve as auto-ethnographic data to illustrate these frameworks and the relationship between powerfulness and powerlessness in my experiences of feminine-of-centre feminism. These 'sweaty moments' are reflections of the ways these tensions between femininity and feminism are experienced viscerally with respect to embodiment.

'Sweaty moments:' analysis strategy

My cheeks redden and my throat gets dry when a feminist student comments that she understands how eye make-up can involve artistry and could be powerful but that no self-respecting feminist can 'justify' wearing foundation; it is just a blatant adherence to patriarchal oppression. I worry I am sweating through my own foundation, leaving it patchy or streaked. I fear the post-birth-control-syndrome-driven acne and bright red scarring are breaking through my melting foundation, juve-nilizing me and, I worry, undermining my legitimacy as an instructor as quickly as my vocal fry. The student's assertion demonstrated the elements of the recuperation framework: (1) demands to justify femininity in order to maintain a feminist identity; (2) the rejection of femininity apart from reclaimed portions, affects, or identities; (3) appeals to a masculinised value system to recuperate femininity piecemeal; and (4) questioning the possibility of feminism and femininity co-existing.

An upper-level feminine-of-centre cisgender woman student confesses that she shaves her legs, using an embarrassed tone that suggests she has committed a crime against feminism. My classroom becomes embroiled in a tense conversation surrounding body hair. Where is the line between patriarchal pressures and individual choice, they demand? They ask me how they can know if they are enjoying something because they enjoy it or because, at least in some way, they are *supposed* to enjoy it? I shift in my seat, suddenly acutely aware of my smooth legs rubbing against one another beneath a tea-length dress. I think of the sensation of slipping just-shaven legs into fresh sheets in the summer – Luxurious; a pleasurable tactile experience I refuse to give up. I think of my preteen self, bleeding in the shower, knicks marking my legs as I learn to remove the dark hair that has sprouted, deemed culturally repugnant for an almost-woman. I offer the students the best answer I have; that there is no answer. There is no place of uninterrupted feminist transcendence, no perfect feminist identity marked by constant gender euphoria, finally free from the impact of patriarchal socialisation. Perhaps, I urge them, this is actually the wrong question. Rather, perhaps the weight of gender equity does not rest on any razor as no individual choice will single-handedly undermine nor uphold patriarchal oppression. After all, I point out to them, no one has demanded that their masculine-of-centre cis and trans men colleagues attempt to recuperate their gendered routines of razor usage in order to prove their feminism, despite their freshly shaven faces seated around our conference table. They have simply been accepted as feminist, despite their gender-normative masculinity.

In opposition to the recuperation framework, I argue for an acceptance framework regarding femininity, which, as this example illustrates, is arguably already present with respect to masculinity and feminism. An acceptance framework for femininity within feminism would entail the following elements: (1) using intersectional self-reflexivity to deliberately resist masculinist assertions and assumptions within feminism; (2) judging feminine-of-centre feminists based on their work, activism, and ethical commitments regardless of gender presentation or identity; and (3) rejecting the use of gender identity or expression as a barometer of feminism. Using this framework, all feminists could breaking down the assumption that feminist consciousness demands particular embodiments or that particular embodiments imply feminist consciousness.

Finally, the rejection of femininity in the name of remaining authentic to feminism is understood as a politics of feminine feminist respectability. Building upon existing frameworks for respectability politics (Pitcan et al., 2018; Schippers, 2007; Story, 2017), rejecting femininity increases the palatability of feminism to a broader audience by remaining in line with patriarchal culture.

Reframing femininity: the simultaneity of powerfulness and powerlessness

The goal of the current paper is not to offer a re-framing of femininity that is necessarily universalizable and all-encompassing. Certainly, I am decidedly against perpetuating conceptualisations of femininity that draw essentialist, racist, colonialist, classist, heterosexist, ableist, sizeist, and cissexist boundaries around who can or should consider themselves feminine (Hoskin, 2020; Hoskin & Taylor, 2019; McCann, 2018; Schippers, 2007). Although I reference specific experiences of femininity here to ground my analysis, these experiences and gendered practices should not be construed as prescriptive requirements for femininity. I argue that powerfulness and powerlessness occur simultaneously within femininity and that recognition of this reality cultivates more theoretical space to appreciate powerlessness. As a result, the vast and varied experiences of feminine-of-centre folx within feminism can be more accurately conceptualised and re-valued.

Challenging the partial recuperation of femininity within feminism

The sound of high heels. That click-clack noise. For me, it is the sound of power. The sound always takes me back to elementary school when I would hear the teacher coming down the hallway and watch a hush fall over the classroom before she even got there – the power to silence a room before you enter it. When I click-clack through the building to teach university classes I imagine that my students feel similarly when they hear me coming down the hallway. I have never felt as authoritative as when I hear a classroom falling silent as my heels approach the room, before I get there, without having to say or do anything. As a short, young, femme woman who is often asked where the 'real' professor is, it can be hard to command authority. Much like Story (2017), describes her accomplishments being attributed to other, more 'credible' faculty members, I find myself needing to continuously remind students that I am, in fact, the instructor. I have experienced harassment, threats, and generally sexist and homophobic behaviours in my encounters with students, particularly those who are white cisgender heterosexual men. I have found that the physical effects of wearing heels – that I am more likely to be able to look someone in the eye or be taller than them and that my movements command more attention and take up more audible space – can change these interactions.

At the same time, and perhaps paradoxically, I feel physically more vulnerable when I wear high heels. Wearing heels impacts my mobility and they hurt. Cobblestone has never gone out of fashion on U.S. college campuses, and my heels routinely get stuck in them. There is often a great deal of walking required to get around campus. This paradox, the ways one becomes powerless to the experience of wearing high heels while wielding the power of wearing them, illustrates that the powerfulness of femininity does not exist without powerlessness. To recuperate only the powerful portions of this experience, such as the ways that wearing high heels can feel empowering and exert authority over a space, is to ignore the heart of feminine-of-centre experiences by framing femininity through recuperation. Doing so ignores the ways that such powerfulness relies upon embracing powerlessness, such as, in this case, the concomitant physical vulnerability of wearing heels.

My experiences of vulnerability and powerfulness, both in this instance of high heels and throughout this piece, do not necessarily hold true for everyone. For example, I feel powerful, not uncomfortably spotlighted, by the attention that my high heels garner when I am standing in front of a classroom. However, I am a white, cisgender, femme, physically able-bodied woman. Despite my queerness, I am perceived as normatively feminine. What I experience as powerful related to femininity may very well be experienced as powerlessness or victimising by others (Hoskin & Taylor, 2019). Feminised visibility is paradoxical in this way. It will mean something very different for black and brown folx and, trans women, for example, often falling into what Story (2017), describes as simultaneous hypervisibility and invisibility (p. 418).

Indeed, this inconsistency occurs at the individual level. Piepzna-Samarashina (2015), for example, describes the inconsistency of experiences of fem(me)ininity, powerfulness, and powerlessness in conjunction with bodily changes such as navigating chronic illness. To build upon this description, on days that I am experiencing a chronic illness flare-up, being physically constrained within form-fitting feminine clothing, putting on makeup, and manoeuvring the campus in heels may simply be too taxing. I am left feeling vulnerable, without the powerful authority of my preferred forms of femininity, and (seemingly) paradoxically spotlighted through their absence, angry red marks surging forth undeterred on my skin, my short, vulnerable body on full display. The ways that the intersections of visibility, powerfulness, powerlessness, and vulnerability are experienced inconsistently across interactions with femininity underline the need to challenge a recuperation framework for femininity rooted exclusively in powerfulness by demonstrating that powerfulness and powerlessness are intertwined and non-universal.

Additionally, the inseparability of powerfulness and powerlessness encourages a reconsideration of the treatment of the 'routine' within feminist femininity. For example, like Stelly (2009), some days I revel in the ' ... feeling of my eyelashes heavy with mascara' (p. 22). However, some days I will put my make-up on more out of routine than active pleasure. Sometimes these are different moments in the same day. Building upon Stelly (2009), 'not every femme mannerism is intentional or conscious' (p. 21) and the reality of banality within experiences of femininity, including powerlessness, has too often been relegated to the realm of the unspeakable. This is because, within the recuperation framework, anything other than active enjoyment, where femininity appeals to the masculine value of powerfulness, can be construed as simply internalised oppression (Barton & Huebner, 2020; Dahl, 2016; Hoskin, 2020; McCann, 2018). Extending Gay's (2014) argument, faced with this reality feminine feminists are consistently waiting for and/or fearing an 'aha moment' that proves someone is a 'bad feminist.' 'Bad feminist' moments serve to reify the exhausting, evolving, and inconsistent litany of individual aesthetic and behavioural choices that delegitimize someone as a feminist (Dahl, 2015; Gay, 2014; Hoskin, 2017; McCann, 2018; Schwartz, 2018; Scott, 2019). As a result of these tensions, the embrace of a practice like wearing high heels or routine femininity, is an embrace of powerlessness alongside powerfulness and is a threat to the feminine feminist politics of respectability through recuperation.

Feeling like a feminist failure: embracing powerlessness

One of the times in my life when I have felt the most joy in my body was wedding dress shopping. Everyone I went shopping with was a feminist, the majority of the group was queer, and everyone there had a Ph.D. We kept obscuring from view or ignoring all of the signage that said 'Mr. & Mrs.' but otherwise there was nothing obviously feminist or queerly different about us as a group and our experience compared to the other shoppers at the bridal boutique that day. Contrary to some femme writing on the subject (Albrecht-Samarasinha, 2014; Schwartz, 2018), we did not necessarily stand out from the rest of the (perceived) heteronormative shoppers. Or if we did, the shop owner, motivated by a queer-friendly politic or a capitalistic impulse for commission, did not let on. I felt powerless to the desire to be beautiful as dresses were placed onto me, clipped and adjusted with panel inserts to show how they could fit if they were purchased in the appropriate size, and I was put onto a pedestal to look at dresses with my group.

The desire to be beautiful was happening in spite of myself, and in spite of being a feminist. Indeed, this desire arose in spite of knowing how oppressive and reductionist the category of beauty is and how constant appearance-based judgements are for feminine-of-centre folx. This desire ran counter to my knowledge of the wedding industry as overpriced, exploitative, and anti-feminist (Boden, 2003). I think perhaps it was the surprise of it; that, after a lifetime of body hatred issues and not being 'sample size' I expected wedding dress shopping to be the epitome of a terrible shopping experience. But there was joy in being rendered powerless to feeling beautiful. There was also joy knowing that harnessing this feeling would make me feel powerful on my wedding day – not just an ornament to be observed by attendees, but a boldly beautiful bride claiming attention.

I felt as though on the one hand I was living my peak feminist life, revelling in my body and knowing that it was a queer relationship that was going to be solidified while I wore this dress. It felt powerful to actually feel beautiful within an oppressive structure that endlessly tells feminine-of-centre folx to seek beauty while knowing full well they can never achieve it and should never actually feel beautiful. I felt that I was experiencing what feminist and femininities scholars have argued; that enjoying our bodies and our embodied experiences, as feminist-of-centre folx, is an act of resistance to patriarchal femininity (Dahl, 2011, 2012; Hoskin, 2019a, 2019b; Scott, 2019; Stelly, 2009).

Simultaneously, this moment greatly troubled me. I felt as if I was at my least feminist and my least queer. I had succumbed to this oppressive expectation of being beautiful and I had (assumedly) disappeared as a queer person. To onlookers, I was just another normatively feminine bride-to-be, interchangeable with countless others. In admitting a deep-seated desire to feel beautiful, I admitted a deep-seated slippage into wanting to feel desirable to an imagined other (Dahl, 2016; Hoskin & Taylor, 2019; McCann, 2018). I felt as though admitting a desire to feel beautiful was akin to deeming acceptable the use of beauty as an oppressive tool and the objectification and harassment feminine-of-centre folx routinely encounter. As I reflected upon this question, I was reminded that I heard fellow feminine-of-centre feminists debating variations of this question with alarming regularity as part of the feminist politics of feminine respectability. By contextualising this question within the practice of femininity itself (e.g., could I call myself a feminist and want to feel beautiful) rather than the oppressive structures through which femininity is enacted and experienced (e.g., the expectations of patriarchal femininity within a broader cultural context are oppressive), such questioning continues to render femininity and feminine-of-centre folx as the problem. By contrast, I have never encountered similar theoretical handwringing over whether it is possible, as a feminist, to aspire to feel strong or assertive (normatively masculine traits). When my students, for example, assert a desire to feel attractive in a suit, I have not encountered a similar conversation around justifying such desires in order to demonstrate one's feminism.

Feminist politics of feminine respectability further extend patriarchal victim-blaming rhetoric by implying that if feminine-of-centre folx are properly feminine-while-feminist by rejecting femininity and recuperating only that which can be made valuable and powerful, they can escape the oppressive expectations of patriarchal femininity (Dahl, 2015; Hoskin, 2017; Lazar, 2006; McCann, 2018). However, adhering to feminist politics of feminine respectability will not erase the inescapable powerlessness that accompanies powerful experiences and practices of femininity nor will it undermine patriarchal oppression. This is illustrated in the ways that feminised bodies are constantly consumed by others. Feeling authoritative and powerful does not prevent me from being harassed on the street while I walk to work or from being touched without my consent in public. My high heels end up in my teaching evaluations instead of, or alongside, actual commentary on my pedagogy. These experiences of powerlessness and powerfulness are co-constitutive. As a result, to be feminine is to be (made) vulnerable, consumable, touchable, criticise-able; it is to be (made) powerless, no matter how feminist you are or how powerful you feel in your femininity (Dahl, 2016; Hoskin, 2019a, 2019b, 2020; McCann, 2018; Piepzna-Samarashina, 2015; Scott, 2019).

Limitations and future research

Given that this piece draws upon autoethnographic data, the 'sweaty moments' outlined here are non-universalizable and future research is needed to continue investigating the nuances of the various embodied experiences of feminine-of-centre feminists in balancing femininity and feminism. Furthermore, my argument for moving towards feminine acceptance within feminism should be understood as a preliminary step, particularly with regards to eliminating masculinism within feminism. For example, recognising that powerlessness and powerfulness are inseparable is not a call to get rid of power. Indeed, that would be both impossible and would further obfuscate that it is the masculinisation of power through the valorisation of powerfulness and the rejection of powerlessness that contributes to the rejection of femininity.

Discussion

Simultaneously embracing both powerfulness and powerlessness is a key step in moving towards a feminist acceptance framework for femininity. Continuing to require justification for femininity is a form of in/out-group discrimination that relies upon the notion that femininity is negative and must adhere to a recuperation framework in order to be (partially) acceptable (Barton & Huebner, 2020; Dahl, 2015; Hoskin, 2020; McCann, 2018, 2020; Scott, 2019; Serano, 2007). One step towards realising the goal of an acceptance framework is to reckon with the fact that femininity has long been considered a tool of the patriarchy within feminism in a way that, strikingly, masculinity has not (Dahl, 2012; Hoskin, 2020; McCann, 2018; Scott, 2019). As Hoskin and Taylor (2019) argue, ' ... perhaps, femininity was never the master's tool after all' (p. 15). If masculine-of-centre feminists are not automatically mindless dupes of the patriarchy even when inhabiting normative masculinity then, perhaps, neither are feminine-of-centre feminists.

Conclusion: moving towards acceptance

To embrace both powerfulness and powerlessness means recognising that perfect, feminist femininity, according to existing masculinist paradigms, does not exist because powerlessness cannot be eradicated. It also means recognising that adhering to the feminist politics of feminine respectability will never allow feminine-of-centre folx to fully escape or single-handedly undermine institutional systems of oppression. Rather than prescribing what feminist femininity can or should be and becoming preoccupied with the individual choices feminine-of-centre feminists make, feminism can more fully recognise that all feminists, regardless of our gender identities and expressions, are negotiating within these systems. Through an acceptance framework, it becomes clearer that all feminists are making calculations in their attempts to carve out space for embodied joy while simultaneously existing within a patriarchal culture designed to steal the possibility of joy from embodiment. The implementation of an acceptance framework within feminism, therefore, offers a preliminary step towards realising a more inclusive feminist future disinvested from masculinism by more fully recognising that experiences of power include powerlessness, and that feminised experiences are not only unavoidable but valuable.

Notes

1. Patriarchal oppression is used to signal interlocking and co-constitutive forms of oppression including, but not limited to, sexism, heterosexism, ableism, racism, classism, colonialism, sizeism, and ageism. Patriarchal femininity and hegemonic masculinity signal coercive gender expectations that support these systems. See Hoskin (2019b) and McCann (2020) for elaboration.
2. This has propped up neoliberal critiques of femininity that contribute to recuperation frameworks (see McCann, 2018, 2020).
3. I maintain a feminine/masculine dichotomy due to the overall masculinisation of androgyny and gender-neutrality (Barton & Huebner, 2020; Scott, 2019; Serano, 2007) and the pushback, hostility, and even violence that trans, nonbinary, and gender non-conforming individuals describe when living betwixt feminine-of-centre and masculine-of-centre expectations (Hoskin, 2019b, 2020; LeMaster et al., 2019), both of which demonstrate the theoretical and practical non-neutrality between femininity and masculinity.
4. Certainly there have been different theoretical treatments of femininity within various forms of feminism (see Dahl, 2012; Hemmings, 2011). However, these theoretical differences do not appear to be translating into markedly different generational differences in the lived tensions between femininity and feminism as associated with various forms of feminism. Additional research is needed to determine a broader range of feminine-of-centre feminist experiences including the role of the recuperation framework within transnational contexts.
5. The recuperation framework represents a masculinist value system within feminism because it leaves uninterrogated the overall negativity associated with femininity. This devaluation of femininity within feminism, including blaming femininity for experiences of sexist discrimination, is in line with masculinist logics addressed by Hoskin (2020) and Serano (2007).

Disclosure statement

No potential conflict of interest was reported by the author.

References

Adams, T., & Herrmann, A. (2020). Expanding our autoethnographic future. *Journal of Autoethnography*, *1*(1), 1–8. https://doi.org/10.1525/joae.2020.1.1.1
Ahmed, S. (2006). *Queer phenomenology: Orientations, objects, others*. Duke University Press.
Ahmed, S. (2017). *Living a feminist life*. Duke University Press.
Albrecht-Samarasinha, L. L. (2014). On being a bisexual femme. In L. Harris & E. Crocker (Eds.), *Femme: Feminists, lesbians, and bad girls* (pp. 138–144). Routledge.
Barton, B., & Huebner, L. (2020). Feminine power: A new articulation. *Psychology & Sexuality*, 1–10. https://doi.org/10.1080/19419899.2020.1771408
Berger, M. T., & Radeloff, C. (2015). *Transforming scholarship: Why women's and gender studies students are changing themselves and the world* (2 ed.). Routledge.
Boden, S. (2003). *Consumerism, romance, and the wedding experience*. Palgrave Macmillan.

Dahl, U. (2011). Femme on femme: Reflections on collaborative methods and queer femme-inist ethnography. *SQS-Journal of Queer Studies in Finland, 5*(1), 1–22. https://doi.org/https://journal.fi/sqs/article/view/50871

Dahl, U. (2012). Turning like a femme: Figuring critical femininity studies. *NORA-Nordic Journal of Feminist and Gender Research, 20*(1), 57–64. https://doi.org/10.1080/08038740.2011.650708

Dahl, U. (2015). Sexism: A femme-inist perspective. *New Formations: A Journal of Culture/Theory/Politics, 86*, 54–73. https://doi.org/https://www.mjuse.jhu.edu/article/604489

Dahl, U. (2016). Femmebodiment: Notes on queer feminine shapes of vulnerability. *Feminist Theory, 18*(3), 35–53. https://doi.org/10.1177/1464700116683902

Gardiner, J. K. (2002). *Masculinity studies & feminist theory.* Columbia University Press.

Gay, R. (2014). *Bad feminist.* Harper Perennial.

Halberstam, J. (1998). *Female masculinity.* Duke University Press.

Hemmings, C. (2011). *Why stories matter: The political grammar of feminist theory.* Duke University Press.

Hooks, B. (2015). *Feminism is for everybody: Passionate politics* (2 ed.). Routledge.

Hoskin, R. A. (2017). Femme interventions and the proper feminist subject: Critical approaches to decolonizing western feminist pedagogies. *Cogent Social Sciences, 3*(1). https://doi.org/10.1080/23311886.2016.1276819

Hoskin, R. A. (2019a). Can femme be theory? Exploring the epistemological and methodological possibilities of femme. *Journal of Lesbian Studies, 25*(1), 1–17. https://doi.org/10.1080/10894160.2019.1702288

Hoskin, R. A. (2019b). Femmephobia: The role of anti-femininity and gender policing in LGBTQ+ experiences of discrimination. *Sex Roles, 81*, 686–703. https://doi.org/10.1007/s11199-019-01021-3

Hoskin, R. A. (2020). 'Femininity? It's the aesthetic of subordination:' Examining femmephobia, the gender binary, and experiences of oppression among sexual and gender minorities. *Archives of Sexual Behavior, 49*, 2319–2339. https://doi.org/10.1007/s10508-020-01641-x

Hoskin, R. A., & Taylor, A. (2019). Femme resistance: The fem(me)inine art of failure. *Psychology & Sexuality, 10*(4), 281–300. https://doi.org/10.1080/19419899.2019.1615538

Lazar, M. M. (2006). 'Discover the power of femininity!' Analyzing global 'power femininity' in local advertising. *Feminist Media Studies, 6*(4), 505–517. https://doi.org/10.1080/14680770600990002

LeMaster, B., Shultz, D., McNeill, J., Bowers, G., & Rust, R. (2019). Unlearning cisheteronormativity at the intersections of difference: Performing queer worldmaking through collaged relational autoethnography. *Text and Performance Quarterly, 39*(4), 341–370. https://doi.org/10.1080/10462937.2019.1672885

McCann, H. (2018). *Queering femininity: Sexuality, feminism and the politics of presentation.* Routledge.

McCann, H. (2020). Is there anything 'toxic' about femininity? The rigid femininities that keep us locked in. *Psychology & Sexuality.* https://doi.org/10.1080/19419899.2020.1785534

Pascoe, C. J. (2011). *Dude, you're a fag: Masculinity and sexuality in high school.* (2 ed.). University of California Press.

Piepzna-Samarashina, L. L. (2015). *Dirty river: A queer femme of color dreaming her way home.* Arsenal Pulp Press.

Pitcan, M., Marwick, A. E., & Boyd, D. (2018). Performing a vanilla self: Respectability politics, social class, and the digital world. *Journal of Computer-Mediated Communication, 23*(3), 163–179. https://doi.org/10.1093/jcmc/zmy008

Schippers, M. (2007). Recovering the feminine other: Masculinity, femininity, and gender hegemony. *Theory and Society, 36*(1), 85–102. www.jstor.org/stable/4501776

Schwartz, A. (2018). Low femme. *Feral Feminisms, 7*, 5–14. https://feralfeminisms.com/low-femme/

Scott, J. B. (2019). What do glitter, pointe shoes, & plastic drumsticks have in common? Using femme theory to consider the reclamation of disciplinary beauty/body practices. *Journal of Lesbian Studies, 25*(1), 36–52. https://doi.org/10.1080/10894160.2019.1689329

Serano, J. (2007). *Whipping girl: A transsexual woman on sexism and the scapegoating of femininity.* Seal Press.

Stelly, A. (2009). Transition. In J. C. Burke (Ed.), *Visible: A femmethology* (Vol. 1, pp. 21–22). Homofactus Press, L.L.C.

Story, K. A. (2017). Fear of a black femme: The existential conundrum of embodying a black femme identity while being a professor of black, queer, and feminist studies. *Journal of Lesbian Studies, 21*(4), 407–419. https://doi.org/10.1080/10894160.2016.1165043

Tong, R., & Botts, T. (2017). *Feminist thought: A more comprehensive introduction* (5 ed.). Routledge.

Radical vulnerability: selfies as a Femme-inine mode of resistance

Andi Schwartz ⓘ

ABSTRACT
In Western philosophy, vulnerability and femininity have been positioned as subordinate and weak. Reparative readings of selfies can offer a way to reclaim both vulnerability and femininity as generative, connective, and political. In this paper, I examine femme selfies collected during an online ethnography of femme Internet culture on Instagram. I draw from critical feminist scholarship on vulnerability and reparative readings of selfies to argue that selfies are a practice in vulnerability, and therefore a mode of embracing the feminine and feminine resistance. Using visual discourse analysis to read the selected selfies, I argue that femmes strategically mobilise vulnerability via selfies to (re)shape femme identity, create femme communities, and to make political claims about femme lives.

Introduction

The term "selfie' first appeared in 2002 on an Australian online forum (Murray, 2015, p. 491). In the simplest terms, a selfie is a self-portrait taken in the technocultural context of smartphones and social media platforms. Meese et al. (2015) argue the selfie is further defined by stylistic conventions including: the conflation of subject and photographer, the subject's domination of the foreground, and the use of high angles. What these descriptive definitions of 'selfie' do not reveal, however, is the cultural value and meaning of selfies; selfies themselves rarely receive such neutral treatment. Some differentiate between a selfie and a self-portrait, going so far as to say that selfies stigmatise self-portraiture (Murray, 2015). Selfies are often considered an expression of narcissism and are pathologized as a result (Senft & Baym, 2015). Perhaps unsurprisingly, the judgement of selfies is also gendered. The combination of selfies' association with young women and the cultural devaluation of young women perpetuates the negative perception of both in an endless cycle: women are narcissistic because they take selfies, selfies are narcissistic because women take them (Maddox, 2017). In this article, I follow existing scholarship on selfies to offer a reparative reading[1] of femme selfies, positioning them as both a representational tool and a communicative act. I argue that selfies are a practice in vulnerability, a practice that is strategically mobilised by femmes to (re)shape femme identity, create femme communities, and to make political claims about femme lives.

I define 'femme' as a queer identity marked by a critical engagement with femininity that manifests in one's style and values. Femme has origins in the lesbian bar culture of the 1940s (Nestle, 1992), as well as in the drag and ball scene that started in Harlem in the 1960s (Bailey, 2014). Femme has been conceptualised many ways, including as a queer and subversive gender (Brushwood Rose & Camilleri, 2002; Dawson, 2017; Duggan & McHugh, 1996; Hollibaugh, 2000), a site or mode of queer and feminist resistance (Dahl, 2012; Galewski, 2005; Hemmings, 1999; Hoskin & Taylor, 2019; S. F. Lewis, 2012), a source of pleasure and healing (Cvetkovich, 2003; McCann, 2018;

Nestle, 1987; Tinsley, 2018) and as a producer of culture (Brightwell & Taylor, 2019; Cheng, 2019; Connell, 2012; Schwartz, 2016, 2018a, 2018b). Significant for this paper is femme's link to vulnerability.

My understanding of vulnerability is informed by Mackenzie et al. (2013) taxonomy of vulnerability and Petherbridge's (2016) parsing out of vulnerability as constituted by corporeal openness, psychological openness, and an openness to the other. Femme vulnerability has been theorised in similar ways. Femme's corporeal openness (or vulnerability) has been discussed via femme sexuality, sometimes described as surrendering control to the other (Hollibaugh & Moraga, 1992), or as a 'hunger,' that must be enacted with careful consideration (Albrecht-Samarasinha, 1997). Femme's psychological openness has also been understood through sexuality, such as in Cvetkovich's (2003) theorisation of butch/femme sexuality as site of healing from psychological trauma. Femme's openness to the other has been theorised through the desire for platonic femme intimacies, or a desire to belong to a community of femmes (Dahl, 2017; McCann, 2018). I further link femme to vulnerability by considering the ties both have to femininity.

Vulnerability is feminised in Western culture (Mackenzie et al., 2013) and, like all other feminised objects and subjects – including femmes – is often dismissed and discounted. The corporeal dimension of vulnerability is often seen as the potential for experiencing injury or harm and, obviously, resisted. Bodily needs and the body itself are associated with the feminine in Western culture. This stems from the Cartesian mind/body binary, or the idea that, in its superiority, the mind can (and should) conquer the body. Along with rationality, masculinist Western ideology favours independence, and thus the psychological and social aspects of vulnerability (that is, that one is made vulnerable by their social human needs) are necessarily repressed to construct an autonomous, independent self (Mackenzie et al., 2013). Expressing emotions or the desire for interdependence is then understood in terms of pathology and becomes feminised (for example, 'crazy,' 'clingy,' or 'needy').

As feminine subjects, femmes experience a similar framing in Western culture and are subsequently subject to femmephobia. Hoskin (2017) has defined femmephobia as a prejudice, discrimination, or antagonism against someone who is perceived to identify with, embody, or express femininity. This also extends to objects that are gendered femininely (Hoskin, 2017). Femmephobia plays out in a number of ways against femmes. In mainstream culture, femmes receive the same treatment as other feminine people: they are subjected to sexism and misogyny; face discrimination, harassment, and violence; and are seen as vapid, frivolous, and the property of men. In queer culture, the same attitudes towards femininity and feminine people apply, but femmes are also seen as suspect, as not really queer, or not queer enough (Blair & Hoskin, 2015; Brightwell, 2017; Hemmings, 1999). According to Brightwell (2017), queer culture and theory has been defined through antinormativity. Androgyny has been seen as resistant, subversive, and political, whereas femininity has been viewed as antifeminist (Brightwell, 2017). This has meant that femininity is not coded as queer through the discourse of antinormativity. Further, Hoskin (2017) has argued that the devaluation of femininity has meant that femmephobia is excluded from oppression discourse, including intersectionality. In sum, femmes are marginalised in mainstream, feminist, and queer cultures. Mapping femmes' subordinate position is essential for understanding why selfies are a meaningful tool of representation. In this context of femmephobia, self-representation becomes essential for re-writing the negative narratives and images of femmes. Following existing scholarship, this essential self-representation can be achieved through selfies.

Scholars like Murray (2015) and Pham (2015) situate selfies within discussions of art and resistance to argue that taking selfies are one way that marginalised communities do the political work of representation. While young women are called narcissistic for taking selfies, they often see their selfies as empowering and as a radical act of resistance in a male-dominated culture (Murray, 2015). Murray (2015) considers the overarching patriarchal context to argue that young women's selfies can be seen as an 'aggressive reclaiming of the female body' and a 'radical colonization of the digital realm' (p. 490). Murray reads selfies as a postfeminist self-representational strategy. Like Murray

(2015) and Pham (2015) situates selfies in feminist politics, particularly the women-of-colour feminist perspective that political movements are informed by embodied experiences and 'situated knowledges' (p. 224). She acknowledges that selfies are a practice in vanity, albeit *networked* vanity, meaning that while vanity serves an individual's social needs, it is also strategically deployed to build social and political movements. Following these scholars, I argue that selfies are a mode of femme representation. In particular, I argue that, via selfies, femmes strategically mobilise the feminised concept of vulnerability to assert their own femme narratives.

In taking, posting, and sharing selfies, femmes make themselves vulnerable by laying bare not only their faces and bodies (demonstrating corporeal openness), but their experiences and emotions, too (demonstrating psychological openness). Analysing how femmes' bodies are adorned and presented in selfies, as well as which experiences and emotions are shared through selfie captions, enables a discussion of femme aesthetics and politics. Analysing femme selfies through these frameworks of vulnerability leads me to argue that femmes utilise what have been called sources of vulnerability in Western culture (that is, bodies and emotions) to define femme aesthetics, form femme connections, and articulate femme politics through selfies. My argument, then, is that vulnerability is one of the critical axes of femme internet culture. As noted above, vulnerability has long been a fundamental aspect of femme subjectivity, and its overt recuperation is gaining new momentum in contemporary femme culture.

Method

For this research, I conducted a six month online ethnography of femme internet culture on Instagram. Ethnography is characterised by long engagements with a research field and long relationships with research participants (Buch & Staller, 2014) and this traditional method has been adapted for an online context, retaining the foundational principles of immersing oneself in a culture for an extended period of time and recording one's observations about the daily practice and values that are gleaned from participant observation (Hine, 2017). This research was approved by the Office of Research Ethics at York University. I created a public researcher account and declared my intention to use the account to research femme internet culture through both the account's description and by making an introductory post. I included my email and a link to my personal Instagram account for the sake of transparency and accountability, which I saw as an important component of building trust with my participants.

I followed other femme accounts that I located through searching #femme hashtags and a snowball method of finding femme accounts through other femmes (Dahl, 2011). I sought to follow a diverse array of femme Instagram accounts, and looked specifically for femme accounts that focused on intersecting marginalised identities, like racialisation, disability, fatness, and, trans gender identities. As a participant-observer, I posted on my researcher Instagram account, followed other accounts, liked and occasionally commented on other posts, chatted with other users using the Direct Message (DM) function, and eventually set up formal interviews. Building rapport with participants is a critical aspect of ethnography (Buch & Staller, 2014; Dahl, 2011), so participating in femme internet culture in these ways was important to me and my method. Over the course of my fieldwork, I made four posts, acquired 79 followers, and followed 114 users.

I made notes on my observations, took screen captures of relevant posts, and interviewed seven femme Instagram account operators. I did not ask my interviewees to describe their social/cultural identities – apart from explaining their relationship to femme – but, of course, these social/cultural identities came up throughout the interviews and in their online activity. Of my seven interviewees, one was straight and six were queer (two also used the term 'lesbian' in addition to 'queer'); four were white (three of whom had ties to specific white ethnic identities, such as Italian), two were Black, and one was mixed race (Black and Latinx); four were cis women, one was a trans woman, and two were non-binary (none identified as men); two did not mention mental illness or other disability and five talked openly about their disabilities and mental health struggles; five did not mention their body size and two self-described as fat. In what follows, I examine a selection of femme selfies collected during my study to draw out the specifics of contemporary femme aesthetics, and the politics behind them. Some of the selfies discussed were taken and posted by femmes I interviewed, and all selfies are used with permission.

Privacy is one major ethical hurdle in online research. It is possible to conceptualise content posted and conversations conducted online as public, and therefore, 'fair game' for researchers. However, online researchers have developed more nuanced guidelines to navigate internet privacy. Eynon et al. (2017) emphasise being sensitive to the values, aims, and expectations of privacy in the specific online context of study. Though users may not use technological means (for example, passwords and other privacy settings) to keep their posts and conversations hidden, this does not necessarily negate the expectation of privacy. In contexts where there is a higher expectation of privacy, the more like human subjects the online representations should be treated (as opposed to treated as texts); conversely, the more public the online representations and expressions are, the more the posters and posts can be treated as authors and texts, rather than as human subjects. Lee et al. (2017) advise seeking informed consent in instances of high expectations of privacy. I followed Dahl's (2011) femme-inist ethnography methodology that conceives of participants as co-producers of theory and adds the third version of 'citing' to the feminist ethnographic principles of 'siting' and 'sighting' (Dahl, 2011, p. 10), so my approach is more in line with treating online representations as authors and texts. However, I still asked for permission to use specific selfies in my analysis.

Data analysis

To frame this study, I followed Hine's (2017) method for online ethnography. Since the online world is a central site of human experience now, conducting ethnography online is seen as legitimate and necessary (Hine, 2017). According to Hine (2017), there are three general approaches to online ethnography, the most current being a 'multimodal approach,' which contextualises the online world within the offline world, and considers the internet as more than just as a textual media. First, framing my study of femme Instagram and specifically femme selfies as significant can only be achieved when following Hine (2017) and contextualising these visual texts in an offline world or social context that is masculinist, white supremacist, and colonial (among other things); only then can narratives that counter femmephobia, for example, be understood as vital. Secondly, Hine's (2017) multimodal approach is particularly apt for studying Instagram, a platform that is both textual and visual.

To adequately analyse the content produced on Instagram, I also draw from visual discourse analysis as outlined by Traue et al. (2018). Traue et al. (2018) call for a mode of analysing images that considers semiotics as well as principles of design, as images are part of an interdiscursive world. They propose an approach they call sociology with the image, an approach that seeks to resist both logocentrism (the primacy of language) and iconocentrism (the primacy of images). They see the image as a cultural product worth understanding on its own, but also insist on the importance of studying the process of producing the image, and considering how the image then produces society. Visual discourse analysis, as it is rooted in a Foucauldian understanding of discourse, is concerned with issues of power; Traue et al. (2018) consider what is 'visible' in an image is determined by existing social discourse. In this framing, 'visibility' is akin to 'sayability' (Traue et al., 2018, p. 329), meaning it is intelligible and legitimate.

I have found this approach critical for engaging with femme selfies on Instagram. Disregarding the captions of the selfies would mean disregarding femmes' own framing of their selfies, risking the misinterpretation of the images and, thus, undoing the important work of self-representation. Considering the text alongside images, especially the use of the #femme hashtag and other identifications like 'nonbinary,' are imperative for resisting the impulse to extend normative readings of femininity to the category of femme. Without these explicit textual claims to femme and other categories, my own assumptions of what a femme looks like would take precedence and alter the present sample. Relatedly, the images along with the text are crucial for illustrating the gender and racial variance within the femme category, which became instrumental to one of my key arguments around visibility and vulnerability, which I will discuss below.

Results and discussion

My findings are organised around corporeal vulnerability, psychological and social vulnerability, and the political potential of vulnerability. In my discussion of corporeal vulnerability, I explore the connection between vulnerability and visibility in femme Instagram culture. I find that femmes use selfies to illustrate femme aesthetics – close readings of which offer insight into what 'femme' means. In my discussion of psychological and social vulnerability, I explore the vulnerability expressed through sharing feelings, especially negative ones, and receiving emotional support on Instagram. I see selfies circulating in femme internet culture as a common way to make oneself vulnerable and to share this vulnerability with others. Finally, I explore how corporeal, psychological, and social vulnerability are used to theorise femme lives and make political claims on Instagram. I argue that femme selfies are a practice in vulnerability – vulnerability that is engaged strategically and politically mobilised.

Vulnerability and visibility: Femme selfie aesthetics

My results reveal that femmes often used selfies to show off their outfit or make-up of the day. Posts like these signal what can be understood as vulnerable about selfies: if vulnerability is understood to stem from the body, and all vulnerability is experienced in the body (Mackenzie et al., 2013), then displaying and drawing attention to the body in such deliberate ways is, I argue, a mode of mobilising vulnerability.

Feminist scholars have drawn a complex and often ambivalent portrait of vulnerability by weighing its limitations as well as strengths (Dahl, 2017; R. A. Lewis, 2016; Petherbridge, 2016). As noted above, vulnerability has been a critical component in theorising femme sexual agency (Albrecht-Samarasinha, 1997; Hollibaugh & Moraga, 1992) and femme attachments (Dahl, 2017; McCann, 2018). For femmes, vulnerability is made further ambivalent and fraught when it is tied to visibility, as it inevitably is. While femmes' queerness is often rendered invisible, femininity is also hypervisible and, therefore, hyperregulated (see for example, S. F. Lewis, 2012; McCann, 2018). Non-normative embodiments of femininity carry an increased risk of surveillance and regulation, as do feminine bodies that are read as racialised, disabled, trans, fat, or working-class. This is to say that while the vulnerability of selfies is a tool for increasing femme visibility and is often deployed in the politics of representation, visibility can make femmes vulnerable in undesirable and unintentional ways. While some, like femme scholar McCann (2018), consider representation to be politically limiting (that is, relating to interpersonal issues rather than broader issues of injustice), considering femmes' social positioning means recognising that the vulnerability offered by visibility is an important means of connection where femmes perhaps have too few. At the same time, embodying or performing vulnerability is not always a choice, and does not always result in finding a supportive community. Visibility is tricky. Like vulnerability, it is not experienced equally, but remains a fraught and ambivalent category.

The urgency around femme visibility is heightened for femmes of colour, who are paradoxically both invisible as femmes and hypervisible as racialised subjects (S. F. Lewis, 2012; Hill, 2017; Story, 2017). Even to a queer eye, femmes of colour may not read as such; femme is often imagined as a white category because of its visual references to normative femininity, which are coded as white. Black feminists have long argued that Black women have been positioned outside of womanhood or femininity. The famous speech delivered in 1851 by Sojourner Truth and Davis (1981) parsing out of Victorian womanhood demonstrate that vulnerability has long been central to constructing white women as delicate and precious, and Black women as strong, aggressive, and angry. hooks (1981) and Collins (2004) have further unpacked this 'Strong Black Woman' stereotype, which functioned to justify Black women's enslavement in North America and still works to masculinise and dehumanise Black women today. More recently, S. F. Lewis (2012) has argued that Black women's bodies are continually queered by racist discourse, as well as by discourse of racial and class respectability. Hill (2017) has also argued that Black bodies are automatically read as queer, a reading that has often elided her actual lesbian sexual identity. She wrote, 'my queer performance and lesbian identity is in actuality what [my students] deem a typical performance of Black femininity. Accordingly, the compounding of race and gender render Black femininity a queer and already non-normative representation of femininity' (Hill, 2017, p. 436). The implication of this mapping of gender, race, and sexuality is that white women are seen as 'unmarked' or normative while Black women are marked as queer, further implying that femininity is always already white, and white femme-ininity reads as 'unmarked' or normative – in other words, straight – in cisgender women.

One of the femmes in my study frequently uses selfies to discuss the complications of visibility as a nonbinary femme of colour. On, Trans Day of Visibility, they posted a selfie that demonstrates the common femme aesthetic of pulling from both the traditionally masculine and traditionally feminine (Cheng, 2019; Nicholson, 2014). The photo showed this femme dressed in a hot pink and teal floral-patterned jacket, which lays open to reveal chest hair. One hand fluffed their curly, pastel-pink hair, and they are further adorned with pastel purple lipstick, a nose piercing, and dangling earrings. Accompanying this selfie is this caption:

> today is, trans day of visibility #TDOV ! & I just want to thank all of the good lighting i have found this past year for allowing me to gift the world such exquisite & masterful selfies!!! representation is hard work! every day gender non-conforming people are putting ourselves at grave risk with little to no concern for our safety & dignity. we are constantly punished & ridiculed for being ourselves, and yet we still persist! this world is trying its best to disappear us, but bitch i am still here living my best transgenderly life taking my multivitamins & pulling looks!!! take that!!! #trans #nonbinary #queer #girlslikeus

The overt identification as a gender non-conforming person works to, importantly, insert racialised, genderqueer or nonbinary subjects into the category of femme. Laying claim to the femme identity as a trans person makes it possible for other trans people to do so, pushing the boundaries of femme wide enough to include trans, genderqueer, and nonbinary people. While this conceptualisation of femme seems to be largely accepted, it does signal a transformation, or at least shift, from the dominant understanding of femme as a lesbian identity, especially that embodied by cis women. While many other queer women who do not identify as lesbian, as well as men and nonbinary queers, have laid claim to the femme identity since at least the 1990s, debates about whether non-lesbians are welcome under this categorical umbrella continue in contemporary forums like Tumblr. The caption also refers to the complexity and sometimes precarity of visibility. While this bright, genderqueer ensemble works to (re)shape femme aesthetics and the category of femme itself, this aesthetic has also seemed to invite discrimination, harassment, and violence from a cissexist, transphobic, racist, and femmephobic public. Here, visibility as a gender non-conforming femme of colour creates a kind of vulnerability that is undesirable, that demonstrates the actual danger, violence, and wounding that is a risk of living in a human body – especially a non-normative one. This femme's response is informed by contemporary femme Internet politics, as they take up the practice of sharing their vulnerabilities with their audience of followers, thus making them public.

This femme makes themself vulnerable by naming the violence they endure, but also employs a flippant, flamboyant attitude, like when they 'thank all of the good lighting i have found this past year for allowing me to gift the world such exquisite & masterful selfies!!!' Celebrating the transfeminine body in this way while simultaneously naming the violence it endures is both an act of femme representation and a way of transforming vulnerability into an act of resistance to transphobia, cisnormativity, racism, and femmephobia (especially as they explicitly attribute this violence to cissexism and transphobia). This political act utilises the feminist strategy of laying bare one's body and lived experiences, and connecting these experiences to larger social systems. It is by connecting individual experiences to systemic oppression that selfies become political. Otherwise, expressive practices like art therapy or consciousness raising are limited, embodying what Cloud (1998) calls the therapeutic: 'a set of political and cultural discourses that have adopted psychotherapy's lexicon – the conservative language of healing, coping, adaptation, and restoration of a previously existing social order – but in contexts of sociopolitical conflict' (p. xiv). The function of this rhetoric, according to Cloud, is to encourage individuals to focus on their private lives rather than on reforming systems of power (Cloud, 1998, p. xiv). The political analysis of the selfie presented here certainly goes beyond the personal to connect individual experiences with structures of power. This femme further politicises their selfie as they explicitly refer to the representational work the selfie does to hopefully, ultimately combat this oppression, and acknowledges both the importance and difficulty of this work in the current cultural climate. It is clear that femmes are wise to the representational potential of selfies, and are savvy enough to use selfies as a political platform. Here, aesthetics are not neutral but rather signal belonging within the category of femme, as well as within society more broadly.

The femme selfie aesthetic outlined here can be read as constituting a femme gaze, similar to the female gaze identified in post-feminist selfies by Murray (2015). In post-feminist selfies, Murray found that young women use nude, revealing, or sexualised images of their bodies to challenge sexism and represent women's perspectives and feminist concerns. If, as Murray interprets, post-feminist selfie aesthetics can be understood as re-appropriating a symbol or form often used to perpetuate women's oppression – women's objectified bodies – then posting a celebratory, appreciative image of a transfeminine body while overtly challenging cissexism, transphobia, and femmephobia can be read as similarly flipping or challenging the gaze which objectifies femme bodies, here specifically a nonbinary, femme of colour body. We can then read selfies posted by femmes that challenge femmephobia through a combination of politicised rhetoric of vulnerability and brazenly feminine figures as constituting a critical femme gaze: an aesthetic sensibility derived from con-temporary femme politics.[2]

Feeling and 'Lqqking'[3]: Soft Femme Aesthetics

While femme is an aesthetic identity category, it is arguably also an affective one, one based on feeling.[4] Aesthetics and feelings often become intertwined. For example, Dahl (2014) examines the 'feeling of vintage' in femme movements. Femme is further conceptualised as an affective category, one structured by feelings and attachments. McCann (2018), for example, is critical of the focus in femme scholarship on representation, agency and resistance, and aims instead to consider femme as sensate, pleasurable, and capacitating. Elsewhere Dahl (2017) argues that the femme is understood as not only marked by a feminine aesthetic but by an orientation towards some objects and bodies and not others, mirroring Duggan and McHugh (1996) claim that femme only desires queer masculinities. Femme is known for its affective attachments, be they vintage clothes, mascara wands, or butch lesbians.

Not only is femme partially constituted by the shared experience of vulnerability – corporeal and psychological – but femme Internet culture is constituted by sharing these vulnerabilities with each other through selfies. Several scholars say a critical aspect of selfies is that they are shared on social media (Maddox, 2017; Meese et al., 2015). Being social, seeking belonging and acceptance, like femmes do through posting selfies and tagging them as 'femme,' are ways in which they are rendered vulnerable (Dahl, 2017). It follows, then, that selfies are already premised on, not only the vulnerability of exposing the body, but the vulnerability of desiring and seeking sociality and other forms of interdependence. Selfies that communicate femme feelings reveal multiple types of vulnerability – physical, social, and psychological – and do so productively and, I argue, strategically. Like the connection femmes have often found in butch-femme relationships,[5] sharing one's vulner-abilities has proven to forge much-needed connections online. In particular, crying selfies are useful tools to forge femme connections.

Crying selfies fit the definition of selfies as outlined by Meese et al. (2015) with the major exception that the subject of the photograph is crying or has been crying recently. Like funeral selfies, crying selfies may be considered a 'debased' form of the selfie, as they are capturing an unhappy moment, one many would say is inappropriate or narcissistic to capture (Meese et al., 2015). Nonetheless, crying selfies are increasingly common. One white, nonbinary femme in my study often posts crying selfies, marked by visual signifiers like smeared eye make-up and visible tears. The caption on crying selfies will often provide clues as to why the subject is crying: for example, in the caption of one of their crying selfies, this femme wrote 'today's lqqk/things have gotten violent at home again (i need to survive another week before i leave)/lots of public crying 2day #radicalvulner-ability #crybaby #sensitive #softfemme #femmemagic #publiccrying.' Meese et al. (2015) argue that 'selfies often function as communication and are in fact communicating important affective informa-tion about a person's emotional circumstances' (Meese et al., 2015, p. 1825). Indeed, this femme uses a selfie to communicate with their followers the particular difficulties of their current context, including the negative affects they are experiencing. In turn, the crying selfie signals to this femme's followers that the user is in need of emotional support, and offers an opportunity to provide it.

In a study of death and digital media, Internet researchers Lagerkvist and Andersson (2017) find that social media becomes a 'lifeline' for many after they experience significant illness or the death of a loved one. They see the selfie as 'a gestural economy of affection': for example, the hospital selfie offers a way to elicit encouraging messages from others (Lagerkvist & Andersson, 2017, p. 558). Conceptualising the selfie as a gestural economy of affection is useful for theorising crying selfies. The crying selfie in discussion prompted 33 likes and two comments, containing many emojis.

The crying selfie also functions as an indication of a soft femme politic and aesthetic, and highlights the strategic use of vulnerability in femme internet culture. In this post, the femme, perhaps ironically, refers to their crying image as 'today's lqqk' (look) and uses the hashtag #soft-femme, indicating that posting a crying selfie is an aesthetic choice, part of a 'soft femme' aesthetic that stands in contrast to 'hard femme.' The hashtags #radicalvulnerability #femmemagic and #publiccrying indicate how being vulnerable or open with others about one's negative feelings is positioned as a radical act that disrupts the status quo.[6] The deliberate framing of the crying selfie as radical and disruptive suggests that posting one's crying image is a *political* choice as well as an aesthetic one – a political choice intended to challenge the myth of the autonomous, independent adult subject.

Feminist theorising of vulnerability enables us to think of the crying selfie as demonstrating a universal interdependence, an emotional neediness; it gestures to others that their encouragement and support is needed, that they are needed. While documenting and sharing distressing moments on social media has been pathologized (Meese et al., 2015) and can call into question the authen-ticity of such emotional displays,[7] I see the conscious and deliberate performance of this type of vulnerability as evidence of femmes' Internet savvy. Through selfies, particularly the crying selfie, femmes transform what is understood as vulnerable (that is, the body, emotions) – and therefore negative – into something empowering, connective, and productive. The crying selfie becomes a medium through which social and psychological needs can be met. The crying selfie reveals femme to be an aesthetic and affective category, as also articulated through the femme scholarship cited above. Further, the crying selfies demonstrate that vulnerability is the very basis of femme Internet culture: it shapes the aesthetic, the politics, and the network itself.

Selfies as Femme-inist theory

Bost (2008) uses the term 'shared vulnerability' to argue that bonding over shared corporeal boundary states, like illness, may build more powerful alliances than identity politics can offer. Bost's work enables a reading of vulnerability as political as well as aesthetic and affective. If vulnerability is political, and selfies are inherently vulnerable (through their use of bodies and emotions, and their mobilisation towards interpersonal connections), then selfies, too, can be read as political. And, since I read selfies as deeply connected to the feminine because they are associated with young women and vulnerability, selfies become a promising political tool for femmes. If femme politics are about recuperating the feminine and insisting on its value, then a practice rooted in femininity, like selfies, lends itself easily to furthering femme politics. All iterations of femme have in common a political take on femininity – reclaiming it, deconstructing it, or queering it. This means that in addition to being an aesthetic and affective category, femme is a political category and a mode of political critique, as is also articulated through femme scholarship (Dahl, 2012; Galewski, 2005; Hemmings, 1999; Hoskin & Taylor, 2019; S. F. Lewis, 2012).

In her research on technology's impact on emotional styles, Turkle (2011) has observed that younger generations who have 'grown up tethered' – meaning grown up with the level of connectivity made possible and normalised through mobile devices and social media – will share emotions, usually via text message or social media, before they are fully formed or felt. Previously, this impulse to share would have been interpreted as pathological, but Turkle suspects this is becoming a generational style. Meese et al. (2015) corroborate this observation, noting that social media is increasingly where we go to process our inner thoughts and feelings. Our hyperconnectivity does not enable us to cultivate the ability to be alone and reflect on feelings in private, but rather it enables us to cultivate collaborative selves.

Relatedly, Duggan and McHugh (1996) have said that collaboration is a vital aspect of femme science, further suggesting that collaboration is a decidedly femme-inine approach to understanding both one's self and the world. Selfies (perhaps especially crying selfies) can be read as employing the feminised emotional style enabled by social media: selfies illustrate Turkle (2011) and Meese et al.'s (2015) understanding of social media as a way to collaboratively process or make sense of emotions and experiences. This is how bell hooks understands theorising as well – as 'making sense out of what was happening,' (hooks, 1991, p. 2). Femmes also use selfies and their captions to make sense out of what is happening – to unpack, reflect, and explain recent feelings or experiences. In other words, femmes use selfies to theorise, using personal experiences, images of their bodies or faces, and political analysis. Femme selfies, then, are a feminised mode of knowledge production as well as a form of 'presencing' (meaning inserting oneself into a certain context and sharing that context with others) (Meese et al., 2015), a mode of communication, and a gestural economy of affection.

One femme Instagrammer, burlesque dancer, and arts worker from my study posted a photo of herself and wrote about reflecting on deep and complex conversations about race, art, and navigating life. The black-and-white image shows this femme outside, holding a strong pose against the trunk of a tree. She wears a black cropped tank top and a flowing black skirt, hiked up to reveal the skin of one of her legs. Her gaze passes above and beyond the camera, intentionally looking to the distance with determination and confidence. The caption reads:

Reflecting on the conversation tonight on art, access, vulnerability, black bodies, the spaces we navigate, the construction of always being seen. I am still digesting all the things that were said. And on the beautiful and complicated ways we create, make art and performance and tell stories with our whole selves.

I don't think there are any easy answers. And maybe there never will be. But I am so grateful to be in that space with those brilliant artists. And so inspired by the beauty, resilience and resistance of African, Indigenous, Latinx, Caribbean, South Asian, disabled visionaries. And so comforted and proud of our wild magic that continues in spite of everything.

#storyteller #artheart #storiesmatter #create #vision #shapeshifter #magic #witchlife #selflove #performer #artistlife #creativelife #workingartist #heartwork #healing #crafting #dreams #visioning #thejourney #believe #hearthealing #gottahavefaith #thegodinme #survivorship #thrive"

This post takes up a critical position that recognises marginalised groups' oppression as well as their resilience. Pointing to the history and current reality of resistance and resilience in the face of racism positions this Black femme as vulnerable to the effects of white supremacy, colonisation, and patriarchy. Following the Western understanding of bodies as sites of vulnerability, she also appears vulnerable in the photo, as the skin of her arms and one leg is exposed. However, this vulnerability is matched by strength in her stance and her gaze which seems to look confidently into the future and is thus transformed. She appears strong and hopeful, combining vulnerability and strength through both her words and self image – the very embodiment of resilience. Further, the hashtags used describe art as 'heart work,' as healing, perhaps especially for survivors of colour, demonstrating that this femme accesses multiple vulnerabilities in her work. Accessing vulnerability becomes a strategy through which to theorise, or make sense of (hooks, 1991), the role of art in healing, the material impact of racism, colonisation, and patriarchy, and the resilience and value of racialised and disabled communities. This post also reveals that these ideas (that art can be healing, the notion that racism, colonisation and patriarchy have a material impact, and the insistence that racialised and disabled communities are resilient and valuable) stem, at least partially, from conversations with others, signalling the collaborative nature of this knowledge and the femme-inist politic behind its creation.

This example demonstrates how femmes access vulnerability strategically to create and share knowledge. Following hooks (1991) understanding of theorising as 'making sense out of what was happening,' femmes draws on their own experiences and bodies to make sense of the specificities of the current social context. Using the tools at their disposal – in this case, selfies and Instagram – femmes circulate their theories. This kind of lo-fi and collaborative knowledge production is made possible by the shift to feminine emotional styles that Turkle (2011) witnesses and ascribes to 'growing up tethered,' meaning growing up with the level of connectivity made possible and normalised through mobile devices and social media. Selfies, then, usher in new ways to produce social theory that is rooted in traditionally feminine values and traits, like vulnerability and collaboration.

Limitations and directions for further research

While I have argued that femme selfies are useful to the politics of representation and even go beyond representation to become tools of communication, connection, resistance and theorisation, the limits of both representation and social media should be noted. McCann (2018) notes that framing femme identification or representation as political is only effective when the femme presentation in question challenges dominant norms of femininity. This encourages the dismissal of presentations of femininity that are not perceptively subversive, which has been a noted problem of femme theory (Galewski, 2005; VanNewkirk, 2006; Walker, 2012). Further, she notes the impossibility of representing all femmes adequately, and that debates surrounding representation can lead to interpersonal issues within femme communities rather than strategies for fighting oppression in society more broadly (McCann, 2018).

I have not framed femme selfies solely as a representational tool (they are tools of communication as well), but social media more broadly has been found to be limiting in its political scope. In a study of a fat femme fashion blog, Catherine Connell (2012) found that while the blog was successful in circulating counterdiscourse, it was less successful in unseating hegemonic discourse in a grander sense. The focus on this paper has been on femme Internet culture itself, rather than its effect on larger society, but future studies of femme Internet culture could explore this relationship.

I have argued that femme selfies are practices in vulnerability, meaning that femmes use what is deemed vulnerable (that is, bodies, emotions) to develop connections and circulate counterdiscourse on Instagram. While posting crying selfies, for example, does reveal certain vulnerabilities, it also reveals femmes' Internet savvy. All selfies, but these especially, can be read as performative and intentional. An area of further research may inquire how accessing vulnerability strategically can be read either as authentic or inauthentic. Authenticity online has been a concern since the Internet was invented (Turkle, 1997), and this would serve as a contemporary and nuanced way to return to these debates.

Conclusion

In this paper, I have considered the relationship between femme and vulnerability through a study of selfies. Femme vulnerability has already been theorised through sexuality (Nestle, 1992), psychological trauma (Cvetkovich, 2003), and attachments to others (Dahl, 2017). While it is a consistent aspect of femme subjectivity, the negative properties of vulnerability do not affect all femmes evenly. In fact, vulnerability is experienced very differently for femmes of different races and different gender identities, a social fact that alters how each femme strategically accesses vulnerability.

I have argued that selfies are a practice in vulnerability by considering the ways vulnerability has been understood in Western philosophy. Due to the mind/body split, bodies have been seen as vulnerable, needy, and in need of conquering, which has aligned them with the feminine (Mackenzie et al., 2013). As another result of this binary, the mind and rationality have become associated with masculinity, relegating emotions to the feminine, vulnerable realm as well. Frequently, femme selfies draw attention to the (feminine) body and express negative emotions, which can then be understood as embracing what has been deemed vulnerable (that is, bodies and emotions). Selfies can further be understood as aligned with vulnerability and femininity if we consider their association with young women, and how often this association leads to the pathologization of both (Maddox, 2017; Murray, 2015; Senft & Baym, 2015).

Despite their common negative framing, selfies have been re-read as powerful forms of resistance for marginalised groups, like young women and people of colour (Murray, 2015; Pham, 2015). Similarly, I argue that femme selfies are modes of femme-inine resistance. As I detail above, femmes utilise the vulnerability of selfies as a strategy to illustrate femme aesthetics, forge femme connections, and articulate femme politics and theory. Femme selfies can be seen as another way of engaging in femme theory, a body of thought that seeks to challenge the widespread disavowal of the feminine, overturn normative definitions of femininity, and celebrate both feminine subjects and feminine modes of engagement.

Notes

1. This term comes from queer theorist Sedgwick (2003), who offered 'reparative reading' as a way of finding pleasure in texts, rather than seeking only to be critical of them.
2. Cheng (2019) has also used the term 'femme gaze' to describe audience-driven narratives of queer women's desire that transgress lesbian norms in Taiwan.
3. This stylisation originated on eBay.com to attract buyers to online auctions.
4. While the terms are often used interchangeably, Jaggar (1989) suggests we might understand 'feelings' as physiological or sensory, and 'emotions' as more cognitive and socially constructed (p. 153–9). Affect seems to fall somewhere in the middle – defined by its 'in-between-ness' – said to be a pre-cognitive, animating force that refers to 'a body's *capacity* to affect and be affected' (Seigworth & Gregg, 2010, pp. 1–2, emphasis in original).
5. Butches and femmes have had strong alliances since at least the 1940s. They enabled each other to 'pass' as heterosexual couple during the McCarthy era, for example, which was a critical survival strategy during a time of deep queer repression (see for example, Nestle, 1992). Butches and femmes continued to be allies as they were ostracised by lesbian feminism in the 1970s and 1980s for their gender and sexual expression that was said to mimic heteropatriachal norms (see for example, Hollibaugh & Moraga, 1992). Outside of political alliances, butch/femme eroticism has also been described as healing (Cvetkovich, 2003; Nestle, 1992). The strong history of eroticism and allyship has made butch and femme seem inseparable, which some femmes have sought to challenge in order to define femme as a distinct identity (see for example, Brushwood Rose & Camilleri, 2002).
6. The political nature of crying in public is also explored in a study of online femme grieving practices (Schwartz, 2018c).
7. Questions of authenticity have plagued the internet since its invention (see for example, Turkle, 1997).

Disclosure statement

No potential conflict of interest was reported by the author.

ORCID

Andi Schwartz 🆔 http://orcid.org/0000-0002-6433-7409

References

Albrecht-Samarasinha, L. L. (1997). On being a bisexual femme. In L. Harris & E. Crocker (Eds.), *Femme: Feminists, lesbians, and bad girls* (pp. 138–144). Routledge.

Bailey, M. M. (2014). Engendering space: Ballroom culture and the spatial practice of possibility in Detroit. *Gender, Place & Culture, 21*(4), 489–507. https://doi.org/10.1080/0966369X2013.786688

Blair, K. L., & Hoskin, R. A. (2015). Experiences of femme identity: Coming out, invisibility and femmephobia. *Psychology & Sexuality, 6*(3), 229–244. https://doi.org/10.1080/19419899.2014.921860

Bost, S. (2008). From race/sex/etc. to glucose, feeding tube, and mourning: The shifting matter of Chicana feminism. In S. Alaimo & S. Hekman (Eds.), *Material feminisms* (pp. 340–372). In Indiana University Press.

Brightwell, L. (2017). The exclusionary effects of queer anti-normativity on feminine-identified queers. *Feral Feminisms, 7*, 15–24. Retrieved fromhttps://feralfeminisms.com/exclusionary-queer-anti-normativity/ .

Brightwell, L., & Taylor, A. (2019). Why femme stories matter: Constructing femme theory through historical femme life writing. *Journal of Lesbian Studies*, 1–18. Advance online publication. https://doi.org/10.1080/10894160.2019.1691347

Brushwood Rose, C., & Camilleri, A. (Eds.). (2002). *Brazen femme: Queering femininity*. Arsenal Pulp Press.

Buch, E., & Staller, K. (2014). What is feminist ethnography? In S. N. Hesse-Biber (Ed.), *Feminist research practice* (2nd ed., pp. 107–144). Sage Publications.

Cheng, F. T. (2019). Theorizing TL esthetics: Forming a femme gaze through *yes or no 2.5. Journal of Lesbian Studies*, 1–17. Advance online publication. https://doi.org/10.1080/10894160.2019.1689477

Cloud, D. L. (1998). *Control and consolation in American culture and politics: Rhetoric of therapy*. Sage.

Collins, P. H. (2004). *Black sexual politics: African Americans, gender, and the new racism*. Routledge.

Connell, C. (2012). Fashionable resistance: Queer "fa(t)shion" blogging as counterdiscourse. *Women's Studies Quarterly, 41* (1/2), 209–224. https://www.jstor.org/stable/23611784

Cvetkovich, A. (2003). *An archive of feelings: Trauma, sexuality, and lesbian public cultures*. Duke University Press.

Dahl, U. (2011). Femme on femme: Reflections on collaborative methods and queer femme-inist ethnography. *SQS, 5* (1), 1–22. Retrieved from https://journal.fi/sqs/article/view/50871

Dahl, U. (2012). Turning like a femme: Figuring critical femininity studies. *NORA, 20*(1), 57–64. https://doi.org/10.1080/08038740.2011.650708

Dahl, U. (2014). White gloves, feminist fists: Race, nation and the feeling of 'vintage' in femme movements. *Gender, Place & Culture, 21*(5), 604–621. https://doi.org/10.1080/0966369X.2013.810598

Dahl, U. (2017). Femmebodiment: Notes on queer feminine shapes of vulnerability. *Feminist Theory, 18*(1), 35–53. https://doi.org/10.1177/1464700116683902

Davis, A. Y. (1981). *Women, race, and class*. Vintage Books.

Dawson, L. (2017). Playing femme and not playing it straight: Passing, performance, and queering time and place. *Feral Feminisms, 7*, 85–101. Retrieved fromhttps://feralfeminisms.com/playing-femme/ .

Duggan, L., & McHugh, K. (1996). A fem(me)inist manifesto. *Women & Performance, 8*(2), 153–159. https://doi.org/10.1080/07407709608571236

Eynon, R., Fry, J., & Schroder, R. (2017). The ethics of online research. In N. G. Fielding, R. M. Lee, & G. Blank (Eds.), *The SAGE handbook of online research methods* (pp. 19–37). Sage Publications.

Galewski, E. (2005). Figuring the feminist femme. *Women's Studies in Communication, 28*(2), 183–206. https://doi.org/10.1080/07491409.2005.10162491

Hemmings, C. (1999). Out of sight, out of mind? Theorizing femme narrative. *Sexualities, 2*(4), 451–464. https://doi.org/10.1177/136346099002004005

Hill, D. C. (2017). What happened when I invited students to see me? A Black queer professor's reflections on practicing embodied vulnerability in the classroom. *Journal of Lesbian Studies*, *21*(4), 432–442. https://doi.org/10.1080/10894160.2016.1165045

Hine, C. (2017). Ethnographies of online communities and social media: Modes, varieties, affordances. In N. G. Fielding, R. M. Lee, & G. Blank (Eds.), *The SAGE handbook of online research methods* (pp. 1–16). SAGE Publications.

Hollibaugh, A., & Moraga, C. (1992). What we're rollin' around in bed with: Sexual silences in feminism: A conversation toward ending them. In J. Nestle (Ed.), *The persistent desire: A femme-butch reader* (pp. 243–253). Alyson Publications.

Hollibaugh, A. (2000). *My dangerous desires: A queer girl dreaming her way home*. Duke University Press.

hooks, B. (1981). *Ain't I a woman? Black women and feminism*. South End Press.

Hooks, B. (1991). Theory as liberatory practice. *Yale Journal of Law and Feminism*, *4* (1), 1–12. Retrieved from https://digitalcommons.law.yale.edu/yjlf/vol4/iss1/2

Hoskin, R. A. (2017). Femme theory: Refocusing the intersectional lens. *Atlantis*, *38*(1), 95–109. http://orcid.org/0000-0001-9065-980X

Hoskin, R. A., & Taylor, A. (2019). Femme resistance: The fem(me)inine art of failure. *Psychology & Sexuality*, *10*(4), 281–300. https://doi.org/10.1080/19419899.2019.1615538

Jaggar, A. (1989). Love and knowledge: Emotion in feminist epistemology. *Inquiry*, *32*(2), 151–176. https://doi.org/10.1080/00201748908602185

Lagerkvist, A., & Andersson, Y. (2017). The grand interruption: Death online and mediated lifelines of shared vulnerability. *Feminist Media Studies*, *17*(4), 550–564. https://doi.org/10.1080/14680777.2017.1326554

Lee, R. M., Fielding, N. G., & Blank, G. (2017). Online research methods in the social sciences: An editorial introduction. In N. G. Fielding, R. M. Lee, & G. Blank (Eds.), *The SAGE handbook of online research methods* (pp. 3–16). Sage Publications.

Lewis, R. A. (2016). Queering vulnerability: Visualizing Black lesbian desire in post-apartheid South Africa. *Feminist Formations*, *28*(1), 205–232. https://doi.org/10.1353/ff2016.0022

Lewis, S. F. (2012). "Everything I know about being femme I learned from *Sula*" or Toward a Black Femme-nist Criticism. *Trans-Scripts*, *2*, 100–125. Retrieved fromhttp://sites.uci.edu/transscripts/files/2014/10/2012_02_09.pdf .

Mackenzie, C., Rogers, W., & Dodds, S. (Eds.). (2013). *Vulnerability: New essays in ethics and feminist philosophy*. Oxford University Press.

Maddox, J. (2017). "Guns don't kill people … selfies do": Rethinking narcissism as exhibitionism in selfie-related deaths. *Critical Studies in Media Communication*, *34*(3), 193–205. https://doi.org/10.1080/15295036.2016.1268698

McCann, H. (2018). *Queering femininity: Sexuality, feminism and the politics of presentation*. Routledge.

Meese, J., Gibbs, M., Carter, M., Arnold, M., Nansen, B., & Kohn, T. (2015). Selfies at funerals: Mourning and presencing on social media platforms. *International Journal of Communication*, *9*(2015), 1818–1831. Retrieved from http://ijoc.org

Murray, D. C. (2015). Notes to self: The visual culture of selfies in the age of social media. *Consumption Markets & Culture*, *18*(6), 490–516. https://doi.org/10.1080/10253866.2015.1052967

Nestle, J. (1987). *A restricted country*. Cleis Press.

Nestle, J. (Ed.). (1992). *The persistent desire: A femme-butch reader*. Allyson Publications.

Nicholson, N. (2014). Tumblr femme: Performances of queer femininity and identity. *Carolina Communication Annual, 30* (2014), 66–80. Retrieved from https://carolinascommunication.files.wordpress.com/2018/02/2014-carolinascommunicationannual.pdf

Petherbridge, D. (2016). What's critical about vulnerability? Rethinking interdependence, recognition, and power. *Hypatia*, *31*(3), 589–604. https://doi.org/10.1111/hypa.12250

Pham, M. T. (2015). "I click and post and breathe, waiting for others to see what I see": On #FeministSelfies, outfit photos, and networked vanity. *Fashion Theory*, *19*(2), 221–242. https://doi.org/10.2/52/175174115X14168357992436

Schwartz, A. (2016). Critical Blogging: Constructing Femmescapes Online. *Ada: A Journal of Gender, New Media, and Technology*, *9*, n.p. Retrieved fromhttp://adanewmedia.org/2016/05/issue9-schwartz/ .

Schwartz, A. (2018a). Locating femme theory online. *First Monday*, *23*(7), n.p. https://doi.org/10.5210/fm.v23i7.9266

Schwartz, A. (2018b). Low Femme. *Feral Feminisms: An Open Access Feminist Online Journal*, *7*, 5–14. Retrived fromhttp://www.feralfeminisms.com/low-femme/ .

Schwartz, A. (2018c). 'Put on all your makeup and cry it off': The function of ugliness in Femme Grieving practices. In S. Rodrigues & E. Przybylo (Eds.), *On the politics of ugliness* (pp. 69–89). Palgrave-MacMillan.

Sedgwick, E. (2003). *Touching feeling: Affect, pedagogy, performativity*. Duke University Press.

Seigworth, G. J., & Gregg, M. (2010). An inventory of shimmers. In G. J. Seigworth & M. Gregg (Eds.), *The affect theory reader* (pp. 1–25). Duke University Press.

Senft, T. M., & Baym, N. K. (2015). What does the selfie say? Investigating a global phenomenon. *International Journal of Communication*, *9*(2015), 1588–1606. http://ijoc.org

Story, K. A. (2017). Fear of a Black femme: The existential conundrum of embodying a Black femme identity while being a professor of Black, queer, feminist studies. *Journal of Lesbian Studies*, *21*(4), 407–419. https://doi.org/10.1080/10894160.2016.1165043

Tinsley, U. (2018). *Beyoncé in formation: Remixing Black feminism*. University of Texas Press.

Traue, B., Blanc, M., & Cambre, C. (2018). Visibilities and visual discourses: Rethinking the social with the image. *Qualitative Inquiry, 25*(4), 327–337. https://doi.org/10.1177/1077800418792946

Turkle, S. (1997). *Life on the screen: Identity in the age of the internet.* Simon & Schuster.

Turkle, S. (2011). *Alone together: Why we expect more from technology and less from each other.* Basic Books.

VanNewkirk, R. (2006). "Gee, I didn't get that vibe from you": Articulating my own version of a femme lesbian existence. *Journal of Lesbian Studies, 10*(1/2), 73–85. https://doi.org/10.1300/J155v10n01_04

Walker, L. (2012). The future of femme: Notes on femininity, aging and gender theory. *Sexualities, 15*(7), 795–814. https://doi.org/10.1177/1363460711417482

"But where are the dates?" Dating as a central site of fat femme marginalisation in queer communities

Allison Taylor 🆔

ABSTRACT

Drawing on interviews with fifteen queer fat femme women and gender nonconforming individuals, I explore queer fat femmes' negotiations of dating in contemporary queer communities in Canada. Using thematic analysis to analyse the interviews, I identify how queer fat femmes' experiences of dating in queer communities are often characterised by rejection and fetishisation. These experiences have significant and negative impacts, generating feelings of undesirability, fear, and failure. I connect the marginalisation of queer fat femmes in queer dating contexts to the reproduction and circulation of fatphobia and femmephobia in queer communities. Finally, I suggest that queer fat femmes' responses to their marginalisation in queer dating contexts reflect resilience, as they find ways to navigate their oppressions and fulfill their needs.

Introduction

Under colonial constructions of beauty and desire, being fat and brown and queer and femme … means feeling unlovable, being unlovable, and no one disagreeing. Being fat and brown and colonised means to value, desire, and prioritise romantic love – a love that doesn't want you, that will never have you (Luna, 2014).

In their essay, 'On Being Fat, Brown, Femme, Ugly, and Unlovable,' Caleb Luna (2014) articulates the ways in which romantic desires are shaped by and through the intersections of colonialism, white supremacy, fatphobia, heteronormativity, misogyny and femmephobia. Social scientific research echoes Luna's (2014) assertions that desire and romantic love are political, suggesting that racism (A. Han, 2006; Patel, 2019), transphobia (Blair & Hoskin, 2019), classism (Canoy, 2015; Heaphy, 2011), ableism (Vaughn et al., 2015), and other oppressions significantly impact marginalised individuals' experiences of dating in contemporary, Western queer communities.

The slur 'no fats, no femmes,' pervasive in gay male culture, highlights how oppression operates in the contexts of desire and dating. 'No fats, no femmes,' often followed by 'no Asians,' reflects fatphobic, misogynistic, femmephobic, and racist, at the very least, dating and sexual 'preferences' by excluding fat, femme, and Asian individuals from consideration for dating, sex, and love (C. Han, 2008; Liu, 2015; Pyle & Klein, 2011). While the intersection of fatness and fem(me)ininity is explored via 'no fats, no femmes,' in the context of gay male culture, emergent scholarship suggests that anti-fat and femmephobic attitudes also exist in queer women's and gender nonconforming individuals' navigations of desire, dating, romance, and sex (Blair & Hoskin, 2015, 2016; Hoskin, 2019; Luis, 2012; Maor, 2012; Taylor, 2018).

Drawing on interviews with fifteen queer fat femme women and gender nonconforming individuals, I explore queer fat femmes' negotiations of dating in contemporary queer communities in Canada. Queer fat femme refers, loosely, to individuals negotiating their intersecting queerness, fem(me)ininity, and fatness, alongside other identities such as race and disability (Taylor, 2018). Specifically, I examine how queer fat femmes' experiences of dating in queer communities are often characterised by rejection and fetishisation and, therefore, have significant and negative impacts. I connect the marginalisation of queer fat femmes in queer dating contexts to the reproduction and circulation of fatphobia and femmephobia in queer communities. I suggest that queer fat femmes' responses to their marginalisation in queer dating contexts reflect resilience, as they find ways to navigate their oppressions and fulfill their needs.

Critical femininities, femmephobia & (queer fat) femmes

Critical femininities challenges ubiquitous framings of femininity as 'subordination, sexualization, objectification, and superficial narcissism' (Dahl, 2012, p. 61). Instead, critical femininities rethinks feminine subjectivities, resisting patriarchal conceptions of femininity to explore 'femininity as a genre in all its variations, representations, and materializations' (Dahl, 2012, p. 61). Therefore, critical femininities research centres complex, hopeful, and recuperative approaches to femininities, theorising 'the queerness of (all) femininity as well as relations between femininities' (Dahl, 2012, p. 58).

An emergent branch of critical femininities scholarship explores feminine individuals' experiences of oppression on the basis of femininity. This scholarship deploys the concept of femmephobia, which 'refers to the systemic devaluation of femininity as well as the regulation of patriarchal femininity' (Hoskin, 2019, p. 687). Patriarchal femininity encompasses normative feminine ideals, including whiteness, able-bodiedness, cisnormativity, heteronormativity, youthfulness, and slenderness (Blair & Hoskin, 2015; Hoskin, 2017, 2019). Femmephobia targets people, objects, emotions, and qualities perceived as embodying or expressing femininity, with the effect of devaluing femininity and policing deviations from normative feminine ideals (Hoskin, 2019). Thus, critical femininities scholarship draws on the concept of femmephobia to posit femininity as an axis of oppression and analyse the role of femininity in individuals' experiences of marginalisation (Hoskin, 2019, 2020).

Research on femme-identified queer women and gender nonconforming individuals finds that femmephobia is a salient aspect of their experiences in queer communities (Blair & Hoskin, 2015, 2016; Levitt et al., 2003; Levitt & Hiestand, 2005; Levitt et al., 2012). Femme first emerged as an identity within 1940s and 1950s working-class, racialised lesbian bar culture, primarily in a Western context, among women negotiating the intersection of femininity and non-heterosexuality or lesbianism (Kennedy, 1997). Contemporary femme scholarship maintains femmes' attachments to queer, racialised, and working-class femininities by conceptualising femme as femininities (re)claimed by individuals excluded from dominant cultural conceptions of femininity (Hoskin, 2017; Serano, 2013). Beyond referring only to queer feminine women, femme encompasses all those who 'refuse to and/or do not [or cannot] approximate the ideal norm of what patriarchal femininity constitutes' (Hoskin, 2017, p. 100). Femmephobia informs oppressive understandings of queer femmes as 'inauthentic' and invisible as lesbians and/or queers, passive partners of butches, passing for straight, heteronormative, and assimilationist. Such assumptions marginalise femmes in both queer and mainstream spaces (Blair & Hoskin, 2016; Dahl, 2010; Eves, 2004; Stafford, 2010). Consequently, femme is often perceived as an undesirable and politically invalid or inferior identity within queer communities (Maltry & Tucker, 2002).

Recent scholarship on queer fat femmes thickens critical femininities scholarship by including considerations of fatness and fatphobia in analyses of fem(me)ininity and femmephobia. Rhea Ashley Hoskin (2017) identifies fatphobia – the fear and hatred of fat people (Cooper, 2016) – as one of many oppressions that intersect with femmephobia. Specifically, Hoskin (2017) finds that fatphobia intersects with femmephobia to regulate slenderness as an imperative of patriarchal femininity. Building on this work, in her thematic analysis of queer fat femme women's personal essays, Allison Taylor (2018) explores how queer fat femme women experience and negotiate the intersecting oppressions of misogyny, femmephobia, fatphobia, and heteronormativity, as well as racism, classism, and cissexism. Of particular relevance to the current paper is Taylor's (2018) finding that fat fem(me)ininities are often positioned as unattractive and undesirable in queer communities, in part because fatness deviates from popular conceptions of fem(me)ininity as slender. Therefore, fat femmes are targeted not only for their expressions and embodiments of fem(me)ininity, but also for the ways in which their fatness defies normative fem(me)ininity. Accordingly, fat femmes' fatness and fem(me)ininities, and experiences of femmephobia and fatphobia, are inextricably intertwined (Taylor, 2018). Mary Senyonga's (2020) chapter on 'Black fat queer femme embodiment' deepens this analysis by exploring the ways in which fatphobia is 'intimately tied to the project of white supremacy' (p. 223) and the consequent casting of 'Black fat femme bodies in monstrous contrast to white femininity' (p. 225). Using qualitative data, I build on critical femininities scholarship, previous research on queer fat femmes (Taylor, 2018), and Senyonga's (2020) analysis of intersecting white supremacy, femmephobia, and fatphobia to explore how femmephobia, fatphobia, and other oppressions operate in the context of queer fat femme women's and gender nonconforming individuals' experiences of dating.

Methods

In the current paper, I draw on interviews with fifteen queer fat femme women and gender nonconforming individuals living in Canada. Interviews were part of a larger study exploring if, why, and how queer fat femme embodiments matter to women and gender nonconforming individuals in their experiences of gender, sexuality, embodiment, oppression, and resistance, which was approved by the Office of Research Ethics at York University. To participate in the research, individuals had to identify as queer, fat, and femme, as women or gender nonconforming, and live in Canada. Participants were recruited online through social media groups for fat, queer, and/or femme people, as well as through snowball sampling. Interviews were held in person for local participants, and via video conferencing software for participants living at a distance. Interviews were, on average, one and a half hours in length. Participants were asked to bring three photographs they felt spoke to their experiences of queer fat femme embodiment to the interview. Interviews were conducted with a loose interview guide and participants were also asked to discuss the meanings of their photographs. Photographs complemented and built upon the interview method by invoking different kinds of information, memories, and meanings for participants to create richer accounts of their experiences (Luttrell, 2010).

Fifteen participants took part in the interviews (See Table 1). Twelve participants identified as white (80%), one as Black (6.6%), one as Latinx and white (6.6%), and one as East Indian and white (6.6%). Ten of the fifteen participants identified as disabled (67%). Participants were between the ages of twenty-four and forty-six, with a mean age of thirty-four ($SD = 7$). Eleven participants identified as cis women (73%), one identified as a nonbinary, trans masculine femme (6.6%), one as nonbinary (6.6%), one as a genderfluid femme (6.6%), and one as a genderqueer woman (6.6%). The average income range for participants was twenty to forty thousand dollars per year. One participant identified as between small fat and fat (6.6%), ten as fat (67%), one as midsize fat (6.6%), and three as fat to superfat (20%). A majority of participants were university educated and held graduate degrees (53%, N = 8), while the rest held bachelor's degrees (47%, N = 7).

Thematic analysis (Braun & Clarke, 2006) was used to identify, organise, describe, and analyse themes within the interview data. The research question guiding the analysis was: how do femme-phobia, fatphobia, and other oppressions work together in queer fat femmes' experiences of dating in contemporary queer communities in Canada? Rather than focusing on prevalence, themes were identified based on their importance to the research question in an effort to highlight marginalised experiences (Ferguson, 2013). Queer, feminist, fat, and femme theoretical approaches were used to

Table 1. Participants' characteristics table.

Pseudonym	Gender Identity	Race	Education (Degree)	Fat Identity	Income ($/year)	Disabled (Y = yes)	Age
Allison	cis woman	white	bachelor's	fat	20–40,000	Y	33
Kat	nonbinary	white	bachelor's	fat	under 20,000	Y	25
Alex	genderfluid femme	white	master's	fat	40–60,000	Y	28
Joanna	cis woman	white	bachelor's	fat	40–60,000		26
Meena	cis woman	East Indian and white	bachelor's	fat to superfat	20–40,000		34
Kristy	cis woman	white	master's	fat	20–40,000	Y	46
Lauren	cis woman	white	PhD	midsize fat	under 20,000	Y	31
Ngina	cis woman	Black	master's	small fat to fat	over 80,000		30
Rio	nonbinary, trans masculine femme	Latinx and white	bachelor's	fat	40–60,000		27
Sookie	genderqueer woman	white	master's	fat	20–40,000	Y	35
Stéphanie	cis woman	white	machelor's	fat	under 20,000	Y	24
Tracy	cis woman	white	master's	fat to superfat	20–40,000	Y	44
Liz	cis woman	white	bachelor's	fat to superfat	over 80,000	Y	41
Vanessa	cis woman	white	bachelor's	fat	20–40,000		39
Rachel	cis woman	white	master's	fat	60–80,000	Y	43

identify themes, and the interview data was coded according to the specific research question (Braun & Clarke, 2006).

Findings & discussion

When asked in what spaces or contexts they felt excluded, discriminated against, and/or oppressed on the basis of queerness, fatness, and fem(me)ininity altogether, participants overwhelmingly mentioned dating. Joanna (cis woman, white, fat, 26) says that 'I really do think a lot of these identifiers solidify when I'm thinking about dating.' Similarly, Alex (genderfluid femme, white, fat, disabled, 28) describes how

> I've been on a bunch of not great online dates, and you hear so many horror stories. That's where I feel like those three things would inherently intersect most. Online dates and blind dates … is where I feel like those three are most likely to intersect in a negative way.

Ngina (cis woman, Black, small fat, 30) agrees: 'I just find those intersections, when it comes to dating, is probably the place where I find the discrimination or whatever else the most.' Kat (nonbinary, white, fat, disabled, 25) calls dating 'the big elephant in the room' for queer fat femmes, elaborating on how negative experiences of dating are a point of commonality amongst the queer fat femmes zey know. Lauren (cis woman, white, midsize fat, disabled, 31) suggests that queer fat femme marginalisation may be acute in dating contexts because of 'the sexual capital thing,' referring to the ways in which sexual desires, attitudes, and behaviours reflect and reproduce larger social inequalities (Gonzales & Rolison, 2005). For participants, intersecting fatphobia and femmephobia are the larger social inequalities reflected and reproduced in queer dating contexts, suggesting that queer fat femmes do not hold much sexual capital in contemporary, Western queer communities.

Via my analysis of participants' interviews, I find that queer fat femmes' experiences of dating in queer communities are often characterised by rejection and fetishisation, and that this exacts a heavy toll on queer fat femmes. Their oppressive experiences in queer dating contexts are shaped heavily by superficial engagements with fat politics, and femmephobia and its intersections with fatphobia. However, queer fat femmes are resilient in the face of their marginalisation, finding ways to navigate dating spaces. I discuss the above themes in turn.

Rejection

Participants' dating experiences in queer communities were largely characterised by rejection. Participants felt that they were often ignored as sexual subjects and, therefore, overlooked or rejected as viable dating or sex partners. Kat explains that 'it's a nightmare dating and trying to get people to do that stuff.' Joanna describes how, on dating websites,

> I feel like I never really [have] had anyone message me first ... I definitely get matched with a lot less in general ... [my thin best friend] goes out on a lot of dates with people who she's like ... they messaged me, whatever. And I feel like I never get that.

Kat articulates a similar experience, detailing how 'on dating websites I do message people ... I see who responds and it's bleak ... it's always this quiet silence.' Kat also narrated zer experiences with a 'queer cruising Facebook page':

> I joined, and one of my dates joined as well and then left, and I was like, why? And they're like, because I saw everyone else going after skinny, white, typical queer people and not fat femmes ... I would respond to ads and people wouldn't respond, or I would post an ad and no one would respond.

Stéphanie (cis woman, white, fat, disabled, 24) echoes these sentiments:

> I could write the same bio on Tinder as someone else and not get any matches ... I'm just reminded by how people treat me ... that I'm Other as a woman and I'm Other as a fat woman ... and I'm not concerned with certain aspects of their lives, like romance or sex ... our wants and needs are not considered a thing.

Rachel's (cis woman, white, fat, disabled, 43) experiences with weight gain highlight the rejection of queer fat femmes in queer communities:

> it was a real adjustment to go from someone who could always reliably pick up whenever I went out to noticing that I was no longer involved with a lot of the people who I would have thought I would have been able to date or wanted to date.

Where zey have gotten responses to online messages, Kat states that, often, zey will 'show up to the date and the person's like, oh, and it's like, great.' Similarly, Liz (cis woman, white, fat to superfat, disabled, 41) discusses 'having that person [she was flirting with on a dating website] see a full body photo and dropping the conversation.' These excerpts demonstrate that queer fat femmes' dating experiences frequently involve being overlooked, ignored, and/or rejected. Participants' experiences are consistent with fat studies scholarship that explores the desexualisation of fat people, especially fat women, because of the ways in which they deviate from the (hetero)normative sex and gender ideals that shape cultural understandings of bodily un/desirability (Gailey, 2014; White, 2016).

Interviews also suggest that race mediates queer fat femmes' experiences of rejection in dating contexts. Ngina states that

> because I am very open about the fact that I'm queer, I'm fat, here is how I dress, and then just by presenting myself as Black, it leads to a smaller pool of people that I can date or who want to date me, because there is still a preference out there among certain communities for people who look like them ... they're interested in someone who is of the same ethnicity as them.

Ngina's comments highlight how sexual racism (Bedi, 2015) can further limit dating opportunities for queer fat femmes of colour, and the ways in which the intersections of racism, femmephobia, and fatphobia reproduce Black, queer, fat, and fem(me)inine bodies as especially undesirable in relation to those of white queer fat femmes (Senyonga, 2020).

Fetishisation

When participants were not overlooked, ignored, or rejected outright, they were often treated in ways that felt fetishising. Kat says that 'even when people are attracted to you ... it's always a mixed bag, you're always wondering, are they dating me for diversity points?' Ngina expands on Kat's question:

> I was dating this person ... and looking back on it, I definitely do wonder very strongly whether this person was just dating me because they wanted to say, 'oh yeah, I'm dating a Black girl' ... [Is] the only reason that you're dating me so you can check a bunch of boxes off of your diversity card or whatever else?

Ngina further describes how

> the intersections of queerness, Blackness, femme, and fatness all lead to this aspect where ... I get people who are only interested in one of those aspects as a fetish of sorts ... a distinction has to be made about, like, are you interested in me because you're looking for something 'exotic'? Or is it a fetishization of my looks? Or are you genuinely interested in me as a person, and you want to actually build a relationship based on that? I've found ... more of the former than the latter.

Lauren, too, discusses being 'fetishised or admired but not a viable dating candidate.' Participants' narratives of fetishisation further suggest that queer fat femmes are not seen as subjects worthy of dating, respect, or love, but rather as objects to be sexualised and dehumanised. Participants' experiences of fetishisation are consistent with fat studies scholarship that analyzes the hypersexualization of fat people, especially fat women, because of associations of fatness with uncontrollability and excessiveness (LeBesco, 2004). Black feminist scholarship teaches that, for Black women and queer fat femmes, hypersexualization is especially pronounced because of racist associations between Black women's bodies and 'the primal, the erotic, and the exotic' (Shaw, 2006, p. 49).

Negative impacts

These experiences of marginalisation in dating contexts take a serious toll on participants. For Joanna: 'for a while, I wasn't dating at all. And I was like, I just don't understand the point of dating, I'm going to be alone forever.' Joanna articulates that 'I feel like I'm a less sexual being because I'm fat.' Meena (cis woman, East Indian and white, fat to superfat, 34) describes how

> I have a bit of a fear of dating, because it's so much easier to get hurt as a fat woman, because there's so much being treated as a joke ... And then there's also the fear of being fetishized. So there's a lot ... of fear, and I don't think it's unfounded. I think it's valid.

Similarly, Rio (nonbinary, trans masculine femme, Latinx and white, fat, 27) expresses

> how stressful and scary it is to try to go into a queer space and flirt with someone because fatphobia, in fact, does not end in the queer community. Which I think is hard to wrap my head around sometimes because I want the queer community to be all things good, and it fails in this way so radically, so often.

From feeling hopeless and alone, to questioning their desirability, to fearing dating, to ultimately being let down by their own communities, these comments reveal the ways in which queer fat femmes are significantly and negatively affected by the oppression they experience in queer dating contexts.

Superficial queer engagements with fat politics

Queer communities' superficial engagements with fat politics was cited as a reason behind queer fat femmes' marginalisation in dating contexts. Participants discussed how efforts towards addressing fatphobia in queer communities are often superficial, and that the context of dating highlights the limits of those efforts. Kat states that 'people are like, look at these cute fat models, and then you're like, hey, and they're like, nope, sorry. So, it's the surface level versus what's actually going on.' Kat refers to fat acceptance in queer communities as 'lip service' and 'tokenisation.' Zey further discuss how

> queerness, even in the city, is very white, in particular, and very, very, very skinny and body based. People will pretend that it's not, and they'll speak intersectionality till their face goes blue, but people don't often talk about fatphobia at all when they talk about intersectionality.

Lauren describes how

> it felt like, when I was first entering queer spaces … there were ways that I was elevated or sexualized as being this beautiful, fat femme. But that was just show-y or talk. And I was like, but where are the dates though … Because you could just be like, 'oh my god, look at how voluptuous she is' or whatever … but it's just like, where's the follow through?

Expanding on this, Lauren states that:

> I feel like the idea that fatness is accepted or welcome or loved in queer spaces is a theoretical one … there's still some shitty rules, or there's some talk that doesn't translate into who you're fucking, which is super political and important … are you fucking fat people? Have you ever fucked fat people? If you haven't, those are some red flags there.

Tracy explains that

> in the last decade … people are more aware of fat politics and what fatphobia is, and so people are kind of hooking onto it as … a thing to know about if you're a 'woke', politicized person. There's a lot of touting fat inclusion or being anti-fatphobia and not a lot of actual real work being done around what that really means or even what it means to have a fat fucking friend.

Participants highlight how, although fat and femme bodies may be acknowledged or even celebrated on a surface level in queer communities, there is still uninterrogated, underlying fatphobia circulating in queer communities that reproduces the exclusion of queer fat femmes in dating contexts.

Participants hypothesised that this superficial engagement with fat politics results from a lack of recognition of and engagement with how desire is political. Kat explains that 'people don't talk about how their attraction plays into things.' Zey further describe how

> everyone's super into 'all bodies are good bodies', and then … how it plays out in the community [doesn't follow through]. It's the same with racism, and it's the same with transphobia … people are not willing to critique their attractions or their preferences, and it becomes frustrating.

Sookie (genderqueer woman, white, fat, disabled, 35), too, discusses 'this lack of recognition that desire is always political … I think there's this failure to interrogate our desires.' Indeed, popular ideas about desire, love, and romance posit them as a matter of individual 'preference' and, therefore, separate from politics and issues of inequality (Bedi, 2015). Dating thus makes sense as the context in which participants felt most marginalised. Participants' experiences of dating in queer communities exemplify how failing to acknowledge the political nature of desire actively perpetuates queer fat femmes' marginalisation.

Femmephobia and fatphobia

Femmephobia was another significant, overarching factor in participants' articulations of why they faced discrimination in dating contexts. Sookie describes how 'there is this … privileging of masculinity and additional desire for butchness in partner choice.' The privileging of masculinity and resulting desire for a butch or masculine of centre partner was contextualised by other participants' comments about femmephobia in their experiences of dating in queer communities. Kat explains that 'queer and femme historically interacted in shitty ways.' For example, Kat describes how 'a lot of femme people have difficulty being read as queer.' Meena, too, suggests that 'queerness is represented as kind of at odds with the way femme is represented,' citing masculinity or androgyny, slenderness, and whiteness as central to popular representations of queerness. Both Kat's and Meena's comments speak to the phenomenon of femme invisibility, whereby femmes are excluded from consideration for dating because they are not read as queer (Blair & Hoskin, 2015, 2016). Femme invisibility connects to the privileging of masculinity in queer communities because, insofar as popular conceptions of queerness are predicated upon masculinity, fem(me)inine individuals are unintelligible as queer (Maltry & Tucker, 2002).

Relatedly, participants discussed being treated as and feeling 'inauthentic' as queers because of their fem(me)ininity. Vanessa (cis woman, white, fat, 39) describes how people 'always just assumed that because I'm femme, I was just gonna go back to a dick anyway. So it was really, really hard ... to date women.' Meena agrees, narrating how 'anyone who sees me is just going to assume I'm a tourist, you know, like I'm taking up space in a queer space. Like, maybe she doesn't belong here,' tying notions of invisibility and inauthenticity together. Ultimately, Meena suggests that 'if I weren't so femme, it [dating] might be somehow easier.' According to participants, femmephobia reproduces queer fat femmes as undesirable dating partners.

More specifically, participants' experiences of dating in queer communities reflected intersecting femmephobia and fatphobia. For some participants, fatness and fem(me)ininity produced fraught experiences of in/visibility. Sookie describes how 'given that femininity, within a misogynistic, patriarchal system, [is] so always and forever reviled, the visibility that comes with fatness, and the intersection of fatness with femininity is a particular site of violence.' Vanessa echoes Sookie's sentiments, describing how 'fat does put a target on us because we are more visible, we take up more space.' For Sookie and Vanessa, their fatness makes their queer and femme bodies more visible and, therefore, especially vulnerable to intersecting femmephobic and fatphobic violence in dating contexts, such as harassment and fetishisation. Conversely, Kat finds that, although 'people talk about the double burden of hyper visibility and invisibility ... I find it's more invisibility. I find fatness de-sexualises, and then femmeness makes you invisible, and then, in the queer area, it's hard to be seen as anything.' Relatedly, Joanna highlights how the femmephobic privileging of masculinity in conceptualising queerness intersects with fatness in reproducing queer fat femme invisibility: 'there's a very typical idea of someone who's a woman who's into women like, very butch, especially [a] butch [who's] fat, that's a big stereotype ... And if I don't look like that, it's like, then, what is she?' In Kat's and Joanna's experiences, femmephobia and fatphobia work together to create conditions of invisibility or unintelligibility for queer fat femmes.

Further, intersecting femmephobia and fatphobia generate exclusionary conceptions of femme in queer communities. Kat unpacks how 'femme and fat don't always interact well. There's this concept of what femme should look [like and] what femme shouldn't [look like].' Similarly, Sookie suggests that 'because we live in this cis and heterosexist hellscape, a lot of the time, folks, even within the queer community have a very specific idea of what femme-ness does or doesn't look like or encompass.' Kat and Sookie both suggest that femmeness does not encompass fatness. Indeed, Stéphanie states that, because of their fatness, 'I'm not what comes to mind when people think of queer femmes.' For Kristy (cis woman, white, fat, disabled, 46), 'fat meant that femme was impossible.' Rachel also describes how 'gaining weight originally made me feel like not really part of it [femme] because my desirability shifted. Femme ... was about a certain kind of aesthetic, and so I just remained femme-identified but I didn't necessarily feel [femme].' For example, in Kat's experience, '[with] femme bodies, you're often expected to take up less space, so being bigger is often difficult and it doesn't quite mesh with ... the queer concept of femme.' These participants identify how even queer conceptions of fem(me)ininity are exclusionary of fatness and illuminate how fatphobia works together with femmephobia to reproduce slenderness as a normative fem(me)inine ideal within queer communities.

Consequently, participants identified a hierarchy of desirability amongst femmes, with queer fat femmes being lower on this hierarchy than normatively sized and shaped femmes. Rio describes how 'for a skinny femme ... everyone is happy to see you ... within the queer community, thin femmes do fine. They're doing good.' While normatively sized and shaped queer femmes encounter femmephobia in queer communities, and that femmephobia is mediated via other oppressions, Rio highlights how fatphobia can amplify femmephobia, creating uniquely marginalising conditions for queer fat femmes in dating contexts. Similarly, Rachel discusses how, in her queer circles, 'you can't help but notice the hierarchy of desirability in terms of body size.' She elaborates, describing how

> there was definitely a hierarchy of who was the hottest femme. And it was two or three specific women who were all pretty thin. Not thin-thin but, like, tits and ass, a certain shape. And so, when you were outside of that ... I see now the ways that we can make the fat femmes of that community more like ... the cute, not hot, [femme].

For Rio and Rachel, femmephobia and fatphobia work together to position femme and fat queers as especially undesirable. Not only do queer fat femmes not measure up to fem(me)inine norms of body shape and size, but their fem(me)ininity also renders them less desirable in queer communities. Therefore, queer fat femmes are particularly undesirable queer dating partners.

Resilience

Despite their oppressive dating experiences, participants' interviews revealed their resilience. With their strategic use and negotiation of the label 'queer fat femme,' participants were able to create less oppressive dating environments. Some participants used 'queer fat femme' in a protective manner, labelling themselves as such to prevent interactions that would make them feel badly. Kat narrates how

> a lot of it [coming to queer fat femme] was a practical thing. It was like, I don't want to go on dates with these people who make me feel shitty, and who aren't interested in my body. So, around that time [I realized that] people see me as fat, so, I am fat .... So dating was really when it was like, okay, I guess I really do have to start saying this and identifying as this, otherwise I'm going to have shitty dates endlessly. And it was a really quick filter ... it's sort of like, okay, this is an identity that people are going to see, so this is how I have to refer to myself ... so all my dating sites or profiles always feature like 'I am fat, and cuddly'. I always have at least one full body photo, which, it's a lot to have that, but I do.

Similarly, Liz says that 'I try to get full body photos of myself out there on dating sites, and just anywhere that me being fat might be a factor in people deciding whether they like me. I want to be up front with it.' For Kat and Liz, using the label of queer fat femme – whether explicitly by calling themselves this on their dating profiles, or implicitly by posting full body photographs – is a strategic decision. Kat and Liz strategically use 'queer fat femme' to identify themselves to others in hopes of warding off fatphobic and/or femmephobic encounters. Their strategic employment of 'queer fat femme' in dating contexts helps to make their navigations of dating slightly less fraught.

Interviews also highlighted how participants use the label of 'queer fat femme' to make themselves intelligible and create space for themselves in dating contexts. Joanna describes how

> [queer fat femme is] definitely something that I've started embracing more recently. At least when I'm on dating apps and stuff, it's definitely clear that that is what I am, and [it's] easy to see other people who are also like that.

Sookie uses 'lady bear' to challenge

> this idea that bear culture is specifically this masculine thing because, within queer men's culture, there's space that's carved out, that pre-exists, the existence of fat, hairy bodies that now are coming into that space. And I don't find that that space has been carved out when it comes to fat queer femininity.

Both Joanna and Sookie use 'queer fat femme' (and, for Sookie, 'lady bear') to challenge the invisibility that intersecting femmephobia and fatphobia create for queer fat femmes in dating contexts. They use 'queer fat femme' to identify themselves to others, carving a niche for themselves in a community and broader culture that has denied them intelligibility and space. Further, their use of 'queer fat femme' offers language for others to express a desire for fat and fem(me)inine bodies. 'Queer fat femme' therefore provides queer fat femmes with a positive means of self-identification to negotiate dating spaces.

Implications, limitations, & future directions

Queer fat femmes' narratives highlight the importance of taking fatness and femininity seriously as sites of oppression. Further, their narratives emphasise that dating is a site of intensified oppression for marginalised individuals in queer communities. It is, therefore, imperative that queer scholars and communities politicise their understandings of attraction and desire to interrogate who is marginalised in queer dating communities and why. My finding that queer fat femmes experience rejection and fetishisation, particularly in relation to race, highlights how broader, oppressive cultural ideas about marginalised bodies – in this instance, fatphobic notions of queer fat femme individuals as desexualised and/or hypersexualized – operate in dating contexts.

The underrepresentation of queer fat femmes of colour in this paper is notable and, as a result, my findings are limited in the extent to which they reflect the embodied experiences of queer fat femmes of colour. Critical femininities research demonstrates that, within a colonial and white supremacist Western context, whiteness is central to normative notions of femininity (Deliovsky, 2008). Similarly, emerging fat studies scholarship explores how fatphobia is inherently tied to racism, as fatness is and has historically been constructed as indicative of racial inferiority (Strings, 2019). Consequently, future scholarship should specifically address the intersection of racism, femmephobia, and fatphobia to chart how queer fat femmes of colour's dating experiences in queer communities are shaped by white supremacy. Future research should also explore how other oppressions such as ableism and ageism affect queer fat femmes' dating lives. Examining how queer fat femmes' experiences are mediated by other axes of identity and oppression is necessary to avoid reproducing a dominant representation of queer fat femme as white, able-bodied, young, fat 'in the right places,' cisgender, and otherwise privileged.

Moreover, in focusing on dating contexts, this paper does not consider alternative formations of desire and relationality that queer fat femme lives may highlight. Because of their exclusion from (hetero)normative conceptions of family (e.g. marriage, childrearing), queer and fat people alike often create alternative kinship networks (McFarland et al., 2018). Therefore, future research should explore the diverse and resistant ways of reconceptualising desire, kinship, and relationality that queer fat femmes may create to make their lives more livable and find community and connection.

Conclusion

Queer fat femmes' experiences of dating in queer communities are largely characterised by rejection and fetishisation and have negative impacts. These experiences are shaped by the intersecting prejudices of fatphobia and femmephobia that circulate in queer communities, as well as broader culture. Although queer fat femmes experience marginalisation in queer dating contexts, they are resilient, using 'queer fat femme' to make dating less difficult and to create space for themselves.

Sociologist Jeannine Gailey (2014) writes that

> fat women are hyperinvisible in that their needs, desires and lives are grossly overlooked, yet at the same time they are hypervisible because their bodies literally take up more physical space than other bodies and they are the target of a disproportionate amount of ... judgement (p. 7-8).

This argument rings true for queer fat femmes, too, as their experiences with dating highlight the ways in which they are simultaneously invisible – overlooked, rejected, and marginalised as desiring and sexual subjects – and hypervisible – especially vulnerable to fetishisation, harassment, and other forms of violence. In both ways, queer fat femmes experience intense marginalisation in the area of dating as a result of intersecting fatphobia, femmephobia, and other oppressions. Scholars need to recognise that fatphobia and femmephobia, alongside other oppressions, affect queer individuals, too, and consider how queer fat femmes experience and resist their marginalisation as desiring and desirable subjects.

Disclosure statement

No potential conflict of interest was reported by the author.

Funding

This work was supported by the Social Sciences and Humanities Research Council of Canada (SSHRC).

ORCID

Allison Taylor (iD) http://orcid.org/0000-0001-8825-714X

References

Bedi, S. (2015). Sexual racism: Intimacy as a matter of justice. *The Journal of Politics*, *77*(4), 998–1011. https://doi.org/10.1086/682749

Blair, K. L., & Hoskin, R. A. (2015). Experiences of femme identity: Coming out, invisibility and femmephobia. *Psychology & Sexuality*, *6*(3), 229–244. https://doi.org/10.1080/19419899.2014.921860

Blair, K. L., & Hoskin, R. A. (2016). Contemporary understandings of femme identities and related experiences of discrimination. *Psychology & Sexuality*, *7*(2), 101–115. https://doi.org/10.1080/19419899.2015.1053824

Blair, K. L., & Hoskin, R. A. (2019). Transgender exclusion from the world of dating: Patterns of acceptance and rejection of hypothetical trans dating partners as a function of sexual and gender identity. *Journal of Social and Personal Relationships*, *36*(7), 2074–2095. https://doi.org/10.1177/0265407518779139

Braun, V., & Clarke, V. (2006). Using thematic analysis in psychology. *Qualitative Research in Psychology*, *3*(2), 77–101. https://doi.org/10.1191/1478088706qp063oa

Canoy, N. A. (2015). "Intimacy is not free of charge": An intersectional analysis of cultural and classed discourses of intimacy among gay and transgender identities". *Sexualities*, *18*(8), 921–940. https://doi.org/10.1177/1363460713516786

Cooper, C. (2016). *Fat activism: A radical social movement*. HammerOn Press.

Dahl, U. (2010). Femme on femme: Reflections on collaborative methods and queer femme-inist ethnography. In K. Browne & C. J. Nash (Eds.), *Queer methods and methodologies: Intersecting queer theories and social science research* (pp. 143–166). Ashgate.

Dahl, U. (2012). Turning like a femme: Figuring critical femininity studies. *NORA*, *20*(1), 57–64. https://doi.org/10.1080/08038740.2011.650708

Deliovsky, K. (2008). Normative white femininity: Race, gender and the politics of beauty. *Atlantis: Critical Studies in Gender, Culture & Social Justice*, *33*(1), 49–59. https://journals.msvu.ca/index.php/atlantis/article/view/429/422

Eves, A. (2004). Queer theory, butch/femme identities and lesbian space. *Sexualities*, *7*(4), 480–496. https://doi.org/10.1177/1363460704047064

Ferguson, J. M. (2013). Queering methodology: Challenging scientific constraint in the appreciation of queer and, trans subjects. *The Qualitative Report*, *18*(25), 1–13. http://www.nova.edu/ssss/QR/QR18/ferguson25.pdf

Gailey, J. (2014). *The hyper(in)visible fat woman: Weight and gender discourse in contemporary society*. Palgrave Macmillan.

Gonzales, A. M., & Rolison, G. (2005). Social oppression and attitudes toward sexual practices. *Journal of Black Studies*, *35*(6), 715–729. https://doi.org/10.1177/0021934704263121

Han, A. (2006). I think you're the smartest race I've ever met: Racialised economies of queer male desire. *Australian Critical Race and Whiteness Studies Association*, *2*(2), 1–14. https://espace.library.uq.edu.au/data/UQ_229149/UQ229149_OA.pdf?Expires=1600100859&Key-Pair-Id=APKAJKNBJ4MJBJNC6NLQ&Signature=LTN5g6GaOdjHQMaxZoUFpkGLaIy2biQJpb~YI4Nr8EE5~kmTRDrA4k7ByDGykVpF3learSTHCCPAZGrtVDpX05ua8qlyUt7npbrtahsT6AJnkH1xRR~ITEPzlzV1TBZx~1RpB4lQJ5oGDK-fJZyjm57h~oDiYdgfszHLI~rsrH0qWjaQmj1SoB8-v8x5vIui~a78-pfD~mDxCXBjbvN33gw~

Han, C. (2008). No fats, femmes, or Asians: The utility of critical race theory in examining the role of gay stock stories in the marginalization of gay Asian men. *Contemporary Justice Review*, *11*(1), 11–22. https://doi.org/10.1080/10282580701850355

Heaphy, B. (2011). Gay identities and the culture of class. *Sexualities*, *14*(1), 42–62. https://doi.org/10.1177/1363460710390563

Hoskin, R. A. (2017). Femme theory: Refocusing the intersectional lens. *Atlantis*, *38*(1), 95–109. https://journals.msvu.ca/index.php/atlantis/article/view/4771/95-109%20PDF

Hoskin, R. A. (2019). Femmephobia: The role of anti-femininity and gender policing in LGBTQ+ people's experiences of discrimination. *Sex Roles*, *81*(11–12), 686–703. https://doi.org/10.1007/s11199-019-01021-3

Hoskin, R. A. (2020). "Femininity? It's the aesthetic of subordination": Examining femmephobia, the gender binary, and experiences of oppression among sexual and gender minorities. *Archives of Sexual Behavior*. Online First. https://doi.org/10.1007/s10508-020-01641-x

Kennedy, E. L. (1997). The hidden voice: Fems in the 1940s and 1950s. In L. Harris & E. Crocker (Eds.), *Femme: Feminists, lesbians, and bad girls* (pp. 15–39). Routledge.

LeBesco, K. (2004). *Revolting bodies: The struggle to redefine fat identity*. University of Massachusetts Press.

Levitt, H. M., Gerrish, E. A., & Hiestand, K. R. (2003). The misunderstood gender: A model of modern femme identity. *Sex Roles*, *48*(3), 99–113. https://doi.org/10.1023/A:1022453304384

Levitt, H. M., & Hiestand, K. (2005). Enacting a gendered sexuality: Butch and femme perspectives. *Journal of Constructivist Psychology*, *18*(1), 39–51. https://doi.org/10.1080/10720530590523062

Levitt, H. M., Puckett, J. A., Ippolito, M. R., & Horne, S. G. (2012). Sexual minority women's gender identity and expression: Challenges and supports. *Journal of Lesbian Studies*, *16*(2), 153–176. https://doi.org/10.1080/10894160.2011.605009

Liu, X. (2015). No fats, femmes, or Asians. *Moral Philosophy and Politics*, *2*(2), 255–276. https://doi.org/10.1515/mopp-2014-0023

Luis, K. N. (2012). Karma eaters: The politics of food and fat in women's land communities in the United States. *Journal of Lesbian Studies*, *16*(1), 108–134. https://doi.org/10.1080/10894160.2011.605007

Luna, C. (2014, July 21). *On being fat, brown, femme, ugly, and unloveable*. BGD. https://www.bgdblog.org/2014/07/fat-brown-femme-ugly-unloveable/

Luttrell, W. (2010). "A camera is a big responsibility": A lens for analyzing children's visual voices. *Visual Studies*, *25*(3), 224–237. https://doi.org/10.1080/1472586X.2010.523274

Maltry, M., & Tucker, K. (2002). Female fem(me)ininities: New articulations in queer gender identities and subversion. *Journal of Lesbian Studies*, *6*(2), 89–102. https://doi.org/10.1300/J155v06n02_12

Maor, M. (2012). The body that does not diminish itself: Fat acceptance in Israel's lesbian queer communities. *Journal of Lesbian Studies*, *16*(2), 177–198. https://doi.org/10.1080/10894160.2011.597660

McFarland, J., Slothouber, V., & Taylor, A. (2018). Tempo-rarily fat: A queer exploration of fat time. *Fat Studies: An Interdisciplinary Journal of Body Weight and Society*, *7*(2), 135–146. https://doi.org/10.1080/21604851.2017.1376275

Patel, S. (2019). "Brown girls can't be gay": Racism experienced by queer South Asian women in the Toronto LGBTQ community". *Journal of Lesbian Studies*, *23*(3), 410–423. https://doi.org/10.1080/10894160.2019.1585174

Pyle, N. C., & Klein, N. L. (2011). Fat. Hairy. Sexy: Contesting standards of beauty and sexuality in the gay community. In C. Bobel & S. Kwan (Eds.), *Embodied resistance: Challenging the norms, breaking the rules* (pp. 78–87). Vanderbilt University Press.

Senyonga, M. (2020). Reading and affirming alternatives in the academy: Black fat queer femme embodiment. In M. Friedman, C. Rice, & J. Rinaldi (Eds.), *Thickening fat: Fat bodies, intersectionality, and social justice* (pp. 219–229). Routledge.

Serano, J. (2013). *Excluded: Making feminist and queer movements more inclusive*. Seal Press.

Shaw, A. E. (2006). *The embodiment of disobedience: Fat black women's unruly political bodies*. Lexington Books.

Stafford, A. (2010). Uncompromising positions: Reiterations of misogyny embedded in lesbian and feminist communities' framing of lesbian femme identities. *Atlantis*, *35*(1), 81–91. https://journals.msvu.ca/index.php/atlantis/article/view/175/182

Strings, S. (2019). *Fearing the black body: The racial origins of fat phobia*. New York University Press.

Taylor, A. (2018). "Flabulously" femme: Queer fat femme women's identities and experiences. *Journal of Lesbian Studies*, *22*(4), 459–481. https://doi.org/10.1080/10894160.2018.1449503

Vaughn, M., McEntee, B., Schoen, B., & McGrady, M. (2015). Addressing disability stigma within the lesbian community. *Journal of Rehabilitation*, *81*(4), 49–56. https://d1wqtxts1xzle7.cloudfront.net/43888838/Lesbian___Disability.pdf?1458395051=&response-content-disposition=inline%3B+filename%3DAddressing_Disability_Stigma_within_the.pdf&Expires=1600104742&Signature=gaO-2h0b0ET5gkCb4FsTTcNFI5IdGu0V6RsxvGF0mIvVUKOxInjhY-Z9C8OaqAH9qQyTPnyz255SVzo7t8Da61eh6OcD38AGHqcTHcNk4iCZsijRymoUM8~KzA~mLvLlUhTNhpQfZPQWBewSCR0-hsynPBl~eQ6C0rHJtt~EmE8nu1H-ckiN8KvWqlngfosS00g5X6bUPsqu4ndpvpZ8P6sAOmIuAtI545drMKPYZXVdx8lP~hhOjFMw1dbnwFi8TLgeoPZE~ln88nWbfWnwZNzTRqCJbldKfJ8nxtqbcD2Czh~NjqyQrM6yfGtitK86HgbYyk0AxWF5PNkATA~0hg___&Key-Pair-Id=APKAJLOHF5GGSLRBV4ZA

White, F. R. (2016). Fucking failures: The future of fat sex. *Sexualities*, *19*(8), 962–979. https://doi.org/10.1177/1363460716640733

Stacys, Beckys, and Chads: the construction of femininity and hegemonic masculinity within incel rhetoric

Lauren Menzie

ABSTRACT

This paper explores the discursive constructions of femininity and masculinity expressed by incels. Situated within a new wave of misogyny, incels blame feminism for disrupting a natural order whereby women and broader societal structures are organised around heterosexual, monogamous couplings. Using femmephobia as a lens, I consider how incels employ heteropatriarchal conceptions of emphasised femininity to both devalue women and describe pervasive social conditions that force them to remain celibate. Femmephobia casts feminine expressions as inherently performative and directed towards a masculine subject. Through an online ethnography of incel-identified subreddits and a deep-reading of Elliot Rodger's manifesto, this paper situates incel discourse within contemporary work on critical femininity. It finds that incels use gendered actors to illustrate and explain their status as incels. Further, these actors all operate within heteropatriarchal understandings of gender, and operationalise femininity or hegemonic masculinity for social capital. Through the use of these actors, incels demonstrate how they view sexual access and relationships as a unique form of capital that they are denied. Taking gender as its starting point, this paper contributes to the emerging field of critical femininity through an understanding of the misogyny and femmephobia expressed by incels through the use of gendered actors.

The involuntary celibate (incel) movement has received heightened public attention and concern. The Fifth Estate described this movement as a 'real and present threat,' and the majority of scholarship has been concerned with the violent and extremist ideology expressed within these groups (Nagle, 2016; The Fifth Estate, 2019; Zimmerman et al., 2018), or focused on the motivation behind incel-identified political violence (Baele et al., 2019). Although public attention to incel rhetoric has grown with killings by Elliot Rodger, Alek Minassian and others, there is limited consideration of incel discussions taking place in the manosphere, and most of the critical attention is focused on politically motivated violence and its rationalisation, or on the perpetrators of extremist violence. This paper emerges from a deeper need to consider the quotidian rhetoric surrounding gender within incel communities. In focusing predominantly on the violence committed by self-identified incels, we fail to fully capture the diverse and disparate nature of these communities and leave significant gaps in our understanding of online femmephobia (i.e., the systemic devaluation and regulation of femininity; R. Hoskin, 2017b, 2019).

Attending to online conversations within incel-identified spaces that do not incite violence or plan for socio-political change, this paper hones in on the practical implications of gendered constructions by incels. Using critical femininity as a theoretical lens, this paper considers rhetoric expressed by members of online incel communities to explore the ways in which incel communities spread femmephobia but, unlike many other systematic expressions of femmephobia that reject femininity to maintain masculine superiority, incels also reject and denigrate more traditional performances of masculinity (Myketiak, 2016). This article examines discussions emerging from incel-identified subreddits, and supplements the discussion using Rodger's manifesto *My Twisted World: The Story of Elliot Rodger* (Rodger, 2014). It considers, at the forefront, the symbolic actors created by incels post-Rodger (i.e., Stacy, Becky, and Chad) and how these actors are afforded power, agency, and socio-sexual capital through the assumptions put forward by incels.

Critical femininity

Critical femininity is a relatively new field of study that interrogates the nearly ubiquitous ways in which femininity has been socially read as an external imposition or a means of oppressing and subjugating women (Dahl, 2012). It interrogates the ways in which femininity has been cast as a discrete construct, where one is either classified as feminine or not (Blair & Hoskin, 2015; R. Hoskin, 2017a). Critical femininity is both a radical response to the inattention afforded to femininity within the academy, and a critique of how expressions of femininity are denigrated, policed, or cast as performative and societally imposed. For instance, academic work on gender has historically used the term emphasised femininity to describe a feminine presentation that complies with gendered subordination and the accommodation of male desire (Connell, 1987; Connell & Messerschmidt, 2005). In doing so, these scholars also discard the existence of a hegemonic femininity, suggesting that femme identity and presentation can only support a patriarchal power structure.

Schippers (2007) and R. Hoskin (2019) argue that hegemonic femininity does exist and, rather than exerting an authoritative power, can be used to regulate power relations among women. Scholars have also critiqued the concept of emphasised femininity as permitting the subordination of femininity as being enacted for a masculine gaze, arguing that many femmes perform emphasised femininity without being compliant or mindful of a male gaze (Brushwood Rose & Camilleri, 2002; R. Hoskin, 2017b, 2019; Volcano & Dahl, 2008). R. Hoskin's (2017b) work reconceptualises this understanding of emphasised femininity as it complies with conditions set under patriarchal rule. Here, a hyper feminised performance is essentialized and forced upon persons who are assigned female at birth (AFAB; R. Hoskin, 2017b). Accordingly, this construction of femininity must be obedient to the conditions of heteropatriarchy, compliant with the male gaze, and of 'acceptable' form (white, straight, able-bodied, thin, etc.; R. Hoskin, 2017b; Mishali, 2014).

While femininity is always coded as inferior to masculinity within gender hegemony, it becomes further devalued and regulated when deviating from the conditions of patriarchal femininity. As illuminated by R. Hoskin (2017b), the denigration and regulation of various forms of femininity has been widely considered by scholarship, using terms such as: anti-femininity (Eguchi, 2011; Kilianski, 2003; Miller, 2015), trans-misogyny (Serano, 2007, 2013), effemimania (Serano, 2007), femi-negativity (Bishop et al., 2014), sissyphobia (Eguchi, 2011), anti-effeminacy (Sanchez & Vilain, 2012), slut-shaming (Tanenbaum, 2015), misogynoir (M. Bailey, 2014), and femiphobia (M. J. Bailey, 1996). As each of the above expressions are considered a 'failed' model of patriarchal femininity (R. Hoskin, 2017b), they are subjected to femmephobia (Blair & Hoskin, 2016). Femmephobia functions as a widespread system of oppression to dichotomise and police bodies that make use of feminine signifiers outside of patriarchal expectations.

To better understand the devaluation and regulation of femininity within incel spaces, femme-phobia was used as a frame of analysis. For those familiar with the incel movement, it is hardly surprising to hear that community discussions frequently devalue or regulate expressions of femininity and are overtly and deeply misogynistic. Using femmephobia as a frame of analysis does not overlook misogyny; rather, femmephobia provides a specific analytical tool to illustrate and further understand misogyny. Incels frequently express frustration over the perceived challenges they experience in obtaining a romantic partner or sexual access; indeed, the inability to gain sexual access is how they define group membership. In this sense, incels see all women as failing to comply with the conditions of patriarchal femininity. As argued by R. Hoskin (2019), 'to be feminine is to be a passive recipient of male pleasure' (p. 694). Thus, by failing to be sexually available or providing a 'right of access,' the women in incel imaginary are deserving of condemnation, even violence, for subverting gender hegemony.

Critical femininities scholarship has critiqued the emergence of femininity as a 'singular concept,' calling for more work and discussion on relations between femininities (Dahl & Sundén, 2018, p. 270; Dahl, 2012). This paper offers a unique contribution to critical femininities scholarship in its examination between femininities within incel ideology. Using femmephobia as an analytical tool allows for a deeper understanding of the relations between both Stacy and Becky as their expressions of femininity are depicted and subsequently devalued. By attending to how incels view their 'ideal' heteropatriarchal conditions – and, similarly, how women fail to abide by those conditions – we are able to glean insight into the implicit meanings behind the actors Stacy, Becky, and Chad, and how incels conceptualise gender accordingly.

Methodology

With respect to studies in the manosphere, it has been said that 'more attention needs to be paid to the online context, not only because it offers evidence of a widespread and particularly malicious antifeminist men's "movement" but also because these assemblages demonstrate a radical shifting of the parameters of antifeminism' (Ging, 2017, p. 2). This project is a direct engagement with Reddit's incel-identified communities, supplemented by and read alongside Elliot Rodger's manifesto. Rodger's manifesto was included for two reasons: 1) incel-identified communities still reference Rodger and his manifesto, considering him the primary founder of their movement; and 2) the availability of open, public incel-identified communities on Reddit is rapidly decreasing.[1] Illustrating this, back in 2018 when r/braincels was first placed under quarantine, one user commented in r/incelswithouthate that they were, 'disappointed but not surprised ... Eventually there'll be nothing left but a gigantic liberal echochamber where **ANY** discussion of reality viewed outside of their side of the overton window is disallowed.' Rodger's manifesto thus provided a stable, uncensored space for incel ideology and analysis.

The communities were studied through an ethnographic content analysis (ECA) which, to my knowledge, has not yet been done to study gendered constructions in online incel-identified subreddits. ECA allows for the examination and analysis of data while remaining open to the community's culture, nuance, and the development of theory (Altheide & Schneider, 2013). Ethnographic methods support the development of theory and challenge a researcher's preconceived notions set forward by the media and literature (Hammersley & Atkinson, 1983). Incel-identified communities have received prolific media commentary with limited academic attention and, for this reason, ECA allowed this project to avoid outside/media influence wherever possible.

Online ethnographic research procedures will vary somewhat depending on the affordances of the space in question. The research process begins by defining the setting and research perspective, the cultural entrance, then the collection and analysis of data (while ensuring that the interpretations made are trustworthy), and taking steps to conduct ethically sound research (Skågeby, 2011). First, the scope of inquiry was predefined to the following subreddits: r/braincels; r/inceltears; r/incelswithouthate; r/incelistan; r/shortcels; r/inceldense; r/theIncelPill. Each of these settings were defined individually by the community guidelines and rules to account for any variation in the data.

Online observation was the predominant form of data collection for this process. This was conducted through hidden observation, without active participation in the communities. Many online ethnographic projects benefit from including members of the studied community, requesting that they provide feedback to the researcher and comment on findings (Skågeby, 2011). To not involve the community in an ethnographic project rightfully raises some ethical concerns regarding the protection of members, their anonymity, and damage to participant trust. However, due to the nature of this project and the choice to use femmephobia as a lens for analysis, involving self-identified incels was not an option. Instead, I opted to collect minimal physical data that had been produced by community members, anonymise any quotes with the use of pseudonyms, and rely on field notes that were taken during periods of observation to minimise harm. Field notes have received limited coverage as a means of recording online observations for virtual ethnographic research, but are able to provide deep insights for analysis while protecting the researched community (Altheide & Schneider, 2013; Skågeby, 2011).

Reddit is conceptualised best as 'a community of communities' (A. Massanari, 2017, p. 331), and was chosen, in part, to mediate the ethical concerns of covert online ethnographic research. A user from r/braincels commented on how Reddit was a 'megaphone' and provided incels with both visibility and a platform for recruiting new members. There is an awareness that spaces on Reddit have flexible boundaries and can be easily accessed and read by outsiders (Menzie, 2018). Within communities and threads, the presentation of writing on Reddit is disparate and wide-ranging; it includes in-group references, GIF responses, images and stories, links to outside content, and racist and sexist speech (A. Massanari, 2013). This mess of data has been described by A. Massanari (2013) as a 'carnival': chaotic, compelling, revulsive and grotesque (Bakhtin, 1965/1984). A challenge in compiling data from Reddit is sifting through the carnival to represent the original meaning and intention, while preserving the multiple forms of presentation the data might take (Menzie, 2018).

Online observation was conducted through two primary approaches. The first was a targeted search across incel-identified subreddits using the search terms 'Stacy,' 'Becky,' 'femoid,'[2] and 'Chad.' While examining these specific terms only revealed a narrow slice of these communities, they uncovered the most relevant discussions regarding the construction of masculinity and femininity within incel ideology. The second component was immersion within the subreddits identified above for observation. Immersion was maintained from September 2018 until the end of December 2018, and involved spending five hours a week in the above subreddits while varying the dates and times in each space. Content was organised using Reddit's default settings. Immersion helped to provide insight into the daily lives of members, along with their ideology and assumptions surrounding gender (Garcia et al., 2009; Skågeby, 2011).

Findings

From the data, I found five interrelated themes that form the body of this paper. Firstly, incels deploy and create gendered actors to illustrate or explain a perceived sex-deficit that they argue is experienced by most men. They further suggest that incels are the least attractive or desirable men and, therefore, will never be able to legitimately gain sexual access or an intimate partner.

Second, the use of Stacy as an actor demonstrates femmephobia towards women who display a hyper-feminine performance or emphasised femininity. Stacy is critiqued for not embodying all heteropatriarchal conditions as understood by incels (mainly, by not providing sexual access), while benefitting from her femininity. Stacy represents the most attractive women; incels devalue Stacy (and women more generally) by describing her as shallow, unable (or unwilling) to contribute meaningfully to the labour force, and manipulative in using men for resources.

Third, the use of Becky as an actor demonstrates a more flexible femmephobia that can be deployed towards women of varying feminine presentations. Becky is described inconsistently, but is often used to represent women who are average or relatively attractive. Incels will invoke critiques of feminism alongside critiques of Becky, suggesting that she has unrealistic standards and will either date men more attractive than herself, or rely on feminism to cope with being unable to attract the same men that Stacy can.

The fourth theme is how incels understand masculinity through the use of Chad. Chad is a contested and debated figure in incel discussions. Incels are envious of the sexual access and social status they believe results from his appearance. However, many will comment that he is similarly a victim in social conditions that allow women to exploit men (financially or emotionally) for sex.

Finally, I suggest that incels are primarily concerned with the display of a partner as a symbolic form of wealth. Incels mobilise erotic capital to define various actors and their socially ascribed status, while notably rejecting the idea that they hold erotic capital. This theme embodies how they understand their place in society on the basis of being unable to have and display a romantic partner. Here, I adopt Bourdieu and Hakim's understanding of capital to suggest that what drives this femmephobia and preoccupation with a lack of partnership/sexual access is an inability to be seen with a particular type of woman that incels understand to denote social value. The display of a partner as a form of capital runs throughout incel community discussions; I use the term socio-sexual capital to refer to the status that incels ascribe to men with conventionally attractive, hyper-feminine partners.

Contextualising the sex deficit

Incels have developed many interrelated explanations for why social conditions make it impossible for them to attract a romantic partner (see Jaki et al., 2018; Nagle, 2016). Explanations will often blame feminism for disrupting what they see as a natural order whereby women and broader societal structures would be organised around heterosexual and monogamous couplings (Zimmerman et al., 2018). Incels similarly direct hate towards women for not allowing them sexual access or for providing them with companionship (Myketiak, 2016). This can be conceptualised as a widely held, in-group misogynistic femmephobia, whereby the particular construction of gender held by incels asserts a universal failing by women to comply with the conditions of heteropatriarchal femininity (R. Hoskin, 2017b, 2019).

Incels suggest that women have unrealistic physical standards and collectively all desire the most attractive alpha males, leaving them behind in the sexual marketplace. This sentiment is captured by what incels call the 80 20 rule. Jason, from r/braincels explains this, saying:

> 80% of the effects come from 20% of the causes. What is the effect we're referring to? Sex. What causes sex? Those who take the active role in the mating process: men. So the 80/20 rule as applied to the SMP [sexual marketplace] actually means 20% of the men get 80% of the sex. The difference is subtle, but important. The top 20% of men get the lion's share of what women offer as affection while the bottom 80% get what's left over after hook-up culture has taken its toll.

In using the pareto principle, incels are referring to an uneven distribution. By suggesting that this is unfair or inequitable, the underlying assumption is that women should be a stable resource in the sexual marketplace. Echoing heteropatriarchal assumptions, incels assume that men exclusively initiate sex, but that women elect to only sleep with the top 20% of men who initiate.[3] On r/braincels, Gabriel noted:

> the universal **SEXUAL STRATEGY** is for males to approach, continually, as many females as he can until he finally succeeds with one. Unless you are a very attractive male, you will never be approached, nor will you succeed with many of the females you eagerly talk to, hence the statistical 'getting lucky' element of the whole mating game.

Gabriel is quick to clarify that this is only applicable 'when an average guy gets with a girl.' Under this proposed framework, women would be competing over and choosing from the same group of sexual partners, so some men would have near unlimited sexual access while others, as Jason noted, 'get what's left over.'

The widespread acceptance of an 80 20 rule within incel rhetoric creates three primary type-casts that oppose and cast out incels: the top 20% of men are constructed as alpha males, otherwise referred to as Chad; the women who compete over Chad will be either predominantly successful or occasionally unsuccessful (Stacy and Becky, respectively). As a counterpart to feminism and women's rights movements (Ging, 2017), incels believe that feminism is creating conditions where women have untethered sexual access. In this imaginary, they argue that Chad will always reap the benefits.

Incels thus view emphasised femininity as a means of competing against other women for sexual access to Chad. They do not see themselves having similar power or influence to compete within the sexual marketplace, arguing that too many factors are at play and predetermined. Triston comments on the factors limiting access to the sexual marketplace, writing on r/braincels: 'Face matters. Hair matters. Height matters. Shoulder to hip ratio matters. Your lean muscle mass matters. Your testosterone level matters. Your Dick Size Matters. Your status and your money matters. Being an asshole and not some beta faggot matters.' Most incels see themselves as lacking all forms of power or influence within this new gendered hegemony, consequently believing that the only way to challenge these conditions is through a unified socio-political movement (Connell, 1987; Connell & Messerschmidt, 2005; Schippers, 2007).

Incel rhetoric could alternatively be read through the lens of the 'mismatch problem' developed by evolutionary psychologists (M. Apostolou, 2017, 2018; Crawford, 1998; Maner & Kendrick, 2010) and, perhaps most usefully, through Catherine Hakim's (2011a, 2011b)) conceptualisation of erotic capital and what she has termed the 'sex deficit.' On r/braincels, Derrick comments:

> I hope this makes people realise that the largest gripe of incels isn't women, but the absence of sex. It is subtle, but it is important. It isn't women that incels dislike, it's the deliberate oversight of the hypocritical nature of women that incels dislike more than anything.

The absence of sex is a stable factor that many in the incel community view as fixed and naturalised due to the decisions made by women.

Menelaos M. Apostolou (2018) analysed responses from one thread found on r/AskReddit, a neutral space not aligned with the manosphere. The study organised thread comments into conceptual categories for why men believed that they were single, finding three primary causes: (1) poor looks; (2) little or no capacity to initiate contact/flirt; (3) self-reported low effort (M. Apostolou, 2018). Of these, both poor looks and trouble initiating flirting are recurring themes within the incel community. In a pre-industrial context, where parents would have substantial say, physical attractiveness would be less important to a good match than it is today (M. Apostolou, 2008, 2014; Perilloux et al., 2011).

When parents have primary influence or select mates, such as in a pre-industrial socio-historical context, difficulty flirting and making contact would also not be a barrier to forming a romantic partnership. Incels frequently argue for a shift to more archaic (or even dystopian) systems of governance that place men as primary decision makers over the sexual marketplace in order to escape the sex deficit. Incels see this shift to an extreme form of heteropatriarchy as a means to re-establish hegemonic masculinity through new enacted practices (Connell, 1987, 1995; Connell & Messerschmidt, 2005). A sexual marketplace that affords women no agency in deciding on or agreeing to sexual partnerships would, incels argue, fix the sex deficit. The interests of the incel community would reconfigure gendered performances and feminised essentialism to strengthen the divide between hegemonic masculinity and patriarchal femininity (R. Hoskin, 2017b; Myketiak, 2016). Perhaps dangerously, M. Apostolou's (2018) work affords some legitimisation to the idea that incels 'exist' because of the gains made by women's rights movements and advocacy.

Some feminist scholarship has pointed out that many social customs, cultural norms, and values are enacted to ensure that men have sexual access to women on terms favourable to men (Hakim, 2011b). These social customs, norms and values have been said to make up the 'male sex right' (Pateman, 1988). Incels frequently suggest that women will avoid relationships in order to compete for romantic attention from Chad. R. Hoskin (2019) found that both 'gender hegemony and the heterosexual matrix define femininity as signifying masculine right of access' (p. 693). Incels see women as responsible for subverting the customs, norms, and values concerned with granting *all* men, rather than just men in general, sexual access. Figure 1 was developed by a member of the incel

The overlapped images can be viewed by clicking on the following two links:

https://incels.wiki/w/File:Becky2.png and https://incels.wiki/w/File:Stacy.png

Figure 1. The Becky and the Stacy (r/braincels).

community to describe Stacy and Becky, the two primary typecasts of femininity, performing femininity differently in order to compete for romantic attention.

While Becky is portrayed as 'off the market,' hoping for a sexual relationship with Chad, Stacy is understood as successful and able to maintain multiple sexual relationships with alpha men. Both women are described as performing emphasised femininity and curating their sexuality to appeal to the male gaze (Connell, 1987; Connell & Messerschmidt, 2005; Schippers, 2007). Laura Mulvey's (1989) work is particularly useful here in understanding how incels understand the performance of femininity. Mulvey (1989) looks to the ways in which patriarchal systems cause an ordered sexual imbalance, with a focus on narrative and cinema. She considers how gaze in film assumes a split between the active male and a passive female. Here, the female figure is subjected to a particular fantasy through the male gaze and is styled and instructed to perform accordingly (Mulvey, 1989). For example, Mulvey (1989) argues that 'in their traditional exhibitionist role women are simulta-neously looked at and displayed, with their appearance coded for strong visual and erotic impact so that they can be said to connote to-belooked-at-ness.' (p. 19).

While Mulvey refers specifically to film, her theory of the male gaze is frequently taken up within feminist work to chronicle the ways femininity holds expectations of performance and male desire. Mulvey (1989) considers the function of spectatorship as repressing exhibitionism, not being seen, whilst simultaneously projecting a repressed desire onto the performer. Separate from Mulvey's work, and at the core of incel logic, is the understanding that women hold a particular kind of power over men and broader social structures, and enact this power through performance. Incels also see emphasised femininity as a performance for *some* men, but only those who are able to prove masculine dominance and superiority (Coston & Kimmel, 2012; Myketiak, 2016). This power allows them to 'play life on easy mode,' according to Chris from r/braincels, and easily access economic capital despite being less skilled than men. Incels see this as the deployment of sexuality and desire, while only giving access to select few, thus exclusively regulating supply while ensuring an endless, unmet demand.

Amanda Marcotte, a well-known feminist blogger, suggests that incels imagine that the sexual marketplace *should* operate similarly to a free market economic system where they are disappointed, overlooked, and discriminated against as consumers.

> I think the consumerist model of dating really helps here. The analogy I'd use is if I go into a store, I feel as a customer entitled to a certain amount of selectivity amongst the products … I want to go buy a flower pot. If all the flower pots there are not the shape I like or the colour I like, I'm disappointed. And I'll leave and I'll just be like, well they didn't have the flower pot I wanted … But if I went into a store and I found a flower pot I wanted and I brought one up to the clerk and was like, 'Here's my money.' And they were like, 'We will not accept your money, you are not good enough to shop here,' everyone would be like, 'That's ridiculous. That's discriminatory.' And that's because a flower pot is just an object, right? (Marcotte in Rozsa, 2018)

This framework strongly resonates both with the entitlement in how incels understand heteropatriarchal conditions, and with the overarching sentiment that they have been targeted and identified as 'subhumans' by women on the basis of physical markers and genetics that they have no means of fixing or undoing. Jared creates a post on r/braincels, proclaiming that 'I HAVE FOUND THE SECRET TO BECOMING A CHAD ....,' only to joke in the body of the post that the secret is 'Good genetics.'

In incel imaginary, women have exclusive control over the sexual marketplace and deny access to those deemed unworthy. Hakim (2011a, 2011b)) has similarly argued that women possess and *could* exercise significantly more control over the sexual marketplace, exchanging forms of sexual access for gifts, resources, and firm commitments.[4] Hakim's (2011a, 2011b)) theoretical framework does, at times, advocate for a more transformative socio-political approach to the erotic, where women might strategically mobilise their capital to force equity rather than equality with respect to gendered issues such as pay gaps. She expands upon Pierre Bourdieu's work on capital and considers erotic capital as a fourth category to be considered alongside economic, cultural, and social capital (Bourdieu, 1986; Hakim, 2011a). The conceptualisation of erotic capital is comprised of several interrelated forms of attractiveness.

Hakim (2011a) describes erotic capital as 'a combination of aesthetic, visual, physical, social, and sexual attractiveness to other members of your society, and especially to members of the opposite sex, in all social contexts' (n.p.). Hakim (2011a) is quick to establish as a dominant theme throughout her writing that women have more erotic capital than men and employ it more actively and intentionally. While Hakim argues that erotic capital should be used to achieve equity, the notion of erotic capital *and* the recognition that women have more erotic capital than men has been expressed in a more misogynistic light. Both Rodger's manifesto and popular discourse in incel-identified communities believe that 'women have more power in human society than they deserve, all because of sex' (Rodger, 2014, n.p.).

Stacy

Stacy is described universally across incel communities as having the most erotic capital. Hakim (2011a, 2011b)) suggests that erotic capital is composed of several elements: (1) beauty[5]; (2) sexual attractiveness[6]; (3) social skills or charm; (4) liveliness[7]; (5) social presentation or style/hygiene; (6) sexuality[8]; (7) fertility (Hakim, 2011a, 2011b). While this paper will not unpack the nuances of each facet of erotic capital, it is important to note that incels, where possible, will denigrate particular facets of a woman's erotic capital for not prescribing to their ideal heteropatriarchal conditions; this is not dissimilar to many forms of systemic femmephobia categorised by R. Hoskin (2019). Like transmisogyny (Serano, 2007, 2013), anti-effeminacy (Sanchez & Vilain, 2012), slut-shaming (Tanenbaum, 2015), misogynoir (M. Bailey, 2014), and other forms of systemic femmephobia, incels employ these actors to police and regulate gender with the intention of denigrating femininity and maintaining masculine ascendency (R. Hoskin, 2019). Stacy, despite being imagined as the sexual ideal, is often said to be lacking with respect to her social skills and sexuality. With respect to Stacy, Damian on r/braincels wrote, 'Shes a portable Fleshlight. I doubt it even has a personality at this point, only a chad cock taking algorithm.' In this particular post, an incel was complaining about his younger sister's maturation into 'a Stacy' and her growing disinterest in maintaining a relationship with him.

Stacy, in this context, no longer fosters relationships that do not materially benefit her sexually or financially, and is unwilling to develop interests outside of maintaining her erotic capital and subsequent romantic relationships. Stacy is reduced to and mocked for her feminine presentation because it does not fit within the incel imaginary of hegemonic masculinity. By not conforming to incels' expectations of emphasised femininity accompanying a 'right of sexual access,' women are belittled, hypersexualized, and denigrated. Stacy does not contribute meaningfully to a labour force because she – and women more generally – are purportedly unable to match a man's skills. Here, incels attempt to signal traditional markers of masculinity through authority, strength, intelligence, and value in the labour market (Coston & Kimmel, 2012). In posts concerned with work and school, Stacy is portrayed as 'checked out,' scrolling through dating apps, or otherwise preoccupied with social status (typically via social media) or with her relationships with men. As Markus from r/braincels affirms, 'Stacies get paid for existing.' Figure 1 similarly establishes that Stacy has a '$2000 Gucci bag' while still 'never [working] a day in her life, [she] lives in luxury.'

Stacy is then quite competent at transforming her erotic capital into financial resources. When men in incel communities discuss any success with women, the overarching assumption by the community is that they are being used for money. Incels further do not believe that Stacy could ever be loyal to a 'beta' male. In this sense, self-improvement is a farce, even if it results in some romantic success or conquest. Glen on r/braincels commented that he'd '[spent] his 20s gymcelling[9] but [his] looksmatch[10] eye fucks Chad and won't even look at [him].' Rory from r/braincels attempted to dissuade others in the comments from pining after an attractive woman, saying that 'Stacys make your dick hard but your brain and heart disgusted. They are for hate-faps only.' Exemplifying the disparity in the sexual marketplace, Stacy is resented both for her success in the sexual marketplace and for being unattainable.

Becky

Stacy and Chad are imagined as the central figures controlling the sexual marketplace, while Becky is present and benefitting from the current system. While incels do not have a universal imagining of Becky, she is most commonly understood as another attractive figure (although less attractive than Stacy), who is uninterested in dating them. Incels frequently make comparisons between Becky and Stacy, often reproducing and altering graphics as in Figures 1 and 2, and using comparisons that focus predominantly on (lack of) wealth and physical appearance. Becky's presentation is not always a hyper-feminised; she might intentionally present outside of patriarchal femininity by dying her 'hair green, pink or blue after attending college' (Figure 2), choosing more androgenous 'loose baggy clothing to hide' her body (Figure 1), or being dominant in her relationships (Figure 2). Incels devalue Becky *through* Stacy, exemplifying femmephobic logics by devaluing a feminine presentation that incels see as less worthy of attention, given its deviation from patriarchal norms. Patrick from r/incelswithouthate asked 'Is it just me or Stacies have a better attitude than Beckies. Maybe it is because she doesn't need to deal with "undesirable" men or Beckies try to make up for lack of beauty?' Becky and Stacy almost always appear together, and Stacy acts to devalue Becky's erotic capital as the more attractive counterpart.

Like Stacy, incels devalue Becky's personality and portray her as vapid, 'basic,' and uncomplicated. Jordan on r/braincels describes a group of women as 'basic Beckys who are all the same cookie cutter type who watch the Office, drink Franzia, and get excited for pumpkin spice anything.' This narrative is used to strategically devalue and regulate any perceived interests that Becky would have and

The overlapped image can be viewed by clicking on the following link:

https://cdn.vox-cdn.com/uploads/chorus_asset/file/10732403/WumKAm3.jpg

Figure 2. Another take on the Becky and the Stacy (r/braincels).

mockingly read them as feminine and therefore, less sophisticated than conventionally masculine interests.

Much like Stacy, Becky desires Chad. Unlike Stacy, who mobilises erotic capital for personal gain, Becky is promiscuous, not for resources but, rather, to protest patriarchal gender roles. Becky uses her sexuality as a political tool, something that incels often downplay or insult using slut-shaming rhetoric. Again, by failing to perform patriarchal femininity, women are devalued and reduced to a crude characterisation. The assumption is that, while Stacy is highly desirable and could easily find a monogamous, hypergamous relationship, Becky has to work harder and justifies her trials and errors through a narrative of sexual liberation and empowerment. Here, incels reinforce hegemonic masculinity by drawing attention to the inequalities surrounding casual consensual sex and engaging in femmephobic slut-shaming (Tanenbaum, 2015).

Benji from r/braincels wrote about a university experience, commenting:

> Most girls were taking a minor in gender studies where they discuss how to beat the patriarchy. These girls are on their phones for half the class on Facebook or tinder talking to Chad. And were often major sluts because having a lot of sex was empowering because if Chad can do it, why shouldn't Becky be a ho."

Becky frequently is described as 'working' to gain sexual access with Chad, using dating apps and displaying neediness. While discussing a women's dating advice subreddit on r/incelswithouthate, Dale commented 'that's a becky subreddit, they are super toxic and bitter to the bone, Stacies dont need "strategies" to get chad.' Again, Becky is used to demonstrate that women participate unevenly in the sexual marketplace and that participation, incels argue, is to their detriment and failure in finding a sexual partner.

Becky, unlike Stacy, is assumed to be participating in the labour force. This normally falls under two rationalisations: either Becky cannot exchange enough erotic capital to avoid the labour force because men do not invest in her as much as they do Stacy; or Becky is a feminist who insists in her own participation in the labour force despite. Becky's feminism is often read as a strategic way to mediate any rejection from Chad, and incels understand her feminist ideology as universally off-putting to men and, at times, even to Stacy. In this sense, incels reproduce many of the ideological underpinnings of Connell's (1987) emphasised femininity whereby a particular type of feminine presentation is mobilised to maintain hegemonic masculinity. In Figure 1, it is said that Becky 'thinks guys like the "natural" look.' Here they invoke two tropes of femmephobia: that her femininity is intended for a man and that it is inherently inauthentic (R. Hoskin, 2017b, 2019; Serano, 2007).

Chad

Chad is often understood as the male counterpart to Stacy, or a prototypical alpha male. While Chad is understood as highly desirable, incels do not acknowledge his erotic capital and will instead describe him in ways that would cut down his desirability: as brutish, Neanderthal, and obnoxious. Rather than seeing these qualities as traditionally masculine attributes that reinforce hegemonic masculinity (i.e., seeing Chad as strong, brave, or confident), they position him as mentally inferior (Coston & Kimmel, 2012; Myketiak, 2016). Ashton from r/incelswithouthate comments that 'Chad is programmed from 10,000 years ago to try and impregnate as many women as he can,' demonstrating his belief that Chad is programmed differently from himself. While incels acknowledge that women are attracted to Chad, their attraction is understood as an evolutionary flaw that women collectively hold – a flaw that Rodger and others online argue is animalistic, degenerate, and representative of under-developed thought. For example, in his manifesto Rodgers writes:

> Females truly have something mentally wrong with them. Their minds are flawed, and at this point in my life I was beginning to see it ... All of the hot, beautiful girls walked around with obnoxious, tough jock-type men who partied all the time and acted crazy. They should be going for intelligent gentlemen such as myself. Women are sexually attracted to the wrong type of man. This is a major flaw in the very foundation of humanity (Rodger, 2014, n.p.)

While incels strategically devalue Chad, it is women who are blamed for continuing to pursue him. Chad is a neutral, occasionally contested figure in the sexual marketplace, but is not seen as the reason why incels are forced to remain celibate.

Incels are divided on Chad; Chad is often portrayed as uninterested in the women he sleeps with, but this may be due to manipulation and exploitation by those women. Chad is paradoxically portrayed as a powerful figure with unlimited sexual access, but also an exploited figure who is inherently tied to the women incels hate. This contradiction between both exploited and exploiting exemplifies the strength of their misogyny: women are objects to be used by Chad, but also deny Chad (and all men) reciprocal affection. In this way, women are held accountable both for the existence of Chad and of incels for universally denying love and affection while controlling and affording sexual access to the attractive elite. As Toby explains in r/braincels:

> Chad might get pussy, but in the end he just loses money and any feelings he has for stacy are likely not reciprocated. Chad will end up with his heart broken, and can only cure that broken heart by going through stacy after stacy. and Eventually chads ability to love will be diminished by his promiscuity.

Occasionally incels will view Chad with sympathy, as another victim of the changing sexual market-place or even as an 'in' to social or sexual contact with women. However, many claim that, by nature of existing, Chad must be read as an enemy. Chad exemplifies their concerns with this new gender hegemony whereby he uniquely benefits from their disenfranchisement. Even in misogynistic posts that aim to cut down women and represent Chad as a figure with conventional family values and morals, replies will emphasise the social status that Chad holds and the unending options available to him. For example, Steve wrote that 'Chad will settle with a 6 who has a great personality and good values, raise a family with her while she's in her 20s, any day of the week over a 10 who's all about that roast-beef-life.'[11] In response to Steve's comment on r/braincels, Clark stated that 'Chad doesn't settle.'

Incels

Incel communities measure their collective failure to attract a romantic partner against Chad's per-ceived success. They are deterministic and assume that they have nothing to offer women in exchange for erotic capital based on both their genetics and poor social skills. Genetics often invoke racist sentiments, where an incel might identify as a racialised sub-branch of incel identity,[12] suggesting that their racialised identity is a reason they cannot find a romantic partner. Chad is always imagined as a white figure[13] and, when depicted, has traditionally Aryan features such as blonde hair and blue eyes, and is always muscular and described as over 6' tall. Incels therefore measure their perceived inadequacies against Chad's physical appearance: they are racialised, or too short, or report having an unattractive build or facial features. They rely on pseudo-scientific logic to explain the deterministic nature of the incel status. Just as patriarchal femininity is essentialized (R. Hoskin, 2019), so too do incels see their social status as predetermined and fixed.

Certain physical features are emphasised as 'incel features,' and incels assume that these features display lower levels of testosterone. The suggestion that these physical features are read as beta or less masculine allows incels to maintain a deterministic ideological position where women will never elect to date them and, therefore, any attempt at self-improvement will ultimately fail. Lenny on r/braincels writes that 'wrist circumference is a useful proxy for adolescent testosterone levels. Low test at that stage of development means small penis, narrow shoulders, wide hips, beta skull shape, high-inhibition personality and so on.' Testosterone, as Triston explained above, is one of the many factors that matter and predetermine your success.

Incel community members operate under a logic that they are always mocked by others, especially attractive women or alpha men. They assume that society reads them as not having a romantic partner, and those that are more successful at attaining partners ridicule them as sub-human. Incels see themselves as entirely without erotic capital and, beyond that, do not read erotic capital as something that men can possess and cultivate. Erotic capital intrinsically is part of femininity and, more specifically, a form of hyper-femininity. Instead of being concerned with their celibacy, incels express concern with their ability to display ownership of a mate and sexual success with women. Again, femininity is seen as something to be consumed by men (R. Hoskin, 2019).

Incels are predominantly concerned with social readings of their desirability and their success with women, rather than their erotic capital. They disparage efforts towards self-improvement (like gymcelling) and instead fixate on women as partners to be displayed. Erik from r/incelswithouthate wrote that 'there aren't really that many chads out there ... we are all affected by cognitive biases. Our perception of a man's physical attractiveness is based a lot on if he is seen with a woman (and how attractive she is).' Erotic capital, for incels, does not exist without sexual conquest and displaying that conquest to other men. Rather than assessing a man's erotic capital, incels look more to a visible success in the sexual marketplace as a form of capital, something I would call a socio-sexual capital. This, rather than erotic capital, is central to the incel imaginary.

Because erotic capital and emphasised femininity is seen as a passive process under hegemonic masculinity, incels do not recognise it as belonging to women. Instead, it is conceptualised as a marker of their own desirability. By rereading a woman's erotic capital as something that marks a man as 'successful,' incels read displays of femininity as tools to elevate masculinity. Rodger (2014), while writing on his hope to win the lottery, comments that 'once [he'd] won it, [he'd] be able to have [his] beautiful blonde girlfriend, [he'd] be able to show the world that girls consider [him] worthy, [he'd] be able to show the world how superior [he is]'; he writes that displaying a beautiful girlfriend 'was [his] ultimate purpose in life, [his] reason for living' (n.p.). Femininity is not only devalued because of its association with women (particularly women who deny heteropatriarchal assumptions) but it is also heavily regulated, objectified and used to signal masculinity and status.

Socio-sexual capital

I argue that the specific negotiation of femininity, erotic capital, and romantic partnership that surfaces in incel communities calls for further attention to this phenomenon that I have termed socio-sexual capital. The capacity for objectively[14] desirable romantic partnerships to signal a superior status and form of masculinity may occur in other sociohistorical contexts than incel-identified communities, but perhaps here it is most evident. Socio-sexual capital should be understood as a display of ownership over an attractive sexual partner. Self-presentation and appearance is something incels work to control and foster, displaying a more elite social presentation through material goods where possible. Rodger's manifesto demonstrates a particularly strong obsession with his appearance, both through adopting 'cool' hobbies like skateboarding in his adolescence and through brand-name clothing and expensive cars in his adulthood. He notes that '[he] became more and more obsessed with [his] appearance ... [he] bought new clothes every time [he] visited [his] hometown. [His] favorite brands were Hugo Boss and Armani' (Rodger, 2014, n.p.).

Rodger used these markers of status as a means of demonstrating a superior form of masculinity to that of his peers. He also echoed a common sentiment within incel-identified communities by devaluing certain forms of labour as 'beneath him' and, because of his parents' financial resources, was able to support his lifestyle without working. Rodger (2014) commented on how he felt working a 'menial job,' writing:

> I started a day of working at this new job ... to my horror and humiliation, the job turned out to be a menial custodial job, and I had to clean offices and even the bathrooms. There was no way I would ever degrade myself to such a level. (n.p.)

Particular kinds of work, work without status or the potential for high income, are not considered conducive to winning over a romantic partner. Gaining sexual and romantic access is seen as a product of displays of wealth and power.

Incel-identified communities now hold a fairly stable view that work (financial capital) and fitness or practices of socialisation (erotic capital) are useless. Effectively, they see socio-sexual capital as the ultimate marker of status and do not believe that they can exchange other forms of capital for sexual access. Here, they see themselves as being owed access to women, owed a degree of socio-sexual capital, and do not acknowledge an element of exchange present in the sexual marketplace they envision. While Chad may exchange resources for sexual access, he does so with women who already desire him. The repeated assumption, in Rodger's manifesto and in online incel-identified communities, is that women have prejudged them as unworthy and that they have, in their lifetimes, matched or exceeded efforts made by other men and are therefore destined to fail.

Viewpoints that women are inherently unfaithful and therefore are an unstable form of capital are frequently expressed within the online community. Rodger believed that women could be commodified and purchased, writing that 'being rich will definitely make me attractive enough to have a beautiful girlfriend' (Rodger, 2014, n.p.). These logics, while inherently paradoxical, are often used together which suggests an overarching conception of women as both immoral and as objects. Femininity is seen as something to be controlled by a man, heavily surveilled, monitored, and pacified with expensive gifts.

Rodger, and members of the online community, continually stress that a girlfriend (or sexual access) is something to be displayed. In Rodger's writing, women and sex are conflated (Myketiak, 2016). In incel-identified communities, the relationship between women and sex is more complicated. While incels see the display of a partner as a reflection of their own masculinity (Connell, 1987), they idealise and fantasise about women that, in their eyes, do not exist. Incels idealise and imagine a woman that perfectly embodies patriarchal femininity (R. Hoskin, 2019). Without a girlfriend, incels assume that both feminine presentations and displays of socio-sexual capital are performances intended for a male gaze. As incels feel belittled and insulted by the attractive men and women that they read as sexually active, they betray that, in their imagination, they also fall prey to gaze and are assessed through their ability to perform a particular kind of masculinity. Rodger (2014) writes about how he felt when he was unable to display socio-sexual capital to his father and his roommate:

> My father drove up to Santa Barbara to meet me a few days later. The two of us went to have lunch at a restaurant in the Camino Real Marketplace, an area that I often frequented. When we sat down at our table, I saw a young couple sitting a few tables down the row. The sight of them enraged me to no end, especially because it was a dark-skinned Mexican guy dating a hot blonde white girl. I regarded it as a great insult to my dignity. How could an inferior Mexican guy be able to date a white blonde girl, while I was still suffering as a lonely virgin? I was ashamed to be in such an inferior position *in front my father*. When I saw the two of them kissing, I could barely contain my rage. I stood up in anger, and I was about to walk up to them and pour my glass of soda all over their heads. I probably would have, if father wasn't there. I was seething with envious rage, *and my father was there to watch it all*. It was so humiliating. *I wasn't the son I wanted to present to my father*. I should be the one with the hot blonde girl, making my father proud. Instead, *my father had to watch me suffer in a pathetic position*. (n.p. [emphases added])

> After a few weeks of living with [my roommate], I realized that I had a psychological problem with his presence in my apartment . . . I could hide the details of my lonely, celibate life from the rest of the world, but I could not hide it from Spencer. *The fact that I never had any girls over to my room was clear enough that I was an undesirable outcast*, and I hated it when people knew this about me and judged me for it. (n.p. [emphasis added])

As Rodger illustrates, the primary concern for incels centres on displaying and presenting a romantic partner to demonstrate socio-sexual capital. Much like his reliance on objects like his car and clothing to display a superior status, Rodger saw a particular kind of girlfriend (white, skinny, and blonde or, in Hakim's (2011a) framework, someone with a high degree of erotic capital) as offering similar or greater value to his self-presentation.

Van Valkenburgh (2018) found that other spaces on the manosphere hold assumptions that women can be possessed, exchanged and commodified. I argue that incels are not just concerned about limited sexual access, but also about their inability to display sexual access as a means of demonstrating their own masculinity. Their masculinity is constructed alongside Chad, who serves as an antagonist with access to everything they lack. The depiction of femininity as a construction intended for masculine consumption is a reproduction of many other forms of systemic femmephobia. Femmephobia runs through incel narratives from their imagining of Stacy and Becky as objects, of their femininity as performance, and of their labour as unskilled and devalued.

Limitations

While this project provides substantial insight into online incel-identified communities and their construction and interpretation of gendered actors, it is only a first glance into these spaces and thus these findings are subject to limitations. The significant absence of literature on incel movements, on and offline, limits the ability of this work to build upon past scholarship and theoretical frames. Another limitation comes from the disparate online platforms available to incels to gather and form communities. The current study looked only to incel-identified communities on Reddit and is therefore unable to generalise these constructions across other incel-identified spaces or the manosphere more broadly.

Conclusion

The current study demonstrates a strong (re)production of systemic femmephobia within online incel-identified community rhetoric. It analyzes the symbolic actors created by incels as they perform gender, and places this performance as always occurring before a male gaze. This paper argues that incels desire a prescribed status and power that they believe is earned through having an objectively desirable romantic partner to display their masculinity and attractiveness to other men. Here, women and sex are conflated, and femininity is denigrated for failing to conform to their understanding of patriarchal femininity (R. Hoskin, 2019; Myketiak, 2016). The cited sex deficit creates a deterministic and pessimistic framework for how incels read their socio-sexual capital, inciting their need for social transformation. They see displays of femininity as performative and directed towards a male gaze (R. Hoskin, 2017b, 2019; Serano, 2007), and operationalise Stacy and Becky as tools to elevate the alpha male (R. Hoskin, 2019). The devaluation and regulation of femininity in incel rhetoric is not accidental, but a strategic way to explain their lack of romantic prospects and perceived lack of social value.

Notes

1. My research was initially open to all incel-themed subreddits, but many of these were small groups organised by additional identity markers (e.g., r/shortcels). Larger incel-identified subreddits have been subject to heightened surveillance and have experienced censorship resulting in bans, quarantine, or rules and conditions that have caused users to disband. While several incel-identified subreddits were available during this project, all are now banned with the exception of r/incelswithouthate.
2. This was the most common derogatory term used to generally categorise and discuss women.
3. Incel communities are heterosexist and, for this reason, this paper only examines incel rhetoric on relationships between men and women. While incels very occasionally discussed same-sex and bisexual relationships, as well as, trans or gender non-conforming persons in relationships, these discussions were often hateful. Incels expressed scepticism towards the legitimacy of same-sex partnerships and saw them as a way of escaping from the social conditions with which they take issue.
4. I do not necessarily share Hakim's views on erotic capital, but believe there is enough here to resonate strongly with incel rhetoric. Control over sexual access is something that incels argue is held by women and unfairly distributed to the men who most strongly embody traditional and hegemonic masculinity, although they often use different, more derogatory language to make this point.
5. Beauty is understood as static and is easily captured and recognised in a photo. It changes depending on cultural and temporal context, and is primarily assessed through facial attractiveness (Hakim, 2011a, 2011b).
6. Unlike beauty, sexual attractiveness is dynamic and can be assessed through a person's general sex appeal. This is concerned both with their body and 'a way of being in the world' and particular displays of femininity or masculinity (Hakim, 2011a, n.p.)

7. This quality is concerned with physical fitness and social energy (Hakim, 2011a, 2011b).
8. Sexuality is focused most on sexual competence and performance, specifically in an intimate relationship. Sexual skill, then, may not be immediately recognisable in the same way that other facets of erotic capital are. Sex drive is suggested by Hakim (2011a, 2011b)) to indicate more opportunities to have developed sexual skills and competence, and in this sense, may be a way of demonstrating sexuality to those who are not sexual partners.
9. 'Gymcelling' refers to attempts by those in the incel community to improve their physical appearance through exercise. By tagging it as 'celling,' they affirm that celibacy will still be present regardless of any attempts at self-improvement.
10. 'Looksmatch' refers to a partner or person of equal or relatively equal physical attractiveness.
11. This term is analogous with 'roastie,' and refers to women who have had 'too much' sex. This is never defined, but the assumption is that sex will change a woman's genitals to signal promiscuity, making her less attractive. The portrayal of Chad as a figure who never has to settle and has unlimited sexual access reinforces the importance incels place on erotic capital as a marker of status. Chad is understood as an alpha simply because of his dating options. Chad is rarely, if ever, discussed as someone with power or status through employment, wealth, or physical attractiveness, but is only ever assessed by his ability to attract and have sex with women. In this sense, incels again objectify women and see them as markers of status for men. A woman's erotic capital, in the incel imaginary, is used to connote power to a male figure rather than being a representation of their own worth and status.
12. For instance, Asian-identifying or Indian-identifying incels may refer to themselves as ricecels and currycels respectively.
13. White supremacy was central to many discussions from incel communities. It is worth noting that Stacy and Becky are both always depicted as white women, and Stacy is always blonde.
14. Naturally, objective standards of beauty are hard to assess, but here I refer both to how incels idealise particular bodies and how Hakim (2011a, 2011b)) casts certain bodies as having objectively more erotic capital than others. These bodies are often slim, white, and culturally and temporally situated, however I acknowledge that the conceptualisation of bodies as 'objectively' desirable is a problematic construct. This discussion falls outside the scope of this paper, but more critical work should be done that accounts for the means by which certain bodies are highlighted and praised – even within the academy, as in Hakim's work – over others.

Disclosure statement

No potential conflict of interest was reported by the author.

References

Altheide, D., & Schneider, C. (2013). *Qualitative media analysis* (2nd ed.). Sage Publications.
Apostolou, M. (2008). Parent-offspring conflict over mating: The case of beauty. *Evolutionary Psychology*, *6*(2), 504–518. https://doi.org/10.1177/147470490800600207
Apostolou, M. (2014). *Sexual selection under parental choice: The evolution of human mating behaviour*. Psychology Press.
Apostolou, M. (2017). Why people stay single: An evolutionary perspective. *Personality and Individual Difference*, *111*(1), 263–271. https://doi.org/10.1016/j.paid.2017.02.034
Apostolou, M. (2018). Why men stay single? Evidence from reddit. *Evolutionary Psychological Science*, *5*(1), 1–11. https://doi.org/10.1007/s40806-018-0163-7
Baele, S. J., Brace, L., & Coan, T. G. (2019). From "incel" to "saint": Analyzing the violent worldview behind the 2018 toronto attack. *Terrorism and Political Violence*, 1–25. https://doi.org/10.1080/09546553.2019.1638256
Bailey, M. (2014). More on the origins of misogynoir. Retrieved from https://moyazb.tumblr.com/post/84048113369/more-on-the-origin-of-misogynoir
Bailey, M. J. (1996). Gender identity. In R. C. Savin-Williams & K. M. Cohen (Eds.), *Lives of lesbians, gays and bisexuals: Children to adults* (pp. 71–93). Harcourt Brace.
Bakhtin, M. (1984). *Rabelais and his world*. (H. Iswolsky, Trans.). Indiana University Press. (Original work published 1965)
Bishop, C. J., Kiss, M., Morrison, T. G., Rushe, D. M., & Specht, J. (2014). The association between gay men's stereotypic beliefs about drag queens and their endorsement of hypermasculinity. *Journal of Homosexuality*, *61*(4), 554–567. https://doi.org/10.1080/00918369.2014.865464

Blair, K., & Hoskin, R. (2015). Experiences of femme identity: Coming out, invisibility and femmephobia. *Psychology and Sexuality*, *6*(3), 229–244. https://doi.org/10.1080/19419899.2014.921860

Blair, K., & Hoskin, R. (2016). Contemporary understandings of femme identities and related experiences of discrimination. *Psychology and Sexuality*, *7*(2), 101–115. https://doi.org/10.1080/19419899.2015.1053824

Bourdieu, P. (1986). The Forms of Capital. In J. G. Richardson (Ed.), *Handbook of theory and research for the sociology of education* (pp. 241–258). Greenwood.

Brushwood Rose, C., & Camilleri, A. (2002). *Brazen femme: Queering femininity*. Arsenal Pulp.

Connell, R. W. (1987). *Gender and power: Society, the person and sexual politics*. Polity.

Connell, R. W. (1995). *Masculinities*. Polity Press.

Connell, R. W., & Messerschmidt, J. W. (2005). Hegemonic masculinity: Rethinking the concept. *Gender and Society*, *19*(6), 829–859. https://doi.org/10.1177/0891243205278639

Coston, B. M., & Kimmel, M. (2012). Seeing privilege where it isn't: Marginalized masculinities and intersectionality of privilege. *Journal of Social Issues*, *68*(1), 97–111. https://doi.org/10.1111/j.1540-4560.2011.01738.x

Crawford, C. (1998). Environments and adaptations: Then and now. In C. Crawford & D. Krebs (Eds.), *Handbook of evolutionary psychology* (pp. 275–302). Erlbaum.

Dahl, U. (2012). Turning like a femme: Figuring critical femininity studies. *NORA - Nordic Journal of Feminist and Gender Research*, *20*(1), 57–64. https://doi.org/10.1080/08038740.2011.650708

Dahl, U., & Sundén, J. (2018). Femininity revisited: Refiguring critical femininity studies. Guest editors' introduction. *The European Journal of Women's Studies*, *25*(3), 269–277. https://doi.org/10.1177/1350506818774742

Eguchi, S. (2011). Negotiating sissyphobia: A critical/interpretive analysis of one 'femme' gay asian body in the heteronormative world. *Journal of Men's Studies*, *19*(1), 37–56. https://doi.org/10.3149/jms.1901.37

Garcia, A. C., Standlee, A. I., Bechkoff, J., & Cui, Y. (2009). Ethnographic approaches to the internet and computer-mediated communication. *Journal of Contemporary Ethnography*, *38*(1), 1. https://doi.org/10.1177/0891241607310839

Ging, D. (2017). Alphas, betas, and incels: Theorizing the masculinities of the manosphere. *Men and Masculinities*, *22*(4), 1–20. https://doi.org/10.1177/1097184X17706401

Hakim, C. (2011a). *Erotic capital: The power of attraction in the boardroom and the bedroom*. Basic Books.

Hakim, C. (2011b). *Honey money: The power of erotic capital*. Penguin Group.

Hammersley, M., & Atkinson, P. (1983). *Ethnography: Principles in practice*. Tavistock Publications.

Hoskin, R. (2017a). Femme interventions and the proper feminist subject: Critical approaches to decolonizing western feminist pedagogies. *Cogent Social Sciences*, *3*(1), 1-16. https://doi.org/10.1080/23311886.2016.1276819

Hoskin, R. (2017b). Femme theory: Refocusing the intersectional lens. *Atlantis: Critical Studies in Gender, Culture and Social Justice*, *38*(1), 95–109. https://journals.msvu.ca/index.php/atlantis/article/view/4771/95-109%20PDF

Hoskin, R. (2019). Femmephobia: The role of anti-femininity and gender policing in lgbtq+ people's experiences of discrimination. *Sex Roles*, *81*(11–12), 686–703. https://doi.org/10.1007/s11199-019-01021-3

Jaki, S., De Smedt, T., Gwozdz, M., Panchal, R., Rossa, A., & De Pauw, G. (2018). Online hatred of women in the incels.me forum: Linguistic analysis and automatic detection. *Journal of Language Aggression and Conflict*, *7*(2), 240–268. https://doi.org/10.1075/jlac.00026.jak

Kilianski, S. E. (2003). Explaining heterosexual men's attitudes toward women and gay men: The theory of exclusively masculine identity. *Psychology of Men & Masculinity*, *4*(1), 37–56. https://doi.org/10.1037/1524-9220.4.1.37

Maner, J., & Kendrick, D. (2010). When adaptations go awry: Functional and dysfunctional aspects of social anxiety. *Social Issues and Policy Review*, *4*(1), 111–142. https://doi.org/10.1111/j.1751-2409.2010.01019.x

Massanari, A. (2013). Playful participatory culture: Learning from reddit. *Selected Papers of Internet Research*, *14.0*, 1–7. Retrieved from http://spir.aoir.org/index.php/spir/article/view/803

Massanari, A. (2017). #Gamergate and the fappening: How reddit's algorithm, governance, and culture support toxic technocultures. *New Media and Society*, *19*(3), 329–346. https://doi.org/10.1177/1461444815608807

Menzie, L. (2018). *"ITT: Rape analysts": Hosting negotiations of consent, kink, and violence in virtual space* (Unpublished master's thesis). Carleton University.

Miller, B. (2015). 'Dude, where's your face?' self-presentation, self-description, and partner preferences on a social networking application for men who have sex with men: A content analysis. *Sexuality & Culture*, *19*(4), 637–658. https://doi.org/10.1007/s12119-015-9283-4

Mishali, Y. (2014). Feminine trouble: The removal of femininity from feminist/lesbian/queer esthetics, imagery, and conceptualization. *Women's Studies International Forum*, *44*(1), 55–68. https://doi.org/10.1016/j.wsif.2013.09.003

Mulvey, L. (1989). *Visual and other pleasures*. Palgrave.

Myketiak, C. (2016). Fragile masculinity: Social inequalities in the narrative frame and discursive construction of a mass shooter's autobiography/manifesto. *Contemporary Social Science*, *11*(4), 289–303. https://doi.org/10.1080/21582041.2016.1213414

Nagle, A. (2016). The new man of 4chan. *The Baffler*, *30*, 64–76. Retrieved from https://thebaffler.com/salvos/new-man-4chan-nagle

Pateman, C. (1988). *The sexual contract*. Stanford University Press.

Perilloux, C., Fleischman, D., & Buss, D. (2011). Meet the parents: Parent-Offspring convergence and divergence in mate preferences. *Personality and Individual Differences*, *50*(2), 253–258. https://doi.org/10.1016/j.paid.2010.09.039

Rodger, E. (2014). *My twisted world: The story of Elliot Rodger*. New York Times. https://assets.documentcloud.org/documents/1173808/Elliot-rodger-manifesto.pdf

Rozsa, M. (2018, November 18). *A traumatic vision of masculinity lies at the root of a resentful incel movement*. Salon. https://www.salon.com/2018/11/18/a-traumatic-vision-of-masculinity-lies-at-the-root-of-a-resentful-incel-movement/

Sanchez, F. J., & Vilain, E. (2012). 'Straight-acting gays': The relationship between masculine consciousness, anti-effeminacy, and negative gay identity. *Archives of Sexual Behaviour*, *41*(1), 111–119. https://doi.org/10.1007/s10508-012-9912-z

Schippers, M. (2007). Recovering the feminine other: Masculinity, femininity, and gender hegemony. *Theory and Society*, *36*(85), 85–102. https://doi.org/10.1007/s11186-007-9022-4

Serano, J. (2007). *Whipping girl: A transsexual woman on sexism and the scapegoating of femininity*. Seal Press.

Serano, J. (2013). *Excluded: Making feminist and queer movements more inclusive*. Seal Press.

Skågeby, J. (2011). Online ethnographic methods: Towards a qualitative understanding of virtual community practices. In B. K. Daniel (Ed.), *Handbook of research on methods and techniques for studying virtual communities: Paradigms and phenomena* (pp. 410–428). Information Science Reference.

Tanenbaum, L. (2015). *I am not a slut: Slut-shaming in the age of the internet*. Harper Perennial.

The Fifth Estate. (2019, January 27). Why incels are a 'real and present threat' for Canadians. *CBC News*.

Van Valkenburgh, S. P. (2018). Digesting the red pill: Masculinity and neoliberalism in the manosphere. *Men and Masculinities*, 1–20. Advance online publication. https://doi.org/10.1177/1097184X18816118

Volcano, D. L., & Dahl, U. (2008). *Femmes of power: Exploding queer femininities*. Serpent's Tail.

Zimmerman, S., Ryan, L., & Duriesmith, D. (2018). Recognizing the violent extremist ideology of 'incels'. *Women in International Security Policy Brief*, 1–5. Retrieved from https://www.wiisglobal.org/wp-content/uploads/2018/09/Policybrief-Violent-Extremists-Incels.pdf

How is masculinity ideology related to transprejudice in Turkey: the mediatory effect of femmephobia

Beril Türkoğlu ⓘD and Gülden Sayılan ⓘD

ABSTRACT

Prejudice towards trans women is an under-examined but a critical social problem in Turkey. Patriarchal femininity sanctions women who do not comply with the idealised female bodies and feminine norms. On the other hand, ideals of hegemonic masculinity necessitate that men avoid femininity. In that sense, prejudice against trans women ostensibly stands at the intersection of hegemonic masculinity ideology and femininities that diverge from patriarchal feminine norms. Therefore, this study examines the mediatory effect of femmephobia in the link between masculinity ideology and prejudice towards trans women as measured by negative affect and social distancing motivations. Results indicate that femmephobia significantly mediates the relationship between the endorsement of masculinity ideology and prejudice towards trans women. Among three mandates of masculinity ideology, the endorsement of the antifemininity mandate was the most solid indirect predictor of negative affect and social distance through femmephobia, followed by mandates of toughness and status, respectively. Although participant gender does not have an indirect effect on the outcome variables, it has a direct effect on men's social distancing intentions but not on negative emotions. The results are discussed in the light of existing literature which intersects with the devaluation of femininity.

While attitudes towards transgender people have been changing positively, this has not been the case in Turkey (Gölge & Akdemir, 2019). A recent report revealed that Turkey holds the highest rank related to transgender murders among European Countries (Transrespect versus Transphobia Worldwide, 2018). Besides the murders, transgender people in Turkey encounter discrimination and violence in different forms such as physical, sexual and psychological assaults, public hate speech, and invasion of property. Although transgender people are recognised in the Turkish legal system, they face different forms of institutional maltreatment and human rights violations under the guise of moral sanctions (Red Umbrella Sexual Health and Human Rights Association, 2016). As Göç (2019, pp. 177–178) argues, these kinds of moral sanctions become the means of policing those who deviate from *so-called* universal patriarchal norms. This way, transgender people are prevented their right to enjoy fundamental human rights in education, health, and employment areas (Göçmen & Yılmaz, 2017). This prejudice is also observable in interpersonal relations. Turkish people seem to be socially distant and emotionally hostile about engaging in physical or social contact with trans women compared to cisgender women (Cingöz-Ulu et al., 2016; Sayılan et al., 2020).

Turkey is a country where collectivist and masculine values motivate people's beliefs and behaviours, which is highly observable in conformity to societal norms (Hofstede et al., 2010). From a cultural point of view, Turkish people may see transgender people as a threat to traditional gender norms because of *deliberately* embodiment non-conforming gender identities. Besides transgression of gender norms and conventions as motivating forces behind transprejudice (J. L. Nagoshi et al., 2008; Warriner et al., 2013), endorsement of masculinity ideology may be a more precise predictor of transprejudice. As research reveals, masculinity ideology and practices of manhood are socially constructed through the avoidance and degradation of femininity (Bosson et al., 2005; Kimmel, 1997; Kosakowska-Berezecka et al., 2016). In that sense, trans women pose a threat to masculine superiority and the heteronormative binary division of gender by embracing feminine characteristics and abandoning the masculine ones (Nadal et al., 2012; Norton, 1997; Norton & Herek, 2013).

Although transprejudice (Cingöz-Ulu et al., 2016; Sayılan et al., 2020) and the masculine social structure (Bolak-Boratav et al., 2017; Sancar, 2009) are evident in Turkey, there has been no study targeting this intersection in the Turkish cultural context. Aiming to fill this gap, we suggest that the intersection of masculinity ideology endorsement and devaluation of femininity (i.e., femmephobia) is a critical ground explaining transprejudice, specifically towards trans women. Femme Theory (Hoskin, 2017, 2019) conceptualises *femmephobia* as the devaluation and regulation of femininities, specifically arguing that this construct underlines the backlash against those who deviate from patriarchal norms about ideal femininity. Thus, Femme Theory helps us to move our argument about transprejudice in Turkey beyond the masculinity ideology.

Transprejudice

Many of the research have been using the term transphobia to refer to discrimination and the threat of violence faced by transgender people. More precisely, transphobia is a form of prejudice that refers to hatred towards individuals who violate cisnormative gender expectations of society (Hill & Willoughby, 2005). However, given that the term transphobia may connote *phobia* as a psychopathological concept, we prefer the term *transprejudice*, which is motivated (and thus can be diminished) by socio-cultural beliefs and practices (McDermott et al., 2018). For the purposes of this study, transprejudice is conceptualised as having negative emotions (see Glick et al., 2007) and social distancing tendencies (Cingöz-Ulu et al., 2016; Sayılan et al., 2020) towards trans women, thus capturing the texture of emotional and cognitive bases of prejudice (Herek, 2009).

Rates of transprejudice are often higher towards transgender individuals who are on the male-to-female (MTF; trans women) spectrum compared to those on the female-to-male (FTM; trans men) spectrum. Illustrating the dissimilarity in the ways that trans women and trans men experience prejudice (Bauerband et al., 2019; Winter et al., 2008), trans women report higher rates of everyday discrimination than trans men, non-binary individuals, cisgender women, and cisgender men, respectively (Bauerband et al., 2019). Similarly, compared to trans men, trans women are more discriminated in interpersonal relations such as romantic relations or dating (Blair & Hoskin, 2019; Gazzola & Morrison, 2014; Glotfelter & Anderson, 2017). Serano (2007) argues that this differential treatment is, in part, due to the tendency to see trans women as rejecting masculine superiority by adopting femininity and being women when assigned male at birth, both of which pose challenges to gender hegemony. This critical scholarship drew our attention to examine the role of a devaluation of femininity and how it is motivated by the masculinity ideology.

Masculinity ideology and its relationship to transprejudice

Masculinity ideology refers to social norms that align with hegemonic masculinity, including sanctions about appropriate behaviours, appearance, or relations that guarantee male privilege and status. Thompson and Pleck (1986) define masculinity ideology as an endorsement of status, antifemininity and toughness norms, which also represent the structure of masculinity ideology in Turkish culture

(Lease et al., 2009). Accordingly, *status* is related to one's expectations that men deserve status and respect in the eyes of others while *toughness* underlines the need that a man should be emotionally and physically strong and self-reliant. *Antifemininity*, on the other hand, represents the pressure men feel to avoid feminine characteristics or practices (Thompson & Pleck, 1986). Otherwise, their (precarious) privileged status is jeopardised in the eyes of others and themselves (Vandello & Bosson, 2013; Vandello et al., 2008). Together, these three norms/mandates constitute cultural beliefs about an ideal man and justify male power over women, sexual minorities and non-hegemonic men in the face of gender nonconformity threats (Connell, 1995).

Pursuing status and power in the eyes of others is a touchstone of masculinity ideology, both for men and women (Thompson & Bennett, 2015; Vandello & Bosson, 2013), and has close connections with antifemininity norm. Avoiding femininity serves as a building block of masculinity, prohibiting femininity in men's appearance or behaviours as well as motivating men to humiliate those who hold feminine characteristics (Kimmel, 1997; O'Connor et al., 2017). Men continuously invest in societal power and status, and avoiding femininity is the most salient form of the reconstructive practice guaranteeing status (Brescoll et al., 2012; Rudman et al., 2012; Thompson & Bennett, 2015). Research shows that men feel extreme discomfort about being perceived as gay when given (mock) feedback that they are feminine. In response, the men embraced status beliefs (Dahl et al., 2015) and traditional gender roles more strongly (Kosakowska-Berezecka et al., 2016).

The toughness mandate, on the other hand, is in liaison with antifemininity and status norms by sanctioning men to portray an emotionally and physically tough image. Using violence in times of threat, having a sturdy male body, and engaging in risky behaviours set the ground for being *a tough guy* (Lease et al., 2009; Thompson & Pleck, 1986). In that sense, endorsing the toughness mandate may shed light on people's vigilance in the face of the *femme* (i.e., divergence from traditional femininity; see Hoskin, 2019), which is threatening to men's toughness and so to their societal power.

Masculinity ideology is related to intolerance and negative attitudes towards members of sexual minority groups (e.g., gays and lesbians; Bosson et al., 2005; Falomir-Pichastor et al., 2019; Herek, 2000; Konopka et al., 2019; Parrott, 2009). Additionally, cisgender heterosexual men are more prejudiced towards transgender people compared to cisgender heterosexual women (Glotfelter & Anderson, 2017; J. L. Nagoshi et al., 2008; C. T. Nagoshi et al., 2019; Winter et al., 2008), and their prejudice is more substantial towards trans women than trans men. Cisgender men's transprejudice might be rooted in men's *fear* of losing cisheteronormative male power in the face of gender nonconformity (C. T. Nagoshi et al., 2019). People may interpret trans women's femininity as a symbolically 'giving up' their legitimate power in society (Pulice-Farrow et al., 2017; Serano, 2007). Thus, an attempt to understand power internalised through masculinity ideology and how it shapes people's attitudes by degrading femininity might shed light on prejudice towards trans women.

Femininity has almost been the unique threat manipulation used in masculinity research that guarantees de-masculinisation (Bosson et al., 2005; Kosakowska-Berezecka et al., 2016; Vandello & Bosson, 2013). 'Feminised' men are found to lose their status/tough image and to re-embody their masculinity by demonising and humiliating the *femininity*, especially on gay men (O'Connor et al., 2017; Parrott, 2009). Despite this noticeable relationship, there are very few studies that look directly at the relationship between masculinity ideology and transprejudice (see Konopka et al., 2019). Instead, prior studies examine the relationship between broader gender ideologies and transprejudice (see J. L. Nagoshi et al., 2008; C. T. Nagoshi et al., 2019), or prejudice towards gay men (Falomir-Pichastor et al., 2019; Iacoviello et al., 2020; Parrott, 2009).

Since trans women's ostensible embracing of femininity is read as jeopardising masculine ascendency, femmephobia becomes critical in our analysis. The denigration of trans women or feminine/feminised individuals who are AMAB is not only related to the transgression of masculine gender roles but also to adoption of femininity, which is already demoted in patriarchy (Serano, 2007). Thus, we aim to examine the role of femmephobia on prejudice towards trans women, whose expression of femaleness and femininity is interpreted as a transgression of both patriarchal femininity and hegemonic masculinity

(Hoskin, 2020; Serano, 2007). Attending to each of these, Femme Theory thus provides a useful framework of analysis to examine transprejudice towards trans women.

Femme theory, femmephobia, and its relationship with masculinity

Femme Theory defines *femme* as a self-defined and deliberately embraced feminine identity, independent of the assignment of biological sex (Hoskin, 2017, p. 99). From this point of view, Femme Theory dislocates the understandings of patriarchal femininities by redefining femininity as an independent and powerful form of *being* (free from cultural and biological norms attributed to bodies assigned female at birth). It argues that the *femme* is policed and controlled by the ideals of patriarchal in a given society, the most prominent feature of which is regulating femininity to a female body, biological sex, and anatomy (Hoskin, 2017, 2019).

Even within the feminist discourse, femininity is ideologically positioned as being opposite to strength and power (Serano, 2007; Kimmel, 1987). Research so far has underestimated femininity as an intersection of power and oppression. Pointing to this, Hoskin (2017) suggests a novel term *femmephobia* as 'prejudice, discrimination, or antagonism directed against someone who is perceived to identify, embody, or express femininely and toward people and objects gendered femininely' (Hoskin, 2017, p. 101). Femmephobia is a way of devaluing the stereotypically *feminine* (i.e., nurturance, wearing pink, being emotional and sensitive, looking fragile, and innocent, see Bem, 1974; Rudman et al., 2012; Sakallı Uğurlu et al., 2018; Spence et al., 1975) as well as denoting responses to those transgressing normative femininity ideals of the society (Hoskin, 2017). In the case of trans women, embracing cultural norms related to femininity is a way of passing. Simultaneously, however, they are constantly policed for being both too feminine and not feminine enough (Hoskin, 2019). In other words, deviation from hegemonic masculinity pushes trans women into 'effeminate realm' while at the same time it makes their femininity 'inauthentic' as a way of protecting the boundaries of hegemonic masculinity (Hoskin, 2020, p. 2326).

As critical masculinity researchers have noted, a man can cement his masculinity by showing both himself and others that he is not feminine (Brescoll et al., 2012; Dahl et al., 2015; Kimmel, 1997; Vandello & Bosson, 2013). Embodiment and expressions of femininity are strictly forbidden for boys and men throughout their socialisation (Kimmel, 1997; Rudman et al., 2012), and this intrinsically contributes to the construction of femmephobia. From the beginning of gender socialisation, society rewards boys to the extent that they avoid 'girly' things and punishes them if they present feminine characteristics (Levant, 2011). Moreover, status failure accompanies with men's feminisation in the eyes of others (Sancar, 2009). In that sense, both the construction and deconstruction of masculinity are tied up with femininity, and thus, analyses of masculinity need to incorporate femmephobia (Hoskin, 2017).

Men might feel threatened and have a fear of being perceived as gay, even when they only imagine doing feminine activities such as hair brushing or reading fashion magazines (Bosson et al., 2005). Similarly, even diagnosed with stereotypically feminine health problems (e.g., anorexia, bulimia nervosa, major depression) can evoke the anxiety of being considered less of a man (Michniewicz et al., 2015). In that sense, interacting with a trans woman is a considerable risk for a heterosexual, cisgender man because others may not see him as a *real* man by erroneously labelling him as gay (Butler, 2015). In response to trans women murder rates in the USA, Butler (2015) suggests that the perpetrator men may have felt attacked by a noticeably feminine trans woman.

While antifemininity mandate of masculinity and femmephobia may seem to converge, *femininity* serves different purposes for each concept. One's endorsement of the antifemininity mandate of masculinity ideology reflects their acceptance of the invisible prohibitions of society about men's engagement of feminine roles, behaviours, and tasks. In other words, it is merely about male roles in a given society (Thompson & Bennett, 2015; Thompson & Pleck, 1986). Femmephobia, on the other hand, reflects one's prejudiced and discriminative behaviours towards femininity and thus helps to maintain patriarchal power and male privilege by devaluing the feminine (Hoskin, 2018). In that sense, together with status and toughness, endorsement of antifemininity norm sets a ground for femmephobia, through which people engage in the degradation of femininity.

The current study

In light of the literature, the current study explores the role of masculinity ideology on transprejudice with the mediation of femmephobia in a Turkish sample. We measure masculinity ideology as an endorsement of status, antifemininity and toughness mandates of masculinity (Lease et al., 2009); femmephobia as a devaluation/regulation of femininity (Hoskin, 2017, 2019), and transprejudice as a social distance (Bogardus, 1959) and negative outgroup affect (Stephan et al., 1998) towards trans women.

We prefer measuring affective and behavioural/cognitive components of transprejudice separately, as general measures of prejudice obscure the specific emotions and reactions that people might have towards different societal groups (Cottrell & Neuberg, 2005; Stangor et al., 1991). Moreover, particular social groups may evoke different emotions, and each emotion drives a different kind of reaction towards outgroup members (Mackie et al., 2009). For example, people are found to exhibit disgust and pity towards gay men, while they feel anger for other groups (such as activist feminist). These findings, however, are not observable in the measures of general prejudice related to the target group (Cottrell & Neuberg, 2005).

Research on transprejudice reveals that cisgender men are more prejudiced towards transgender individuals compared to cisgender women (J. L. Nagoshi et al., 2008; Winter et al., 2008). However, focusing on gender differences in prejudice may miss the ideological references behind transprejudice. We suggest that it is not solely the gender category but the acceptance of masculinity ideology that creates a difference in terms of transprejudice. Endorsement of this ideology by both men and women suggests that it is not a group code specific to men; instead, it signifies socially constructed norms about the male gender. Masculine ideology seeps into people's characteristics and affects their everyday behaviours in an interpersonal manner (Thompson & Pleck, 1986). Thus, we include participant gender as a control variable in our models. Also, in line with the view that attitudes may differ across different sexual orientations in the same gender identity group (Bauerband et al., 2019), we included only the heterosexual, cisgender men and women as participants. This considered, we expect high endorsement of the three mandates of masculinity ideology to have a relationship with more robust negative emotions and intention to put greater social distance towards trans women, and for femmephobia to have a mediatory role in this relationship. We do not expect to see the indirect effect of gender on prejudice towards trans women as the endorsement of masculinity ideology would get the variability rather than solely gender.

Method

Participants and procedure

Our sample included 280 self-identified heterosexual and cisgender individuals (175 women and 105 men) whose age ranged from 17 to 29 ($M = 21.71$, $SD = 1.90$).[1] Participants were university students who filled in the online survey in exchange for extra course credits. Data collection started after the local ethics committee for research on human subjects approved the study. Because participants were limited to self-identified heterosexual and cisgender men and women, we removed a total of 14 cases (nine women and five men) from the samples for being either non-heterosexual or non-cisgender. Sample sizes met the minimum expected size estimated as 71 participants in Monte Carlo simulation for a three-predictors model with 99% confidence interval, a large effect size (f^2) of .35, and power of .95 (Faul et al., 2009).

Materials

Demographic and background variables

The demographic information form asked participants' gender identity (man, woman, and other/ rather not say), sexual orientation (heterosexual, gay, lesbian, bisexual, asexual), age, and education[2].

Masculinity ideology

We used the Male Role Norms Scale (MRNS) to measure participants' endorsement of masculinity ideology. The 26-item scale was developed by Thompson and Pleck (1986) and adapted to Turkish by Lease and colleagues (Lease et al., 2009). It has three subscales, namely, status (11 items: e.g., 'Success in his work has to be man's central goal in this life.'), antifemininity (7 items: e.g., 'It bothers me when a man does something that I consider "feminine."'), and toughness (8 items: e.g., 'When a man is feeling a little pain, he should try not to let it show very much.'). The internal consistency coefficients of the subscales were .81 for status, .74 for toughness, and .76 for antifemininity in the original study. For the current sample, they were .86, .78, and .78, respectively. Participants rate the items on a *1* (strongly disagree) to *7* (strongly agree) Likert-type scale. Higher scores indicate a stronger endorsement of masculinity ideology.

Femmephobia

We used nine items of the transphobia and genderism scale (Hill & Willoughby, 2005) to measure fear and devaluation of femininity displayed by men/those AMAB which has already been used to measure femmephobia by Hoskin (2018). These items had already been adapted into Turkish in 2016 as a part of the full transphobia and genderism scale (Cingöz-Ulu et al., 2016). The items are related to attitudes and self-reported violent behaviours towards men embodying feminine characteristics (e.g., 'Feminine men make me feel uncomfortable'). The internal consistency coefficient of the original scale was .90; .88 for Turkish adaptation. Participants rated the items on a 7-point scale ranging from *1* (strongly disagree) to *7* (strongly agree). Higher scores indicate a stronger adherence of femmephobia.

To determine the factor structure of the adapted scale in the current sample, we performed a series of Principal Component Analysis (PCA) with Promax rotation. We decided on the number of factors through the Kaiser criterion of eigenvalues over 1.00, the Cattell scree plot test, Monte Carlo parallel analysis and the interpretability of scores.

The Kaiser-Meyer-Olkin Measure of Sampling Adequacy value was .91, reflecting that the items were suitable for factor analysis. Results of the PCA suggested a one-factor solution explaining 52% of the total variance. The loadings of Item 6 and Item 8 were below the acceptable cut-off value of .45 (Tabachnick & Fidell, 2007). Therefore, we repeated the analysis after removing these items. The final one-factor solution explained 63% of total variance with loadings ranging from .88 to .65[3].

Negative affect

We used the Turkish adapted version (Balaban, 2013) of the negative emotions subscale of the outgroup affectivity scale to measure the emotional reactions of the participants in the case of possible communication with a trans woman. It consists of six items (i.e., hostility, superiority, dislike, disdain, hatred, and rejection) ranked on *1* (strongly disagree) to *7* (strongly agree) Likert type scale. Higher scores indicate greater negative feelings towards trans women.

Social Distance

We measured social distancing tendencies of the participants with the 7-item Bogardus Social Distance Scale (Bogardus, 1959). The original scale recommends using outgroup members as the targets of social distancing, and the Turkish version of the scale adapted the items for, trans women as an outgroup member (Cingöz-Ulu et al., 2016). The participants rated the level of discomfort they would feel in various hypothetical social encounters with a trans woman (e.g., having her kin by marriage, working in the same workplace, or being friends with her). Participants rated each item on a *1* (I would not feel uncomfortable at all) to *7* (I would feel extremely uncomfortable) Likert type scale. Higher scores indicate less comfort/ more discomfort with trans women, implying transprejudice.

Results

Before the analyses, we checked the data in terms of normality, linearity, and homoscedasticity assumptions, and it was valid for multivariate data analyses. Table 1 depicts the descriptive statistics and the correlation coefficients among the variables. All the correlations between study variables were statistically significant and in expected directions ($p < .01$). However, regarding that high correlations between study variables could indicate multicollinearity, we checked variance inflation factors (VIF) for each variable. Both the tolerance values (Menard, 1995) and VIF values (Myers, 1990) were within acceptable limits indicating that multicollinearity is not a problematic issue for the study.

As a further test of whether the similarity between femmephobia and antifemininity dimension of masculinity ideology results from similar wording or a shared sentiment, we conducted a series of Confirmatory Factor Analysis (CFA).[4] Results suggested eliminating Item 9 from antifemininity subscale of masculinity ideology and Item 10 from femmephobia scales; we tested the mediational models with the revised version of the scales.

Another critical point to note was the possible effect of gender on study variables. Previous studies have shown gender to have a measurable impact on transphobia or homophobia (J. L. Nagoshi et al., 2008; C. T. Nagoshi et al., 2019). Thus, we first examined gender difference in the study variables by using an independent samples t-test to see whether controlling for gender ought to be required for further analysis. Independent sample t-test results showed that men's scores were significantly higher than women's scores for all study variables (See Table 2). Thus, we

Table 1. Scale means, standard deviations, reliability coefficients, and correlation coefficients between study variables.

Measure	1	2	3	4	5	6	7
1. Gender	–						
2. Status	.18*	–					
3. Toughness	.28*	.71*	–				
4. Antifemininity	.19*	.62*	.70*	–			
5. Femmephobia	.18*	.59*	.63*	.66*	–		
6. Negative Affect	.21*	.43*	.48*	.55*	.68*	–	
7. Social distance	.27*	.40*	.48*	.55*	.55*	.74*	–
M	1.38	3.91	3.23	2.68	2.80	1.91	2.38
SD	.49	1.13	1.07	1.05	1.41	1.01	1.25
Cronbach a	–	.86	.78	.78	.88	.85	.90

All N's = 280. *$p < .01$.

Table 2. T-test results for comparing men and women on masculinity ideology, femmephobia, and transprejudice.

	Men		Women		
Variables	M	SD	M	SD	t(278)*
Status	4.17	1.02	3.75	1.17	3.06
Toughness	3.62	.95	3.00	1.07	4.93
Antifemininity	2.94	.99	2.53	1.05	3.20
Femmephobia	3.12	1.33	2.61	1.43	2.96
Negative Affect	2.18	1.10	1.74	.91	3.62
Social Distance	2.81	1.34	2.12	1.12	4.68

*$p < .01$.

included participants' gender as an IV in the models as a control variable, letting us see the role of masculinity ideology by eliminating a shared variance.

Mediational models on the relationship between masculinity ideology, femmephobia, and transprejudice

Employing the PROCESS Macro Model 4 (Hayes, 2018) with 95% confidence intervals and 5000 bootstrapped samples, we conducted two sets of mediation analyses for the two measures of transprejudice. The predictor variables were the three dimensions of masculine ideology, namely, status, toughness, and antifemininity; as well as the gender of the participants. The mediator variable was femmephobia, and the outcome variables were the two indicators of transprejudice (i.e., negative outgroup affect and social distance).

In the first model, the total explained variance was 49%, $R^2 = .49$, $F (5, 274) = 51.61$, $MSE = .53$, $p = .00$ on the negative outgroup affect. As presented in Figure 1, only the antifemininity dimension of masculinity ideology ($B = .17$, $SE = .06$, $p = .01$, 95% CI [.05, .30]) had a direct effect on negative affect. As for the indirect effects, all three dimensions of masculinity ideology significantly predicted negative outgroup affect through femmephobia ($B_{status} = .09$, bootstrapped $SE = .03$, 95% CI [.03, .16]; $B_{toughness} = .12$, bootstrapped $SE = .04$, 95% CI [.04, .20]; $B_{antifemininity} = .21$, bootstrapped $SE = .04$, 95% CI [.14, .29]). However, the indirect effect of gender on negative affect was not statistically significant (see Figure 1).

When social distance was the outcome, the same model explained more than half of the variance, $R^2 = .58$, $F (5, 274) = 76.95$, $MSE = .66$, $p = .00$. Similar to negative affect, only antifemininity ($B = .16$, $SE = .07$, $p = .03$, 95% CI [.02, .30]) and participant gender ($B = .38$, $SE = .10$, $p = .00$, 95% CI [.17, .59]) directly predicted social distance towards trans women. As for the indirect effects, results indicated that status ($B = .14$, bootstrapped $SE = .05$, 95% CI [.06, .24]), toughness ($B = .18$, bootstrapped $SE = .06$, 95% CI [.06, .30]), and antifemininity ($B = .33$, bootstrapped $SE = .05$, 95% CI [.22, .44]) mandates of masculinity ideology predicted social distance through the mediation of femmephobia; however, the indirect effect of participant gender was not statistically significant (see Figure 2).

As for the relationships between independent variables and mediator, the three mandates of masculinity ideology explained 51% of total variance in femmephobia, $R^2 = .51$, $F (4, 275) = 70.10$, $MSE = 1.00$, $p = .00$. Results indicated that status ($B = .23$, $SE = .08$, $p = .00$, 95% CI [.08,.38]), toughness ($B = .29$, $SE = .09$, $p = .00$, 95% CI [.11,.47]), and antifemininity ($B = .53$, $SE = .082$, $p = .01$, 95% CI

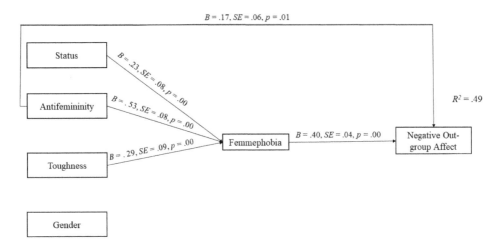

Figure 1. The role of masculinity ideology on negative outgroup affect through femmephobia.
Note. The mediational model presenting the relationship between status, antifemininity, toughness, femmephobia, and negative outgroup affect. Nonsignificant paths are not presented for parsimony, $p < .05$

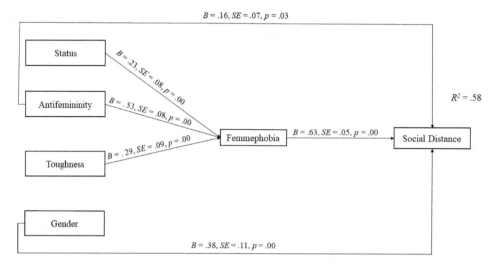

Figure 2. The role of masculinity ideology on social distance through femmephobia.
Note. The mediational model presenting the relationship between status, antifemininity, toughness, femmephobia, and social distance. Nonsignificant paths are not presented for parsimony, *p* < .05.

[.36,.69]) significantly predicted femmephobia for both outcomes. Participants gender, however, had no significant effect in explaining femmephobia.

Discussion

The current research aimed to unveil ideological motivators of prejudice towards trans women in Turkey with a specific focus on masculinity and denigration of femininity. To that end, we tested whether endorsement of status, antifemininity and toughness mandates of masculinity ideology predict (a) negative affect and (b) social distancing tendencies towards trans women with the mediation of femmephobia in Turkish cultural context. We also included participants' gender as a predictor to see whether it played an indirect role on transprejudice after removing the variance of masculinity ideology. Our findings highlighted the mediatory role of femmephobia as an outlet for reducing the perceived gender identity and nonconformity threat of trans women (Hoskin, 2017, 2019).

Our results revealed that the endorsement of masculinity ideology accounts for people's negative emotions towards trans women because of their beliefs devaluing the femininity expressed by a person who is AMAB (i.e., femmephobia). Similarly, the same motivations predicted people's intention to put social distance towards trans women in imaginary social contact situations such as being relatives, friends, neighbours, etc. (Bogardus, 1959). Our findings clearly show that accepted norms of masculinity prevent people from socially interacting with trans women *insofar* as they devalue and police femininity that deviates from the patriarchal norms (Hoskin, 2017, 2018, 2019). Our conceptual models also support that disavowal of the *femme* embraced by the ones who are AMAB stands right at the crossing line of hegemonic masculinity and patriarchal femininity norms (Hoskin, 2020).

Among three mandates of masculinity ideology, the endorsement of the antifemininity mandate is the most solid indirect predictor of negative affect and social distance through femmephobia, and toughness and status mandates, respectively, follow it. This result ascertains the importance of femmephobia as a mediator because it is quite expectable that if people believe that someone AMAB should not be feminine, these beliefs reflect on their attitudes towards a feminine person AMAB in the femmephobia measure. Followers of antifemininity norm, thus, grow negative affect towards and avoid sharing any social/physical environment with trans women who are already demonised in their gender-binary belief system (Butler, 2015; Cottrell & Neuberg, 2005). This result is in line with the research showing that endorsement of antifemininity norm indirectly predicts negative emotions towards feminine gay men

(Parrott, 2009) and the research that used femininity as a source of gender threat to predict sexual prejudice (Bosson et al., 2005; Falomir-Pichastor et al., 2019; Herek, 2000; Konopka et al., 2019).

We can argue that antifemininity and toughness may meet on a common ground of men's concern for *manly* appearance and outlook. Thompson and Pleck (1986) operationalise toughness as physical and emotional sturdiness that present a man as a *tough guy*. On the other hand, they describe antifemininity as avoiding feminine characteristic in personal or interpersonal manners. The endorsement of both norms is related to drawing a good impression upon others (i.e., that he is not a *soft* man). It is parallel with the contemporary gender stereotypes in Turkish culture where being a *tough guy* is a highly desirable characteristic for men (Sakallı & Türkoğlu, 2019; Sakallı Uğurlu et al., 2018). This finding can also be supported by the precarious manhood thesis (Vandello & Bosson, 2013; Vandello et al., 2008). Accordingly, men's status is shaped by others' surveillance, and this creates permanent anxiety about losing manhood status in the face of femininity threat (Brescoll et al., 2012; Michniewicz et al., 2015; Vandello et al., 2008). To be perceived as a *real man*, men have to avoid femininity in their appearance and social relations. Confirming this, trans women who are AMAB report that they experience a decline in social status and power after they transition into womanhood (Cole et al., 2000).

Our analyses indicated that among the gender ideologies previously found connected to transprejudice (J. L. Nagoshi et al., 2008; C. T. Nagoshi et al., 2019), it is the endorsement of masculinity ideology that is susceptible for prejudice towards, trans women. Here, the subject of the prejudice (trans women) collides with the antifemininity mandate of masculinity by threatening male status by ostensibly 'giving up one's male gender identity' (Warriner et al., 2013, p. 1311). Building on this, femmephobia serves as a tool to justify transprejudice because it is nourished by the fear of femininity ingrained in masculinity (Kimmel, 1997; Vandello & Bosson, 2013). Previous research supports that the denigration and abstaining from femininity (via femmephobia) is motivated by men's fear of being seen as gay (Bosson et al., 2005). Hoskin (2017) argues that the backlash of the feminisation among men and those AMAB is a clear indicator of femmephobia, making femininity a key nexus where different forms of oppression intersect. It is this oppression that makes the boundaries of masculinity in the face of the femme (Hoskin, 2020). In our research, femmephobia reconceptualises the backlash against femininity and shows that the practice of feminine devaluation is not specific to men; instead, it is related to people's endorsement of masculinity ideology.

Sexual prejudice is examined under cognitive, behavioural, and affective components. General measures of prejudice obscure specific emotions or attitudes towards different societal groups (see Herek, 2009). In line with this, our research also revealed that prejudice towards trans women could be measured twofold: affective and cognitive/behavioural. Stangor et al. (1991) claim that affective and cognitive sources of prejudice should be examined separately because emotions have the potential to capture mostly self-relevant psychological state that the prejudice-target evokes. However, because cognitive bases of prejudice (i.e., stereotypes) could reflect cultural beliefs about the prejudice-target, it may work as secondary information.

There is a variety of social groups, and each of them may evoke different emotions and behavioural intentions. For example, as stated above, research finds that people feel disgusted towards gay people, and anger towards activist groups (Cottrell & Neuberg, 2005). In the current study, strict followers of three mandates of masculinity ideology had proscriptions about femininity expressed by a body AMAB, and this evoked negative emotions such as hostility, anger, and hate towards trans women. According to Mackie et al. (2009), these emotions may lead to different impulses against the target group. Based on this, we speculate that one's masculinity-rooted femmephobia evoke negative feelings towards trans women, and that these feelings may explain people's future aggression towards trans women in convenient conditions. Thus, future research should focus on negative emotions as a predictor of aggressive behaviours towards trans women.

Considering participants' gender as an independent predictor, we did not expect to see the significant role of gender on any of the outcome measures because of the shared variance with masculinity ideology. In line with our expectations, the direct effect of gender on negative outgroup affect was not significant, but it had a direct effect on people's distancing intentions. The reason why men had greater intention to put social distance could be men's vigilance towards trans women due to their own precarious manhood status (Vandello et al., 2008). 'Feminisation' of a person who is AMAB may have directly elicited a fear that any man can be feminised, which would lead a demolition of conventional masculine status (C. T. Nagoshi et al., 2019). Alternatively, another argument is that this fear could be externalised in the (hypothetical) conditions of being close to trans women, which fuels concerns over protecting precarious manhood status (Vandello et al., 2008) and toughness in the eyes of others (Cheryan et al., 2015). In the case of negative emotions, however, people's feelings can be concealed, which is a central doctrine of masculinity ideology internalised through male socialisation.

Limitations and future suggestions

The current study has some limitations. First, we conducted this study with a student sample aged between 19 and 29. Although the vast majority of research is based on student samples, it would be meaningful to test the same model on different age groups to see whether the same masculinity concerns continue throughout the lifespan. Second, we could have asked participants about the previous contact with transgender people. Norton and Herek (2013) indicate that negative attitudes towards transgender individuals are strictly related to the lack of the previous contact with sexual and gender minorities. College students may lack the experience of the previous contact with a trans woman and build their prejudice via negative stereotypes they have about trans women. Research has already shown that Turkish college students with prior contact with transgender people have more positive attitudes towards transgender people (Gölge & Akdemir, 2019). Thus, future studies may focus on creating imagined or real social contact with transgender people or develop intervention programmes focusing on the similarity between different gender identity groups (i.e., cisgender and trans women and men) in educational settings to diminish transprejudice (see Iacoviello et al., 2020).

Conclusion

In sum, our findings support the existing research that validates the existence of transprejudice in Turkey regarding violent attributions (Cingöz-Ulu et al., 2016) and socio-political and moral attitudes (Sayılan et al., 2020). Undoubtedly, these findings are not isolated; instead, they tend to nourish in the current political atmosphere of the country. As recent reports outline, Turkey is one of the most conservative countries of the Europe region related to attitudes towards sexual minorities (International Lesbian Gay Bisexual, Trans and Intersex Association [ILGA] -Europe, 2019). Thus, providing results from a highly masculine, conservative non-Western country would bring different insights to the existing research using Western samples.

Notes

1. Analyses of the current study were conducted on a merged data set including participants from two samples: a sample with 175 heterosexual-cisgender women and a sample with 105 heterosexual-cisgender men. Apart from gender, the two data sets were identical in terms of study procedures and tested variables.
2. Apart from these, participants were asked about their faith, conservativeness, and political orientation. However, the information on these variables were not included in the scope of this paper as they were not included in the analyses.
3. An overview of the resultant scale can be found in supplementary materials (Table 1) at https://osf.io/abqem/
4. Details of the CFA can be found in supplementary materials at https://osf.io/abqem/

Disclosure statement

No potential conflict of interest was reported by the authors.

ORCID

Beril Türkoğlu (iD) http://orcid.org/0000-0002-4752-5723
Gülden Sayılan (iD) http://orcid.org/0000-0003-0923-1668

References

Balaban, Ç. D. (2013). *The roles of intergroup threat, social dominance orientation and right-wing authoritarianism in predicting Turks' prejudice toward Kurds* [Unpublished Master Thesis]. Middle East Technical University

Bauerband, L. A., Teti, M., & Velicer, W. F. (2019). Measuring minority stress: Invariance of a discrimination and vigilance scale across transgender and cisgender LGBQ individuals. *Psychology and Sexuality*, *10*(1), 17–30. https://doi.org/10.1080/19419899.2018.1520143

Bem, S. L. (1974). The measurement of psychological androgyny. *Journal of Consulting and Clinical Psychology*, *42*(2), 155–162. https://doi.org/10.1037/h0036215

Blair, K. L., & Hoskin, R. A. (2019). Transgender exclusion from the world of dating: Patterns of acceptance and rejection of hypothetical trans dating partners as a function of sexual and gender identity. *Journal of Social and Personal Relationships*, *36*(7), 2074–2095. https://doi.org/10.1177/0265407518779139

Bogardus, E. S. (1959). *Social distance*. Antioch.

Bolak-Boratav, H., Okman-Fişek, G., & Eslen-Ziya, H. (2017). *Erkekliğin Türkiye halleri [Turkish aspects of masculinity]* (1st ed.). İstanbul Bilgi University Publications.

Bosson, J. K., Prewitt-Freilino, J. L., & Taylor, J. N. (2005). Role rigidity: A problem of identity misclassification? *Journal of Personality and Social Psychology*, *89*(4), 552–565. https://doi.org/10.1037/0022-3514.89.4.552

Brescoll, V. L., Uhlmann, E. L., Moss-Racusin, C., & Sarnell, L. (2012). Masculinity, status, and subordination: Why working for a gender stereotype violator causes men to lose status. *Journal of Experimental Social Psychology*, *48*(1), 354–357. https://doi.org/10.1016/j.jesp.2011.06.005

Butler, J. (2015). *Why do men kill trans women? Gender theorist Judith Butler explains*. https://www.vice.com/en_us/article/qkgyqm/man-confesses-to-killing-trans-teenager-with-a-hammer

Cheryan, S., Cameron, J. S., Katagiri, Z., & Monin, B. (2015). Manning up: Threatened men compensate by disavowing feminine preferences and embracing masculine attributes. *Social Psychology*, *46*(4), 218–227. https://doi.org/10.1027/1864-9335/a000239

Cingöz-Ulu, B., Türkoğlu, B., & Sayılan, G. (2016). Kadın şiddet mağdurlarına yönelik tutumlarda mağdurun, trans kimliğinin etkisi [The effect of victim's gender identity on attitudes towards violence victims]. *Türk Psikoloji Yazilari [Turkish Psychological Articles]*, *19* (ÖzelSayı/Special Issue), 94–104. https://www.psikolog.org.tr/tr/yayinlar/dergiler/1031828/tpy1301996120160000m000049.pdf

Cole, S. S., Denny, D., Eyler, A. E., & Samons, S. L. (2000). Issues of transgender. In L. T. Szuchman & F. Muscarella (Eds.), *Psychological perspectives on human sexuality* (pp. 149–195). Wiley.

Connell, R. W. (1995). *Masculinities*. University of California Press.

Cottrell, C. A., & Neuberg, S. L. (2005). Different emotional reactions to different groups: A sociofunctional threat-based approach to "Prejudice". *Journal of Personality and Social Psychology*, *88*(5), 770–789. https://doi.org/10.1037/0022-3514.88.5.770

Dahl, J., Vescio, T. K., & Weaver, K. (2015). How threats to masculinity sequentially cause public discomfort, anger, and ideological dominance over women. *Social Psychology*, *46*(4), 242–254. https://doi.org/10.1027/1864-9335/a000248

Falomir-Pichastor, J. M., Berent, J., & Anderson, J. (2019). Perceived men's feminization and attitudes toward homosexuality: Heterosexual men's reactions to the decline of the anti-femininity norm of masculinity. *Sex Roles, 81*(3–4), 208–222. https://doi.org/10.1007/s11199-018-0985-6

Faul, F., Erdfelder, E., Buchner, A., & Lang, A.-G. (2009). Statistical power analyses using G*Power 3.1: Tests for correlation and regression analyses. *Behavior Research Methods, 41*(4), 1149–1160. https://doi.org/10.3758/BRM.41.4.1149

Göç, M. (2019). Homophobia and queer movement: A political history of subversion and oppression. In A. Öztürk & M. Satici (Eds.), *Living together: Discourses on citizenship in Turkey* (1st ed., pp. 163–182). Nomos. https://doi.org/10.5771/9783845299839-163

Gazzola, S. B., & Morrison, M. A. (2014). Cultural and personally endorsed stereotypes of transgender men and transgender women: Notable correspondence or disjunction? *International Journal of Transgenderism, 15*(2), 76–99. https://doi.org/10.1080/15532739.2014.937041

Glick, P., Gangl, C., Gibb, S., Klumpner, S., & Weinberg, E. (2007). Defensive reactions to masculinity threat: More negative affect toward effeminate (but not masculine) gay men. *Sex Roles, 57*(1–2), 55–59. https://doi.org/http://dx.doi.org/10.1007/s11199-007-9195-3

Glotfelter, M. A., & Anderson, V. N. (2017). Relationships between gender self-esteem, sexual prejudice, and trans prejudice in cisgender heterosexual college students. *International Journal of Transgenderism, 18*(2), 182–198. https://doi.org/10.1080/15532739.2016.1274932

Göçmen, İ., & Yılmaz, V. (2017). Exploring perceived discrimination among LGBT individuals in Turkey in education, employment, and health care: Results of an online survey. *Journal of Homosexuality, 64*(8), 1052–1068. https://doi.org/10.1080/00918369.2016.1236598

Gölge, Z. B., & Akdemir, S. (2019). Trans bireylere yönelik tutum ölçeği'nin türkçe geçerlik ve güvenirlik çalışması [Turkish validity and reliability study of the attitudes toward transgendered individuals scale]. *Psikiyatride Güncel Yaklasimlar-Current Approaches in Psychiatry, 11*(1), 261–275. https://doi.org/10.18863/pgy.621350

Hayes, A. F. (2018). *Introduction to mediation, moderation, and conditional process analysis: A regression-based approach* (2nd ed.). Guilford Press.

Herek, G. M. (2000). SexualPrejudice and gender: Do heterosexual's attitudes toward lesbians and gay men differ? *Journal of Social Issues, 56*(2), 251–266. https://doi.org/10.1111/0022-4537.00164

Herek, G. M. (2009). Sexual prejudice. In T. Nelson (Ed.), *Handbook of prejudice stereotyping and discrimination* (pp. 441–458). Taylor & Francis Group.

Hill, D. B., & Willoughby, B. L. B. (2005). The development and validation of the genderism and transphobia scale. *Sex Roles, 53*(7–8), 531–544. https://doi.org/10.1007/s11199-005-7140-x

Hofstede, G., Hofstede, G. J., & Minkov, M. 2010. *Cultures and organisations: Software of the mind* (Revised and Expanded 3rd Edition). McGraw-Hill.

Hoskin, R. A. (2017). Femme theory: Refocusing the intersectional lens. *Atlantis: Critical Studies in Gender, Culture & Social Justice, 38*(1), 95–109. https://journals.msvu.ca/index.php/atlantis/article/view/4771/95-109%20PDF

Hoskin, R. A. (2018). *Critical femininities: The development and application of femme theory* [Unpublished Doctoral Thesis]. Queen's University.

Hoskin, R. A. (2019). Femmephobia: The role of anti-femininity and gender policing in LGBTQ+ people's experiences of discrimination. *Sex Roles, 81*(11–12), 686–703. https://doi.org/10.1007/s11199-019-01021-3

Hoskin, R. A. (2020). "Femininity? It's the aesthetic of subordination": Examining femmephobia, the gender binary, and experiences of oppression among sexual and gender minorities. *Archives of Sexual Behavior, 49*(7), 2319–2339. https://doi.org/10.1007/s10508-020-01641-x

Iacoviello, V., Valsecchi, G., Berent, J., Anderson, J., & Falomir-Pichastor, J. M. (2020). Heterosexual men's attitudes towards homosexuality and ingroup distinctiveness: The role of perceived men's feminisation. *Psychology and Sexuality, 11*(1–2), 45–61. https://doi.org/10.1080/19419899.2019.1675749

International Lesbian Gay Bisexual, Trans and Intersex Association [ILGA] –Europe. (2019). *Rainbow map 2020.* https://www.ilga-europe.org/sites/default/files/Attachments/ilgaeurope-rainbowmap-2020-interactive.pdf

Kimmel, M. S. (1987). Rethinking „masculinity„: New directions in research. In KimmelM. S. (Ed.), Sage focus editions, *Changing men: New directions in research on men and masculinity* (Vol. 88, p. 9–24). Sage Publications, Inc

Kimmel, M. S. (1997). Masculinity as homophobia: Fear, shame and silence in the construction of gender identity. In M. M. Gergen & S. N. Davis (Eds.), *Toward a new psychology of gender* (pp. 223–242). Taylor & Frances/Routledge.

Konopka, K., Rajchert, J., Dominiak-Kochanek, M., & Roszak, J. (2019). The role of masculinity threat in homonegativity and transphobia. *Journal of Homosexuality.* Advance online publication. https://doi.org/10.1080/00918369.2019

Kosakowska-Berezecka, N., Besta, T., Adamska, K., Jaśkiewicz, M., Jurek, P., & Vandello, J. A. (2016). If my masculinity is threatened I won't support gender equality? The role of agentic self-stereotyping in restoration of manhood and perception of gender relations. *Psychology of Men and Masculinity, 17*(3), 274–284. https://doi.org/10.1037/men0000016

Lease, S. H., Çiftçi, A., Demir, A., & Boyraz, G. (2009). Structural validity of Turkish versions of the gender role conflict scale and male role norms scale. *Psychology of Men and Masculinity, 10*(4), 273–287. https://doi.org/10.1037/a0017044

Levant, R. F. (2011). Research in the psychology of men and masculinity using the gender role strain paradigm as a framework. *American Psychologist, 66*(8), 765–776. https://doi.org/10.1037/a0025034

Mackie, D. M., Maitner, A. T., & Smith, E. R. (2009). Intergroup emotions theory. In T. Nelson (Ed.), *Handbook of prejudice stereotyping and discrimination* (pp. 285–307). Taylor & Francis Group.

McDermott, D. T., Brooks, A. S., Rohleder, P., Blair, K., Hoskin, R. A., & McDonagh, L. K. (2018). Ameliorating transnegativity: Assessing the immediate and extended efficacy of a pedagogic prejudice reduction intervention. *Psychology and Sexuality*, 9(1), 69–85. https://doi.org/10.1080/19419899.2018.1429487

Menard, S. (1995). *Applied logistic regression analysis* (Sage university paper series on quantitative application in the social sciences, series no. 106) (2nd ed.). Sage.

Michniewicz, K. S., Bosson, J. K., Lenes, J. G., & Chen, J. I. (2015). Gender-atypical mental illness as male gender threat. *American Journal of Men's Health*, 10(4), 306–317. https://doi.org/10.1177/1557988314567224

Myers, R. (1990). *Classical and modern regression with applications* (2nd ed.). Duxbury.

Nadal, K. L., Skolnik, A., & Wong, Y. (2012). Interpersonal and systemic microaggressions toward transgender people: Implications for counseling. *Journal of LGBT Issues in Counseling*, 6(1), 55–82. https://doi.org/10.1080/15538605.2012.648583

Nagoshi, C. T., Cloud, J. R., Lindley, L. M., Nagoshi, J. L., & Lothamer, L. J. (2019). A test of the three-component model of gender-based prejudices: Homophobia and transphobia are affected by raters' and targets' assigned sex at birth. *Sex Roles*, 80(3–4), 137–146. https://doi.org/10.1007/s11199-018-0919-3

Nagoshi, J. L., Adams, K. A., Terrell, H. K., Hill, E. D., Brzuzy, S., & Nagoshi, C. T. (2008). Gender differences in correlates of homophobia and transphobia. *Sex Roles*, 59(7–8), 521–531. https://doi.org/10.1007/s11199-008-9458-7

Norton, A. T., & Herek, G. M. (2013). Heterosexuals' attitudes toward transgender people: Findings from a national probability sample of U.S. adults. *Sex Roles*, 68(11–12), 738–753. https://doi.org/10.1007/s11199-011-0110-6

Norton, J. (1997). "Brain says you're a girl, but I think you're a sissy boy": Cultural origins of transphobia. *International Journal of Sexuality and Gender Studies*, 2(2), 139–164. https://doi.org/10.1023/A:1026320611878

O'Connor, E. C., Ford, T. E., & Banos, N. C. (2017). Restoring threatened masculinity: The appeal of sexist and anti-gay humor. *Sex Roles*, 77(9–10), 567–580. https://doi.org/10.1007/s11199-017-0761-z

Parrott, D. J. (2009). Aggression toward gay men as gender role enforcement: Effects of male role norms, sexual prejudice, and masculine gender role stress. *Journal of Personality*, 77(4), 1137–1166. https://doi.org/10.1111/j.1467-6494.2009.00577.x

Pulice-Farrow, L., Clements, Z. A., & Galupo, M. P. (2017). Patterns of transgender microaggressions in friendship: The role of gender identity. *Psychology and Sexuality*, 8(3), 189–207. https://doi.org/10.1080/19419899.2017.1343745

Red Umbrella Sexual Health and Human Rights Association. (2016). *An information note on human rights violations against transgender people living in Turkey*. http://www.kirmizisemsiye.org/SourceFiles/pdf-2018525142539.pdf

Rudman, L. A., Moss-Racusin, C. A., Phelan, J. E., & Nauts, S. (2012). Status incongruity and backlash effects: Defending the gender hierarchy motivates prejudice against female leaders. *Journal of Experimental Social Psychology*, 48(1), 165–179. https://doi.org/10.1016/j.jesp.2011.10.008

Sakallı, N., & Türkoğlu, B. (2019). "Erkek" olmak ya da olmamak: Sosyal psikolojik açıdan erkeksilik/erkeklik Çalışmaları [To be or not to be a "man": Masculinity/manhood studies from social psychological perspective]. *Turkish Psychological Articles*, 22(44), 52–76. https://doi.org/10.31828/tpy1301996120190516m000014

Sakallı Uğurlu, N., Türkoğlu, B., Kuzlak, A., & Gupta, A. (2018). Stereotypes of single and married women and men in Turkish culture. *Current Psychology*. Advance online publication. https://doi.org/10.1007/s12144-018-9920-9

Sancar, S. (2009). *Erkeklik: İmkansız İktidar, Ailede, Piyasada, Sokakta Erkekler*. İstanbul Metis Yayınları.

Sayılan, G., Türkoğlu, B., & Cingöz-Ulu, B. (2020). Keeping my distance: Prejudice towards transwomen and its socio-political and moral predictors. *Psychology and Sexuality*, 11(1–2), 135–149. https://doi.org/10.1080/19419899.2019.1686055

Serano, J. (2007). *Whipping girl: A transsexual woman on sexism and the scapegoating of femininity*. Seal Press.

Spence, J. T., Helmreich, R., & Stapp, J. (1975). Ratings of self and peers on sex role attributes and their relation to self-esteem and conceptions of masculinity and femininity. *Journal of Personality and Social Psychology*, 32(1), 29–39. https://doi.org/10.1037/h0076857

Stangor, C., Sullivan, L. A., & Ford, T. E. (1991). Affective and cognitive determinants of prejudice. *Social Cognition*, 9(4), 359–380. https://doi.org/10.1521/soco.1991.9.4.359

Stephan, W. G., Ybarra, O., Martnez, C., Schwarzwald, J., & Tur-Kaspa, M. (1998). Prejudice toward immigrants to Spain and Israel: An integrated threat theory analysis. *Journal of Cross-cultural Psychology*, 29(4), 559–576. https://doi.org/10.1177/0022022198294004

Tabachnick, B. G., & Fidell, L. S. (2007). *Using multivariate statistics* (5th ed.). Allyn and Bacon.

Thompson, E. H., & Bennett, K. M. (2015). Measurement of masculinity ideologies: A (critical) review. *Psychology of Men and Masculinity*, 16(2), 115–133. https://doi.org/10.1037/a0038609

Thompson, E. H., & Pleck, J. H. (1986). The structure of male role norms. *American Behavioral Scientist*, 29(5), 531–543. https://doi.org/10.1177/000276486029005003

Transrespect versus Transphobia Worldwide. (2018). *TvT TMM update: Trans day of remembrance 2018*. https://transrespect.org/wp-content/uploads/2018/11/TvT_TMM_TDoR2018_Tables_EN.pdf

Vandello, J. A., & Bosson, J. K. (2013). Hard won and easily lost: A review and synthesis of theory and research on precarious manhood. *Psychology of Men and Masculinity*, 14(2), 101–113. https://doi.org/10.1037/a0029826

Vandello, J. A., Bosson, J. K., Cohen, D., Burnaford, R. M., & Weaver, J. R. (2008). Precarious manhood. *Journal of Personality and Social Psychology*, *95*(6), 1325–1339. https://doi.org/10.1037/a0012453

Warriner, K., Nagoshi, C. T., & Nagoshi, J. L. (2013). Correlates of homophobia, transphobia, and internalized homophobia in gay or lesbian and heterosexual samples. *Journal of Homosexuality*, *60*(9), 1297–1314. https://doi.org/10.1080/00918369.2013.806177

Winter, S., Webster, B., & Cheung, P. K. E. (2008). Measuring Hong Kong undergraduate students' attitudes towards transpeople. *Sex Roles*, *59*(9–10), 670–683. https://doi.org/10.1007/s11199-008-9462-y

Breastfeeding, 'tainted' love, and femmephobia: containing the 'dirty' performances of embodied femininity

Lilith A. Whiley, Sarah Stutterheim and Gina Grandy

ABSTRACT

In this conceptual analysis, we theorise breastfeeding as an embodied 'dirty' performance of femininity and draw on Hoskin's (2019a) work on femme theory to propose that women who breastfeed in public, who do so for an 'extended' time, and who enjoy it are subject to femmephobic attacks. We integrate three streams of literature to unsettle the 'taint' of breastfeeding. We first theorise breastfeeding as an act of femininity where women perform gender trouble in line with Butler's work. We also draw on Douglas' work on 'dirt' and Rivera's work on emotional 'dirty' work to theorise that 'taint' is one way in which society stigmatises the phenomenon of breastfeeding. Specifically, we propose that embodied breastfeeding evokes 'tainted' emotions. We then draw on Schippers' work on 'containing' pariah forms of femininity (lest they 'contaminate' patriarchy) by showing how femmephobic stigmatisation limits breastfeeding women's corporeality and presence in shared spaces.

Introduction

"As soon as I start nursing, the area clears. In some ways I am relieved to have the space, but in other ways I feel the repellent behaviour viscerally. I watch people walking by not looking over or quickly turning away. I wonder how long I am able to transgress the normative understandings of the body, and the proper place of the body within this setting. After I leave, is my practice still imprinted in this social space?". (Mathews, 2018, p. 11)

It has been argued that patriarchal femininity must be offered up to the heterosexual male gaze (R. A. Hoskin, 2019a), which serves to restrict the spatial mobility of women and their presence in the world (Fenster, 2005). (Public) breastfeeding is one such 'space' where we see the complexities of these expectations playing out. The World Health Organization (2020) recommends exclusive breastfeeding for the first six months of age and continued breastfeeding up to two years and beyond, and there are a growing number of laws that protect breastfeeding women (*e.g.* the Equality Act 2010 in the United Kingdom (UK), the Fair Labour Standards Act in the United States (US), the Federal Sex Discrimination Act in Australia, the Working Hours Act in the Netherlands). However, despite the public health narrative around *abstract* breastfeeding having many benefits (NHS, 2020; UNICEF, 2019), society still perceives the *embodied* act of breastfeeding as disgusting and shameful. As such, women who breastfeed in public, who do so for an 'extended' time,[1] and who enjoy it are stigmatised (*e.g.* K. Boyer, 2018; Dowling & Brown, 2013; Grant, 2016; Grant et al., 2017; Mathews, 2018; Newman & Williamson, 2018; Tăut, 2017; Tomori et al., 2016). Indeed, KLM's 2019 tweet presents breastfeeding as an activity that makes some people feel 'uncomfortable' and alludes to the possible 'offence' that might be caused:

Breastfeeding is permitted at KLM flights. However, to ensure that all our passengers of all backgrounds feel comfortable on board, we may request a mother to cover herself while breastfeeding, should other passengers be offended by this (KLM, Twitter feed, July 2019).

This, and many other similar incidents draw attention to the need to better understand the contradictions, espoused and felt, about breastfeeding, the stigmatisation surrounding it, and what this means for women who breastfeed. In this conceptual piece, our purpose is to unsettle the, so-called, 'taint' of breastfeeding and theorise breastfeeding as a stigmatised embodied performance of femininity.

To do so, we look to three streams of literature to unsettle taken for granted assumptions about breastfeeding. First, we draw on Butler's (1999) work on gender performance to position breastfeeding as a performance of femininity, and on Hoskin's (2017a; R. A. Hoskin, 2019a) work on femme theory to propose that women who breastfeed in public, who do so for an 'extended' time, and who enjoy it are performing (femme) femininity. They are, therefore, subject to femmephobic attacks (Hoskin, 2017; R. A. Hoskin, 2019b) because they are performing gender trouble (Butler, 1999). We then turn to Douglas (1966) work on 'dirt' and Rivera's (2015) work on emotional 'dirty' work to theorise that 'taint' is one way in which society stigmatises the phenomenon of breastfeeding. Specifically, we propose that embodied breastfeeding evokes 'tainted' emotions. Subsequently, we draw on Schippers (2007) work on 'containing' pariah forms of femininity by showing how femmephobic stigmatisation limits breastfeeding women's corporeality and presence in shared spaces.

In doing this, we want to acknowledge that our position is one of supporting parents in their feeding choices, whether that is to breastfeed, to pump, to formula-feed, to use donor milk, or to combine different feeding methods. We agree that the breast versus bottle 'milk war' (Neely, 2019) detracts from the real systemic issues that prevent women from genuine and authentic equal participation in the world.

The feminist conceptual analysis that we present in this paper is important because, as noted by Kahn, a critique of patriarchy 'must advocate not only the *suppression* (that is, access to birth control and abortion) but also the *expression* of childbearing function, which includes pregnancy, childbirth, *and* lactation' (C. Stearns, 1999, p. 308). It is therefore important for critical femininities to explore the nuances of femininity and, in this paper, we discuss some patriarchal norms that lead to femmephobic stigmatisation of performing femininity via breastfeeding.

Femininity and femme theory

Gender essentialism is the view that masculine and feminine properties are intrinsic, innate, and fixed to bodies' physiological characteristics (Mikkola, 2017). In contrast, Butler (1988) defined gender as something that we do via 'stylised repetition of acts through time' (p. 520). Her view (and we agree) is that gender is not a stable or intrinsic identity 'fact' but a historical idea – a cultural interpretation of one's biological sex. Certain bodily gestures, certain movements, and specific styles of behaviour produce and re-produce what society understands to mean as, so-called, masculine and feminine. It is the materialisation of these repetitive practices that enact, create, and re-create what society believes to be acceptable norms. Patriarchal femininity encompasses (socially agreed) normative ideals of what it means to be feminine. It is entrenched in the notion that femininity is performed for the male gaze and is a product always available for male consumption. Scripts of allowable and disallowed meanings, permeated in sociohistorical context, that femininity is about 'servitude, objectification, and lacking agency' (R. A. Hoskin, 2019b, p. 699), are inherited from previous generations, and compel, legitimise, and enforce gender performances (Butler, 1999).

Femme, originally used to refer to feminine lesbians, offers an alternative theoretical framework that repudiates hegemonic femininity norms and refuses to 'cater to and appease' patriarchal expectations (R. A. Hoskin, 2019a). Femme is about defiance; it is about challenging and renouncing the (socially constructed) idea that femininity is *for* men and that masculine right of access is woven in its very fabric. Femme theory has since evolved from its roots of describing feminine lesbians to encompassing a broader femme identity as femininity in-and-for-itself. It can, therefore, be applied to explore the broader complexities of femininity, such as breastfeeding. We thus contend that, if patriarchal femininity entails regulated performances of femininity for the male gaze and femme is femininity in-and-for-itself, then women who breastfeed in public, who do so for an 'extended' time, and who enjoy it are performing femme. In doing so, they are challenging and re-working norms of femininity that necessitate it as performed for the consumption of patriarchal society.

Our application of femme theory to breastfeeding opens a further avenue of sensemaking via the lens of femmephobia, which R. A. Hoskin (2019b) defines succinctly as the 'fear of the feminine' (p. 687). Women who do not follow the scripted and expected patriarchal femininity social norms, who perform what Butler (1999) calls gender trouble, are punished – they are stigmatised and marginalised. Femmephobia, therefore, maintains the devalued position of patriarchal femininity and, equally, patriarchal femininity is regulated via femmephobia. In our argument, we demonstrate how femmephobia contains performances of femininity psychologically (via 'tainted' emotions) and physically (by regulating women's embodiment in shared spaces). First, we position breastfeeding as a performance of femininity, and breastfeeding in public, for an 'extended' time, and with enjoyment as 'dirty' (femme) femininity.

Breastfeeding as performing femininity

Bartlett (2000) ponders, 'for what other reason could I sit in a theatre with one breast "exposed", unless performing maternity?' (p. 117). Although both men and women have breasts, nipples, and milk ducts, breastfeeding is almost exclusively seen as a feminine activity and is generally practiced as 'an activity corporeally restricted to women'[2] (Bartlett, 2000, p. 179). If we apply the idea of gender performativity to breastfeeding, then we can see how breastfeeding might be considered a feminine gendered act that is materialised through the regular performance of (culturally and historically situated) norms. Breastfeeding is an especially interesting performance because it is a continuous activity that involves the participation of another (the baby); it is also a visual performance because it is often performed in front of others (C. Stearns, 1999). Women who breastfeed in public are thus engaged in a public performance (C. Stearns, 2013) – of femininity.

The lived experience of breastfeeding is also very obviously an embodied act (Newman & Williamson, 2018). It is 'more than the physical and mechanical process of lactation' (Shaw, 2004, p. 105). The embodied *intimate* act of breastfeeding is almost always about much more than simply nourishment for 'when a baby suckles at the breast, it is also about attachment, comfort and love' (Bueskens, 2015, p. 3). Indeed, breastfeeding has been described as being 'embraced in love' (Faircloth, 2011, p. 294). The act of breastfeeding today, in the West is, however, a troublesome performance. Breasts are hypersexualised (Young, 2003) as a sort of 'mass fetish' for male stimulation. Outwardly, lactating breasts might appear even more arousing to some because of their increased size and breastfeeding in public has been construed as analogous to 'indecent exposure' (Bresnahan et al., 2018). Patriarchal femininity expects that breasts, especially arousing breasts, are displayed for the male gaze, and indeed, studies show that an appreciation for larger breasts is associated with sexist attitudes (Swami & Tovée, 2013). Also, breastfeeding involves sucking – a 'gesture full of sexuality' (Tăut, 2017, p. 819). As described by Laplanche (1976):

> Parallel with feeding there is a stimulation of lips and tongue by the nipple and the flow of warm milk. The stimulation is initially modelled on the function, so that between the two, it is at first barely possible to distinguish a difference (Laplanche, 1976, as cited in Grosz, 1994, p. 54)

Sexuality has long been seen as the 'totalising feature of women's personhood' (Bay-Cheng et al., 2018, p. 700). Indeed, women's value has historically been dependent on how her sexual availability is presented. Women are either virgins or sluts, compliant or pariahs (Darwin, 2017; Schippers, 2007); victims, worthy of chivalrous protection, or vamps, who 'knowingly use notions of femininity' to exploit vulnerable men (Schemenauer, 2012, p. 91). Such dichotomous ideologies are one way in which patriarchy is reinforced and sustained. They restrict women's agency and confine their identities to one of two rigid norms: good and chaste, or bad and sexual (Bareket et al., 2018).

The conflict between the (good) maternal feminine body and the (bad) sexual feminine body becomes more obvious when breastfeeding is done in public (C. Stearns, 2013). If the 'proper' (patriarchal feminine) performance of the breast is to sexually entice and excite men (Bartlett, 2005), then women who breastfeed in public, who do so for an 'extended' time, or who enjoy it, are performing femme (femininity in-and-for-itself) and gender trouble (refusing to perform their gender correctly). Breastfeeding in public is thus perceived to be a strategic decision made by calculating 'bad and sexual' women, exhibitionist flashers, who 'unnecessarily' expose their (sexual) breasts to men (Bresnahan et al., 2018; Tăut, 2017, p. 819). Applying the same lens that 'permissible' femininity is performed for the male gaze, then enjoying breastfeeding, especially with non-sexual breasts, is 'non-permissible'.

Clearly, women negotiate gendered expectations by breastfeeding (Mathews, 2018). They simul-taneously perform patriarchal femininity (by engaging with the expression of motherhood), gender trouble (by breastfeeding in public, for an 'extended' time, or by enjoying it), and femme (by refusing the masculine right of access infused in notions of patriarchal femininity). Breast 'performances' that, therefore, fall outside of the patriarchal femininity remit are subject to femmephobic attacks. One manifestation of femmephobia is the propagation of the misogynistic idea that women and their bodies are 'dirty' and that feminine fluids (*e.g.* menstrual blood, lochia, breastmilk) produced by the feminine body are expected to be 'contained and controlled' (Battersby, 2007, p. 102). Another manifestation of femmephobia is the physical restriction of women's equal participation in shared spaces. We first turn to the work of Douglas (1966) and Rivera (2015) to further conceptualise breastfeeding as a performance which evokes 'tainted' emotions.

Breastfeeding as 'dirty' and 'tainted'

Stigmatisation is a socially and culturally constituted process in which a person is labelled as different or deviant, and then devalued, leading to status loss and discrimination (Link & Phelan, 2014; Pescosolido & Martin, 2015). It is one of the means by which society 'punishes' people who contest gender scripts (Butler, 1999). Women who perform patriarchal femininity 'wrong' by breastfeeding in public, for an 'extended' time, or by enjoying it are called deviants (Velding, 2017), inconsiderate nonconformists (Bresnahan et al., 2018), pariahs (Schippers, 2007), shameless hags (Sundén & Paasonen, 2018), and even paedophiles (Newman & Williamson, 2018), for so unabashedly perform-ing unscripted/improv (femme) femininity. Today, in the West, women who breastfeed in public, for an 'extended' period of time, or who enjoy it, are stigmatised through negative attributions, labelling, objectification and depersonalisation, moral criticism, and non-verbal sanctioning beha-viours (Bresnahan et al., 2018).

Stigmatisation reproduces social inequalities and is perpetuated by hegemony and the exercise of power (Scambler & Paoli, 2008).Women are bombarded from a very young age with the (false) norm that they need to discipline, regulate, and even mutilate their bodies to conform to hegemonic standards of femininity. In this context, they need to be able-bodied, youthful, slim, light-skinned, smooth, hairless, and sweet smelling ... lest they be 'gross' (Fahs, 2017), and much of this is 'policed' by other women (Berbary, 2012; Mavin & Grandy, 2015). Others have shown how women's bodies are perceived as 'leaky' and dangerous (Longhurt, 2004), as bodies that 'get in the way' of rational masculine order (K. Boyer, 2012). Breastmilk is seen to be especially 'dirty'; it is perceived as similar to pus (Battersby, 2007), as unhygienic (Tăut, 2017), pollution even (Dowling & Pontin, 2017). As described by a participant in Mahon-Daly and Andrews (2002) study on the breastfeeding experi-ences of women in the UK, 'I felt really dirty if I had leaked, I feel that everyone is looking at it [the stain] and thinking that I'm unclean' (p. 59).

Given how women's bodies during pregnancy are perceived to be 'labouring' bodies (Draper, 2003), how women's work is taken for granted as unpaid labour (Beneria, 2001), and how mother-hood and body work can translate into maternal body work (Gatrell, 2013), we turn to Rivera's (2015) research on emotional 'dirty' work to propose that embodied breastfeeding evokes tainted emo-tions. Although Rivera's research is normally applied to paid employment, we feel it can also be applied in this context because breastfeeding is a form of maternal labour (C. Stearns, 2013); it forms part of women's unseen and unpaid labour in the home.[3] Douglas (1966) defines dirt as matter out of order, matter 'out of place'. Something is socially perceived to be 'dirty' because it is out of its normatively agreed position – it threatens our social norms by being somewhere it should not be. Breastfeeding is especially construed as 'tainted' if the practice is enjoyed by the mother. Blum (1999) notes that some might perceive breastfeeding as akin to adultery, and in Tăut's (2017) study of how narratives of public breastfeeding on Romanian discussion forums are constructed, one post read as follows: 'It is just the mothers' way of clinging to the baby story, to her convenience and *to her personal pleasure*' (p. 821, emphasis added). Breastfeeding is especially 'tainted' if the child is no longer an infant. For example, in Gribble's (2008) study on attitudes towards long-term breastfeeding among Australian mothers, participants reported previously holding negative attitudes towards extended breastfeeding, with one participant stating, 'I found the idea of feeding older children gross and tasteless and a bit off' (p. 7). Additionally, breastfeeding a boy, particularly one that is no longer an infant, is highly 'tainted', as exemplified by one participant's description of her mother-in-law's reaction to extended breastfeeding in Tomori et al. (2016) article on breastfeeding women's experiences in the US and the UK: ' ... ooh ooh, breastfeeding a boy, it's a bit odd, isn't it?' (p. 182).

Rivera (2015) proposes a four-part conceptualisation of 'taint' that evokes objectionable, inap-propriate, excessive, or vulnerable emotions. We extend her work to the context of breastfeeding, and theorise that such emotional performances, by breastfeeding women and the public, are socially constructed and feed off each other. For example, in K. Boyer's (2018) study on breastfeeding in public in the UK, one participant conveyed, 'I don't think others are comfortable with it, which made me feel uncomfortable' (p. 46). Similarly, in Tomori et al.'s (2016) study, a participant explained, 'I feel less comfortable about it, and it is because of potential reactions' (p. 182). Evidently, uncomfortable and out of place emotions are triggered in both the breastfeeding women and those 'observing' breastfeeding, thereby tainting the act and stigmatising those who perform it.

The first category of 'dirty' emotion in Rivera's conceptualisation is objectionable emotions. Objectionable emotions are emotions that are 'viewed as negative or not preferred' (Rivera, 2015, p. 219). Although many women may enjoy breastfeeding, they can also feel ashamed (Thomson et al., 2015), embarrassed, and self-conscious (K. Boyer, 2018) when doing so in public. In K. Boyer's (2018) study, one participant reported that, 'people were really shocked by the fact that you're breastfeeding in public ... I found it really stressful, really embarrassing, really horrible' (p. 46). Similarly, people observing a women breastfeed feel objectionable emotions like disgust, particularly when the child is no longer an infant, as exemplified by a participant in Gribble's (2008) study: 'I must admit that I used to think that it was a bit sick to see someone breastfeed a child who could walk and talk and ask for breastmilk' (p. 7). In fact, disgust and dread are two emotions often connected to women's bodies (Chrisler, 2011; Fahs, 2017). They lead to moral judgements about cleanliness and 'goodness', resulting in prejudice, othering, and stigmatisation.

The second category of emotions is inappropriate emotions. These occur when the 'display is deemed as not matching the event or circumstance' (Rivera, 2015, p. 219). A sense of inappropriateness is especially salient in 'extended' breastfeeding; it was described by a participant in Newman and Williamson (2018) study on the experiences of white women breastfeeding beyond six months in the UK, as 'that's when you tend you get more dirty looks the older your child gets so if they can walk like that's really a no-no, if they can ask for it that's also a bit of a stigma' (p. 243). Significant agency on the part of the child, as manifested in verbal requests to remove clothing, is considered fundamentally inappropriate (C. Stearns, 2011, 2013). For these reasons, some mothers teach their children code words for breastfeeding so that they may engage in the 'shameful' practice of 'extended' breastfeeding while appearing to, as Goffman (1963) calls it, 'pass' in public. Inappropriate emotions are also representative of how people feel about breastfeeding in public in general. In Grant's (2016) analyses of online comments relating to a protest supporting women's right to breastfeed in public on a UK news site, examples included: 'I and many don't want to see you flashing your bits around while we're shopping' (p. 57) and 'Can't bare women like these, all me, me, me'(p. 58).

The third category is excessive emotions. These are experienced when the display is deemed as 'too much or too little emotion related to the work' (Rivera, 2015, p. 219). Excessive emotions can be seen in comments such as, '[emphasis in original quote] This kind of fanatical self-righteousness is what annoys me the most about those who are pro-breast feeding ... And breast feeding is a CHOICE so stop pushing it down everybody's throats' and, 'Regardless of if its feeding or whatever the FACT is to breast feed in public you are exposing a breast in public which is not acceptable, facts are facts regardless of your feeble attempt to justify it ...' (Grant, 2016, pp. 57/58). In this context, women who chose to exercise their right to breastfeed in public are labelled 'breastfeeding mafia', 'holier than thou breastfeeding brigade', and 'lunatic breastfeeding lefty exhibitionists' who are breastfeeding in public for 'cheap points and thrills' (Grant, 2016, p. 56) and to 'cause a stir and fire people up' (Bresnahan et al., 2018, p. 4). Indeed, campaigns such as #FreeTheFreed, virtual lactivism (Boon & Pentney, 2015), and nurse-ins (K. Boyer, 2011) are often perceived very negatively. In Tăut (2017), pro-breastfeeding campaigns were described on Romanian discussion forums as: 'aggressive campaigns, with breasts all over to show' that are 'rather ridiculous, inhibitory and ineffective' (p. 820). Similarly, in Grant's (2016) study, online comments regarding publicly breastfeeding mothers included, 'this bunch are pratting around town trying to "make a point"!' (Grant, 2016, p. 57).

Finally, in Rivera's (2015) conceptualisation, there are vulnerable emotions, and these result from situations where the person 'must admit shortcomings or feel discomfort related to the emotion' (Rivera, 2015, p. 219). Breastfeeding mothers often report feeling vulnerable when breastfeeding, as described by a participant in Thomson et al. (2015), who said, 'I think it is underestimated how vulnerable you feel' (p. 12). The vulnerability is especially the case when trying to find a place to breastfeed, as exemplified by the following participant quote in Newman and Williamson (2018) study: 'Being at an 80th birthday party when it came to breastfeeding I thought "oh I better take myself away"' (p. 13). Similarly, a participant in Thomson et al. (2015) stated, 'I was more concerned with people looking and thinking why is she doing that in public she shouldn't be here, she should be doing that somewhere behind doors, inside in privacy' (p. 39).

Clearly, (public) breastfeeding places women in a vulnerable position. While it can be argued such women 'do gender well' (Mavin & Grandy, 2013) in alignment with exaggerated expressions of femininity, simultaneously, they evoke disgust and perform gender trouble (Butler, 1988). Women are left in a precarious position: They are doing motherhood well in the sense that they are offering the benefits of breastfeeding to their baby. However, at the same time, they experience, and are on the receiving end of, contradictory 'tainted' emotions, and thus are doing 'dirty' femininity. As an embodied act, the performance also blurs the intimate and the public (Smyth, 2008).

We now look to further extend our conceptualisation of breastfeeding as a stigmatised embodied act, and argue that stigmatising the 'space' of breastfeeding is one way through which patriarchy 'contains' femme or 'dirty' femininity via femmephobia.

Femmephobia as 'containing' femininity

Here, we lean on social geography to extend our understanding of breastfeeding because the lived experience of breastfeeding is an embodied act (Newman & Williamson, 2018), which requires negotiating physical space (Grant, 2016). We draw on Schippers (2007) theorising on containing pariah forms of femininity by showing that femmephobic stigmatisation 'contains' breastfeeding women's equal participation in the world by restricting their corporeality (e.g. hiding away their 'dirty' breasts) and limiting their presence in shared spaces (while performing their 'tainted' activity). Schippers (2007) theorises that undesirable forms of femininity – pariah femininities (such as femme) – are contained and managed in society to prevent them from unsettling patriarchal norms of femininity. We see many similarities between Schippers's (2007) work on containment and Butler's (1988) early work on strict punishments, whereby those who deviate from socially mandated performances are stigmatised. We also note how R. A. Hoskin's (2019a) work on femmephobia helps to elucidate Stone and Gorga (2014) containment practices whereby silence is used to exclude lesbian identities, and Tǎut's (2017) notion of permission within boundaries whereby the 'when, where, how and for how long' (p. 820) of breastfeeding is normatively governed. Indeed, femmephobic policing1 (R. A. Hoskin, 2017a) and surveillance (Grant et al., 2017) is often used to prevent breastfeeding in public, as well as 'extended' breastfeeding, forcing mothers to wean by a socially acceptable age (or conceal their 'taint').

According to Phelan et al. (2008), stigmatisation has three functions: to keep people *down* through domination or exploitation, to keep people *in* through norm enforcement, and to keep people *out* as a form of disease avoidance. These are echoed in hegemonic patriarchal scripts of breastfeeding; women are told to cover up, to breastfeed discreetly, to do so in predefined private spaces, and for an approved time only (*e.g.* Bresnahan et al., 2018; Grant, 2016; Newman & Williamson, 2018; Tǎut, 2017). It is not entirely surprising as the feminine form is expected to be small and contained – to take up as little space as possible, to appear powerless (Bartky, 2015), and many women internalise this norm (Tǎut, 2017). However, breastfeeding breasts 'take up space. They [breasts] stick out further than ever before' (Bartlett, 2000, p. 180). Women thus feel that they are breaching this norm when they take up more space in the world than patriarchal femininity permits. The shame is described well by a participant in Gatrell's (2013) study with mothers in the UK: 'I felt really anxious and ashamed of my body, of the visibility of that. I really stood out and then towards the end you know, being the heavily pregnant body in that space was really embarrassing, really shameful' (p. 622). Women who aggressively 'whipped out' '[emphasis in original quote] the WHOLE DANG THING' for 'all and sundry' to see (Jane & Lazard, 2012, p. 21) are seen as being blatantly provocative (Tǎut, 2017). Women therefore self-regulate; the 'leaky and 'dirty' female body is disciplined and controlled to meet the patriarchal norms of modesty (Gatrell, 2013), which is reflected in the following online comment to public breastfeeding in Grant's (2016) study: 'Why can't you use a muslin or shawl when breastfeeding in a public space?' (p. 58). Indeed, Tǎut (2017) notes how covering is about discretion, about 'making sure that public eye remains unoffended and unchallenged by a potentially sexually loaded image' (p. 821).

To protect their modesty, perform the 'permissible' scripted femininity, and 'do gender well' (Mavin & Grandy, 2013), women engage in 'a ritual of positioning themselves' (Mahon-Daly & Andrews, 2002, p. 70). The two main body parts that women frequently feel compelled to hide are the nipple and the stomach (Newman & Williamson, 2018). Exposure is limited by carefully position-ing the baby's head and wearing breastfeeding-friendly clothes, as described by one woman in Mahon-Daly and Andrews (2002): 'I usually wear something I can lift up so I don't show everything' (p. 70). However, this does not seem to be sufficient; in Zhang et al.'s (2018) qualitative study of Chinese women's experience with breastfeeding, one participant reported, 'Even if I use a nursing cloth to cover, people still know what I'm doing' (p. 267). The specific quote really highlights the height of shame and embarrassment that is associated with breastfeeding. Even when the nipple is covered, others still know the hidden 'dirty' act that is taking place. What is it about the nipple, we ask? We certainly live 'in a world of billboards covered in tits' (McNich as cited in Bueskens, 2015, p. 1), so why do women feel compelled to cover up while breastfeeding? We contend that it is because patriarchal femininity is inseparable from the idea of masculine right of access (R. A. Hoskin, 2019b). It is supposed to be performed for and 'offered up' to the heterosexual male gaze (R. A. Hoskin, 2019b), always available and always accessible. When it comes to breastfeeding, the idea of masculine right of access applies as well, even in the West. For example, in Prussia, husbands were the 'arbiters' of the amount of time that wives were allowed to breastfeed (Smith, 2019). As one participant in R. A. Hoskin (2019b) explains, 'Mr. Man owns the public domain, and when [she's] in it he gets to say what's on his mind' (p. 8). Accordingly, if girls and women are hypersexualised and taught to perform their selfhood for male consumption (Ringrose et al., 2019), then women who use their (non-sexual) breasts for an activity that excludes male gratification are out of place and norm defiant. The same can be seen in lesbian stereotypes where 'butch' lesbians are especially vilified (Geiger et al., 2006) but lesbian porn remains highly consumable (see PornHub views).

Women are aware of the conflicted pressures to expose sexual breasts and hide non-sexual breasts. In Jane and Lazard (2012) discursive analysis of internet discussions on breastfeeding, one discussion board post included was, 'I'm pretty damn sure than whenever I breastfed in public then I was baring a lot less than a lot of the girls wandering round wearing their normal summer clothes … ' (p. 22). Similarly, Grant (2016) reported the following online quote: 'Apparently boobs are only allowed to be on show if they are on the 3rd page of a newspaper or some grotty lads mag, but a bit of side boob with no nipple on show is deemed unacceptable' (p. 56). However, despite comments like these, many women still feel the need to physically evict themselves from shared spaces to breastfeed. In Mahon-Daly and Andrews's (2001) study, a participant said, 'I had people to dinner last weekend, and fed her upstairs out of the way' (p. 70).

It is interesting to note how, often, those who oppose breastfeeding in public propose toilets as a more suitable alternative, suggesting that breastfeeding has more in common with 'dirty' defaeca-tion than with 'clean' eating. Indeed, Tăut (2017) notes how even the mere notion that a breast is filled with milk in public evokes feelings of disgust, particularly when present in places where edible products are purchased or consumed (e.g. grocery stores and restaurants). Breastfeeding is a physiological process that involves the excretion of body fluids and, usually, because these sort of processes (urination, defaecation) are perceived to be disgusting, they are deemed as things that should occur in private (Tăut, 2017), as reflected in an exemplary quote from a discussion forum reported in Tăut (2017): 'we don't pass gas around other people' (p. 819). Exposing a breast in public is then equivalent to urinating or defaecating in public, as described in Bresnahan et al. (2018), who conducted thematic analyses of public breastfeeding stigma manifest in online comments. One such comment was, 'Next time, I'll whip it out and pee on the side walk in front of you. Just remember it's a perfectly naturally act. If you don't like, don't look' (p. 5). Others appear to also equate breastfeed-ing with being sick, as exemplified by the following online post included in Jane and Lazard (2012) study: 'Restaurants and other similar public places should have a small area for those who have taken sick, fallen unconscious or for bfding [breastfeeding]' (p. 24). Clearly, devaluation of breastfeeding is demonstrated through the suggestion that these spaces are appropriate spaces for feeding a child.

The apparent best place for 'good' women, who adhere to patriarchal femininity standards, to breastfeed, is a specially designated feeding room. The issue of feeding rooms is quite nuanced. Research shows that most women *do* prefer to breastfeed in such designated spaces (Britton, 2000) and appreciate the seclusion, as reflected by one participant in K. Boyer's (2012) study, who said, 'it was good to be able to go somewhere separate' (p. 557). Indeed, an absence of feeding rooms, especially in the workplace, is often cited as a barrier and a challenge to returning to work (Desmond & Meaney, 2016; Zhang et al., 2018). At the same time, many women report that rooms allocated to feeding or expressing milk are poorly maintained or inadequate.[4] Participants in K. Boyer's (2012) study had much to say about this. One said, 'the air conditioning was never working, and, like, you just used to sit there and sweat in there in the plastic seats, and it was always horrible' (p. 557). Another claimed that the rooms 'can be smelly and cramped or (have) chairs with arms unsuitable for feeding' (p. 557). Additionally, by removing themselves from shared public spaces and going into these secluded areas, women felt 'cut off from what's going on' (K. Boyer, 2012, p. 557). Similar comments were made by participants in Mahon-Daly and Andrews (2002) study, namely that, 'there was a feeling of isolation' (p. 70) and in Bartlett (2000), where a participant said she felt, 'insulted, being locked away out of sight' (p. 181).

Women also engage in strategic planning to ensure they do not take up space with their breastfeeding by timing their outings so that they only leave the home between feeds (C. Stearns, 1999), which seriously restricts the amount of time that breastfeeding women can spend outside of the home and participate in the world. As described by a participant in Tăut (2017), 'If you breastfeed on demand as all big organisations like WHO, UNICEF etc. recommend, you can avoid breastfeeding in public if only you seclude yourself with the baby at home permanently' (p. 821). In this context, only hegemonic feminine bodies ascribed to patriarchal (Western) standards are considered permissible in public; 'the mother's body remains both abject and perverse – disruptive, indiscreet and lacking class' (Bueskens, 2015, p. 5).

Conclusion

"Breasts are a source of food but

they are beautiful in their standing symbol of femininity". (Tăut, 2017, p. 822)

In this paper, we theorise how (public and/or extended) breastfeeding can be understood as a stigmatised embodied act of femininity. In doing this, we looked to four streams of literature to provocatively position breastfeeding in this way. We looked to the work of Butler (1999) to theorise that women who breastfeed in public, who do so for an 'extended' time, and who enjoy it are performing gender trouble. We looked at the work of Hoskin (2017, R. A. Hoskin, 2019a) on femme theory to position breastfeeding as femme and, therefore, subject to psychological and physical femmephobic containment. We also looked to the work of Douglas (1966) and Rivera (2015) to theorise breastfeeding as (unpaid) work that evokes disgust – objectionable, inappropriate, excessive, or vulnerable emotions. Finally, we drew from Schippers (2007) on containing pariah femininity to theorise how shaming (public) breastfeeding serves to restrict women's corporeality and spatial presence. We contend that if we view breastfeeding as a (femme) performance subject to femmephobic attacks, and as 'dirty' femininity work that evokes 'tainted' emotions (for breastfeeding women and the public), then we are in better position to understand why and how breastfeeding women, particularly those who do so in public, those who choose to breastfeed for an 'extended' period of time, and those who enjoy the practice of breastfeeding, are subject to stigmatisation.

Indeed, our conceptual contribution here is framed, and thereby limited, by a Western view of (public) breastfeeding. We acknowledge that, in our theorising, we draw on Western views of patriarchal hegemonic femininity (R. A. Hoskin, 2017b) and that, by doing so, we are engaging in a discourse that simultaneously privileges and marginalises. Patriarchal hegemonic femininity can be defined as 'gender performances […] which act, within a particular context, to uphold a gender binary and maintain traditional social relations between genders' (Paechter, 2018, p. 124). Hegemonic femininity ideals legitimise the dominant as masculine, and subordinate that which is feminine as inferior, as 'other' (Schippers, 2007). Yet, we agree that hegemonic femininity also reinforces 'white heteropatriarchal cisgender standards of able-bodied normativity' (Hoskin & Taylor, 2019, p. 3) and are mindful that there are many intersectional nuances in femininity, such as disability (Malacrida, 2009), race (Cooley et al., 2018), faith (Ferber, 2012), and gender expression (R. A. Hoskin, 2017b).

The research exploring the intersection of culture and breastfeeding is scant (see Street & Lewallen, 2013; Zhang et al., 2018 for exceptions) and we see our analysis as a springboard for future research. We propose that viewing breastfeeding as a biological act that involves exposing the breast, can also carry with it 'undertones of social and racial hierarchies' (Tăut, 2017, p. 819), as exemplified by the following post reported in Tăut (2017): 'Only the gypsies and primitive women breastfeed in public […] Only in Africa you see this fashion' (p. 819). Indeed, in Romania, breast-covered white Western women have traditionally occupied the highest level in the ethnic and social ladder whereas barebreasted dark Non-Western women have occupied the lowest echelons. Similarly, research by Gallegos, Vicca, and Streiner (2015) has explored the ways in which African women who had immigrated to Australia conformed to Western cultural norms. The women, who had breastfed openly and for a long period of time in their home countries, felt that breastfeeding in public in Australia was considered shameful and thus covered up and stopped sooner than they would have. One participant said, 'The way other people were looking, it's like because she's African, that's why she's doing that … Just the look they give you' (Gallegos et al., 2015, p. 731). Clearly, infant feeding practices can be associated with colonialism and with what is deemed 'modern' and reflective of economic status and power (Joseph, Brodribb, & Liamputtong, 2018). Just as stigma is socially, historically, and culturally context specific and changes over time, so is the position and enactment of breastfeeding. Indeed, Paechter (2018) notes that, 'Conceptions of masculinity and femininity change over time and place as interactions and resistances require constant local negotiation and rejustification' (p. 123). Future research should explore further, conceptually and empirically, the contextual and local consideration of our conceptual framing of breastfeeding as a 'dirty' embodied act of femininity.

We conclude that negotiating space and social norms of where and how women should breastfeed not only governs their bodies in space but also contains and restricts their access to shared spaces. Femmephobia, therefore, regulates femininity not only via psychological containment (*i.e.* 'dirt' and 'taint') but also via physical space. As such, standards of patriarchal femininity control and dictate women's spatial mobility and presence in the world (Fenster, 2005). Despite this, we note how women 'simultaneously acknowledge, as well as reject or recalibrate' (Mavin & Grandy, 2015, p. 1108) feminine scripts by performing gender trouble via breastfeeding in public, for an 'extended' time, or by enjoying it – most notably through lactivism but also, simply, by just existing with breasts. Our hope is that in conceptualising breastfeeding as a 'dirty' embodied performance of femininity, albeit in a provocative way, we begin to unsettle taken for granted assumptions that reinforce hegemonic notions of femininity and heterosexuality, which serve to restrict women's ways of being. Our position is not one intended to 'judge' the choices that women make regarding breastfeeding (or not breastfeeding), but rather to critique patriarchal norms which inform how women can do and undo gender.

Notes

1. Breastfeeding beyond 12 months is considered 'extended' breastfeeding (Brockway & Venturato, 2016).
2. Not all women breastfeed, and it is not only cis-gender women who breastfeed; non-binary and trans* persons can also breastfeed or chestfeed. Yet, studies exploring the phenomenon of chestfeeding are extremely limited (e.g. Riggs, 2013) – even those coming from a medical 'lactation' perspective (e.g. García-Acosta, Juan-Valdivia, Fernández-Martínez, Lorenzo-Rocha, & Castro-Peraza, 2020; Jaslar, 2018). We, therefore, urgently call for researchers to explore the phenomenon of chestfeeding and, simultaneously, acknowledge that what we discuss in this paper focuses primarily on the experiences of cis-gender women. Recently, there has also been an interest in cis-gender men breastfeeding. For example, the tech firm Dentsu developed a Father's Nursing Assistant (Marcoux, 2019) that can be worn to allow men to breastfeed and Marie-Claire Springham won the Meaning Centred Design Awards' (2018, pe1) Grand Title Trophy for her chestfeeding device that 'deserves particular attention because it challenges the fundamental meanings of male and female, father and mother, parent and child'.
3. According to the New York Post, being a mother is the equivalent of working 2.5 jobs (Welch, 2018.)
4. See Melk in de meterkast photo project: http://www.floorfortunati.nl/portfolio/photos/melk-in-de-meterkast/.

Disclosure statement

The authors declare that they have no conflict of interest.

Funding

There are no sources of funding to declare

References

Bareket, O., Kahalon, R., Shnabel, N., & Glick, P. (2018). The madonna-whore dichotomy: Men who perceive women's nurturance and sexuality as mutually exclusive endorse patriarchy and show lower relationship satisfaction. *Sex Roles*, *79*(9–10), 519–532. https://doi.org/10.1007/s11199-018-0895-7

Bartky, S. (2015). *Femininity and domination: Studies in the phenomenology of oppression*. Routledge.

Bartlett, A. (2000). Thinking through breasts: Writing maternity. *Feminist Theory*, *1*(2), 173–188. https://doi.org/10.1177/14647000022229146

Bartlett, A. (2005). *Breastwork: Rethinking breastfeeding*. University of New South Wales.

Battersby, S. (2007). Breastfeeding as dirty work in the UK. In M. Kirkham (Ed.), *Exploring the dirty side of women's health*. London: Routledge.

Bay-Cheng, L. Y., Bruns, A. E., & Maguin, E. (2018). Agents, virgins, sluts, and losers: The sexual typecasting of young heterosexual women. *Sex Roles*, *79*(11–12), 699–714. https://doi.org/10.1007/s11199-018-0907-7

Beneria, L. (2001). The enduring debate over unpaid labour. In M. Loutfi (Ed.), *What is equality and how do we get there? Women, gender, and work*, 85-109. International Labour Office.

Berbary, L. A. (2012). "Don't be a whore, that's not ladylike": Discursive discipline and sorority women's gendered subjectivity. *Qualitative Inquiry*, *18*(7), 606–625. https://doi.org/10.1177/1077800412450150

Blum, L. (1999). *At the breast: Ideologies of breastfeeding and motherhood in contemporary United States*. Boston: Beacon Press.

Boon, S., & Pentney, B. (2015). Virtual lactivism: Breastfeeding selfies and the performance of motherhood. *International Journal of Communication*, *9*(1), 1759–1772.

Boyer, K. (2011). "The way to break the taboo is to do the taboo thing" breastfeeding in public and citizen-activism in the UK. *Health and Place*, *17*(2), 430–437. https://doi.org/10.1016/j.healthplace.2010.06.013

Boyer, K. (2012). Affect, corporeality and the limits of belonging: Breastfeeding in public in the contemporary UK. *Health and Place*, *18*(3), 552–560. https://doi.org/10.1016/j.healthplace.2012.01.010

Boyer, K. (2018). The emotional resonances of breastfeeding in public: The role of strangers in breastfeeding practice. *Emotion, Space and Society*, *26*(1), 33–40. https://doi.org/10.1016/j.healthplace.2010.06.013

Bresnahan, M, Zhuang, J, Anderson, J, Zhu, Y, Nelson, J, & Yan, X. (2018). The 'Pumpgate' incident: stigma against lactating mothers in the U.S. *Workplace. Women & Health*, *58*(4), 451-465.

Britton, C. (2000). *Women's experiences of early and long-term breastfeeding in the UK*. Durham University. http://etheses.dur.ac.uk/1228/

Brockway, M., & Venturato, L. (2016). Breastfeeding beyond infancy: A concept analysis. *Journal of Advanced Nursing*, *72*(9), 2003–2015. https://doi.org/10.1111/jan.13000

Bueskens, P. (2015). *Breastfeeding "in public": A personal and political memoir breastfeeding at the bathhouse*. Retrieved July 24, 2019, from Mothers at the margins: Stories of challenge, resistance and love website http://petrabueskens.com/wp-content/uploads/2014/03/Breastfeeding-in-public_A-personal-and-political-memoir2.pdf

Butler, J. (1988). Acts and gender performative: An essay in phenomenology constitution: And feminist theory. *Theatre Journal*, *40*(4), 519–531. https://doi.org/10.2307/3207893

Butler, J. (1999). *Gender trouble: Feminism and the subversion of identity*. http://optics.nuigalway.ie/people/eugenie/Thesis ED.pdf

Chrisler, J. C. (2011). Leaks, lumps, and lines: Stigma and women's bodies. *Psychology of Women Quarterly*, *35*(2), 202–214. https://doi.org/10.1177/0361684310397698

Cooley, E., Winslow, H., Vojt, A., Shein, J., & Ho, J. (2018). Bias at the intersection of identity: Conflicting social stereotypes of gender and race augment the perceived femininity and interpersonal warmth of smiling black women. *Journal of Experimental Social Psychology*, *74*(September2017), 43–49. https://doi.org/10.1016/j.jesp.2017.08.007

Darwin, H. (2017). The pariah femininity hierarchy: Comparing white women's body hair and fat stigmas in the United States. *Gender, Place & Culture*, *24*(1), 135–146. https://doi.org/10.1080/0966369X.2016.1276889

Desmond, D., & Meaney, S. (2016). A qualitative study investigating the barriers to returning to work for breastfeeding mothers in Ireland. *International Breastfeeding Journal*, *11*(1), 1–9. https://doi.org/10.1186/s13006-016-0075-8

Douglas, M. (1966). *Purity and danger: An analysis of the concepts of pollution and taboo*. Routledge & Keagan Paul. https://doi.org/10.1525/aa.1968.70.2.02a00530

Dowling, S., & Brown, A. (2013). An exploration of the experiences of mothers who breastfeed long-term: What are the issues and why does it matter? *Breastfeeding Medicine*, *8*(1), 45–52. https://doi.org/10.1089/bfm.2012.0057

Dowling, S., & Pontin, D. (2017). Using liminality to understand mothers' experiences of long-term breastfeeding: 'Betwixt and between', and 'matter out of place. *Health (United Kingdom)*, *21*(1), 57–75. https://doi.org/10.1177/1363459315595846

Draper, J. (2003). Blurring, moving and broken boundaries: Men's encounters with the pregnant body. *Sociology of Health and Illness*, *25*(7), 743–767. https://doi.org/10.1046/j.1467-9566.2003.00368.x

Fahs, B. (2017). The dreaded body: Disgust and the production of "appropriate" femininity. *Journal of Gender Studies*, *26*(2), 184–196. https://doi.org/10.1080/09589236.2015.1095081

Faircloth, C. (2011). "It feels right in my heart": Affective accountability in narratives of attachment. *Sociological Review*, *59*(2), 283–302. https://doi.org/10.1111/j.1467-954X.2011.02004.x

Fenster, T. (2005). The right to the gendered city: Different formations of belonging in everyday life. *Journal of Gender Studies*, *14*(3), 217–231. https://doi.org/10.1080/09589230500264109

Ferber, A. L. (2012). The culture of privilege: Color-blindness, postfeminism, and christonormativity. *Journal of Social Issues*, *68*(1), 63–77. https://doi.org/10.1111/j.1540-4560.2011.01736.x

Gallegos, D., Vicca, N. & Streiner, S. (2015) Breastfeeding beliefs and practices of African women living in Brisbane and Perth, Australia. Maternal and Child Nutrition, (*11*)4, 727–736. doi: 10.1111/mcn.12034

García-Acosta, J. M, Juan-Valdivia, S, María, R, Fernández-Martínez, A. D, Lorenzo-Rocha, N. D, & Castro-Peraza, M. E. (2020). Trans* pregnancy and lactation: A literature review from a nursing perspective. *International Journal of Environmental Research and Public Health*, *17*(1), 44. doi: 10.3390/ijerph17010044

Gatrell, C. (2013). Maternal body work: How mothers negotiate pregnancy and new motherhood at work. *Human Relations*, *66*(5), 621–644. https://doi.org/10.1177/0018726712467380

Geiger, W., Harwood, J., & Hummert, M. (2006). College students' multiple stereotypes of lesbians: A cognitive perspective. *Journal of Homosexuality*, *51*(3), 225–247. https://doi.org/10.1300/J082v51n03

Goffman, E. (1963). *Stigma: Notes on the management of spoiled identity*. Simon & Schuster.

Grant, A. (2016). "I … don't want to see you flashing your bits around": Exhibitionism, othering and good motherhood in perceptions of public breastfeeding. *Geoforum*, *71*(May), 52–61. https://doi.org/10.1016/j.geoforum.2016.03.004

Grant, A., Mannay, D., & Marzella, R. (2017). "People try and police your behaviour": The impact of surveillance on mothers and grandmothers' perceptions and experiences of infant feeding. *Families, Relationships and Societies*, *7*(3), 431–447. https://doi.org/10.1332/204674317x14888886530223

Gribble, K. D. (2008). Long-term breastfeeding; changing attitudes and overcoming challenges. *Breastfeeding Review: Professional Publication of the Nursing Mothers' Association of Australia*, *16*(1), 5–15. Available at: https://search.informit.com.au/documentSummary;dn=996913581784844;res=IELAPA

Grosz, E. (1994). *Volatile bodies: Toward a corporeal feminism*. Indiana University Press.

Hoskin, R. A. (2017a). Femme interventions and the proper feminist subject: Critical approaches to decolonizing western feminist pedagogies. *Cogent Social Sciences*, *3*(1), 1–16. https://doi.org/10.1080/23311886.2016.1276819

Hoskin, R. A. (2017b). Femme theory: Refocusing the intersectional lens. *Atlantis*, *38*(1), 95–109.

Hoskin, R. A. (2019a). Can femme be theory? Exploring the epistemological and methodological possibilities of femme. *Journal of Lesbian Studies*, 1–17. https://doi.org/10.1080/10894160.2019.1702288

Hoskin, R. A. (2019b). Femmephobia: The role of anti-femininity and gender policing in LGBTQ+ people's experiences of discrimination. *Sex Roles*, *81*(11–12), 686–703. https://doi.org/10.1007/s11199-019-01021-3

Hoskin, R. A., & Taylor, A. (2019). Femme resistance: The fem(me)inine art of failure. *Psychology and Sexuality*, 1–20. https://doi.org/10.1080/19419899.2019.1615538

Jane, C., & Lazard, L. (2012). "Please don't put the whole dang thing out there!": A discursive analysis of internet discussions around infant feeding. *Psychology & Health*, *27*(8), 1–32. https://doi.org/10.1080/08870446.2011.634294

Jaslar, C. (2018). Transgender male breastfeeding after "top" surgery. Journal of Obstetric, Gynecologic & Neonatal Nursing, 47(3), doi:10.1016/j.jogn.2018.04.117

Joseph, J., Brodribb, W. & Liamputtong, P. (2018). "Fitting-in Australia" as nurturers: Meta-synthesis on infant feeding experiences among immigrant women. *Women and Birth*, doi: 10.1016/j.wombi.2018.12.002

Link, B., & Phelan, J. (2014). Stigma power. *Social Science and Medicine*, *103*(February), 24–32. https://doi.org/10.1016/j.socscimed.2013.07.035.Stigma

Longhurst, R. (2004). *Bodies: Exploring fluid boundaries*. Routledge.

Mahon-Daly, P., & Andrews, G. J. (2002). Liminality and breastfeeding: Women negotiating space and two bodies. *Health and Place*, *8*(2), 61–76. https://doi.org/10.1016/S1353-8292(01)00026-0

Malacrida, C. (2009). Performing motherhood in a disablist world: Dilemmas of motherhood, femininity and disability. *International Journal of Qualitative Studies in Education*, *22*(January2015), 99–117. https://doi.org/10.1080/09518390802581927

Marcoux, H. (2019). *Breastfeeding dads are possible with these new devices*. Retrieved July 22, 2019, from Motherly website https://www.mother.ly/Our-Partners/10-pictures-on-the-first-day-of-school

Mathews, V. (2018). Réaménager le corps qui allaite au sein dans les lieux publics urbains. *Social and Cultural Geography*, *9365*(9), 1–19. https://doi.org/10.1080/14649365.2018.1433867

Mavin, S., & Grandy, G. (2013). Doing gender well and differently in dirty work. *Gender, Work & Organization*, *20*(3), 232–251. https://doi.org/10.1111/j.1468-0432.2011.00567.x)

Mavin, S., & Grandy, G. (2015). A theory of abject appearance: Women elite leaders' intra-gender 'management' of bodies and appearance. *Human Relations*, *69*(5), 1095–1120. https://doi.org/10.1177/0018726715609107

Meaning Centred Design Awards. (2018). *Meaning centred design awards*. Retrieved July 22, 2019, from https://www.meaningcentreddesignawards.com/

Mikkola, M. (2017). Gender essentialism and gender non-essentialism. *The routledge companion to feminist philosophy*. London: Routledge.

Neely, E. (2019). *Context is best – A reflection on last week's breast vs bottle uproar*. Retrieved July 16, 2019, from Sciblogs website https://sciblogs.co.nz/guestwork/2019/03/11/context-is-best-a-reflection-on-last-weeks-breast-vs-bottle-uproar/

Newman, K. L., & Williamson, I. R. (2018). Why aren't you stopping now?!' Exploring accounts of white women breastfeeding beyond six months in the East of England. *Appetite, 129*(May), 228–235. https://doi.org/10.1016/j.appet.2018.06.018

NHS. (2020). *Benefits of breastfeeding*. Retrieved April 7, 2020, from https://www.nhs.uk/conditions/pregnancy-and-baby/benefits-breastfeeding/

Paechter, C. (2018). Rethinking the possibilities for hegemonic femininity: Exploring a gramscian framework. *Women's Studies International Forum, 68*(March), 121–128. https://doi.org/10.1016/j.wsif.2018.03.005

Pescosolido, B., & Martin, J. (2015). The stigma complex. *Annual Review of Sociology, 41*(August), 87–116. https://doi.org/10.1126/science.1249098.Sleep

Phelan, J. C., Link, B. G., & Dovidio, J. F. (2008). Stigma and prejudice: One animal or two? *Social Science and Medicine, 67*(3), 358–367. https://doi.org/10.1016/j.socscimed.2008.03.022

Riggs, D.W. (2013). Transgender men's self-representations of bearing children post-transition. In Green, F. & Friedman, M. (Eds.), *Chasing rainbows: Exploring gender fluid parenting practices*. Toronto: Demeter Press.

Ringrose, J., Tolman, D., & Ragonese, M. (2019). Hot right now: Diverse girls navigating technologies of racialized sexy femininity. *Feminism and Psychology, 29*(1), 76–95. https://doi.org/10.1177/0959353518806324

Rivera, K. (2015). Emotional taint: Making sense of emotional dirty work at the U.S. border patrol. *In Management Communication Quarterly, 29*(2), 199–228. https://doi.org/10.1177/0893318914554090

Scambler, G., & Paoli, F. (2008). Health work, female sex workers and HIV/AIDS: Global and local dimensions of stigma and deviance as barriers to effective interventions. *Social Science and Medicine, 66*(8), 1848–1862. https://doi.org/10.1016/j.socscimed.2008.01.002

Schemenauer, E. (2012). Victims and vamps, madonnas and whores: The construction of female drug couriers and the practices of the US security state. *International Feminist Journal of Politics, 14*(1), 83–102. https://doi.org/10.1080/14616742.2011.631277

Schippers, M. (2007). Recovering the feminine other: Masculinity, femininity, and gender hegemony. *Theory and Society, 36*(1), 85–102. https://doi.org/10.1007/s11186-007-9022-4

Shaw, R. (2004). Performing breastfeeding: Embodiment, ethics and the maternal subject. *Feminist Review, 78*(78), 99–116. https://liverpool.idm.oclc.org/login?url=http://search.ebscohost.com/login.aspx?direct=true&db=edsjsr&AN=edsjsr.3874408&site=eds-live&scope=site.

Smith, B. (2019). *Women's studies: The basics*. Abingdon: Routledge.

Smyth, L. (2008). Gendered spaces and intimate citizenship: The case of breastfeeding. *European Journal of Women's Studies, 15*(2), 83–99. https://doi.org/10.1177/1350506808090305

Stearns, C. (1999). Breastfeeding and the good maternal body. *Gender & Society, 13*(3), 308–325. https://doi.org/10.1177/089124399013003003

Stearns, C. (2011). Cautionary tales about extended breastfeeding and weaning. *Healthare for Women International, 32*(6), 538–554. https://doi.org/10.1080/07399332.2010.540051

Stearns, C. (2013). The embodied practices of breastfeeding: Implications for research and policy. *Journal of Women, Politics & Policy, 34*(4), 359–370. https://doi.org/10.1080/1554477X.2013.835680

Stone, A. L., & Gorga, A. (2014). Containing pariah femininities: Lesbians in the sorority rush process. *Sexualities, 17*(3), 348–364. https://doi.org/10.1177/1363460713516336

Street, D. J., & Lewallen, L. P. (2013). The influence of culture on breast-feeding decisions by African American and white women. *Journal of Perinatal and Neonatal Nursing, 27*(1), 43–51. https://doi.org/10.1097/JPN.0b013e31827e57e7

Sundén, J., & Paasonen, S. (2018). Shameless hags and tolerance whores: Feminist resistance and the affective circuits of online hate. *Feminist Media Studies, 18*(4), 643–656. https://doi.org/10.1080/14680777.2018.1447427

Swami, V., & Tovée, M. J. (2013). Men's oppressive beliefs predict their breast size preferences in women. *Archives of Sexual Behavior, 42*(7), 1199–1207. https://doi.org/10.1007/s10508-013-0081-5

Tăut, D. (2017). Breastfeeding (Un)covered: Narratives of public breastfeeding on romanian discussion forums. *International Journal of Behavioral Medicine, 24*(6), 815–826. https://doi.org/10.1007/s12529-017-9687-7

Thomson, G., Ebisch-Burton, K., & Flacking, R. (2015). Shame if you do – Shame if you don't: Women's experiences of infant feeding. *Maternal & Child Nutrition, 11*(1), 33–46. https://doi.org/10.1111/mcn.12148

Tomori, C., Palmquist, A. E. L., & Dowling, S. (2016). Contested moral landscapes: Negotiating breastfeeding stigma in breastmilk sharing, nighttime breastfeeding, and long-term breastfeeding in the U.S. and the U.K. *Social Science and Medicine, 168* (November), 178–185. https://doi.org/10.1016/j.socscimed.2016.09.014

UNICEF. (2019). *Benefits of breastfeeding*. Retrieved July 22, 2019, from https://www.unicef.org.uk/babyfriendly/about/benefits-of-breastfeeding/

Velding, V. (2017). Depicting Femininity. *Youth & Society, 49*(4), 505–527. https://doi.org/10.1177/0044118x14542575

Welch. (2018). *Being a mom is the equivalent of 2.5 full-time jobs*. Retrieved July 23, 2019, from New York Post website https://nypost.com/2018/03/17/being-a-mom-is-the-equivalent-of-2-5-full-time-jobs/

World Health Organization. (2020). *Promoting proper feeding for infants and young children*. Retrieved April 7, 2020, from https://www.who.int/nutrition/topics/infantfeeding/en/

Young, I. (2003). Breasted experience: The look and the feeling. In R. Weitz (Ed.), *The politics of women's bodies: Sexuality, appearance, and behavior,* (215-230). Oxford University Press.

Zhang, Y., Jin, Y., Vereijken, C., Stahl, B., & Jiang, H. (2018). Breastfeeding experience, challenges and service demands among Chinese mothers: A qualitative study in two cities. *Appetite*, *128*(138), 263–270. https://doi.org/10.1016/j.appet.2018.06.027

T(w)een sexting and sexual behaviour: (d)evaluating the feminine other

Antonio García-Gómez

ABSTRACT

This study explores the gendered discourses of youth sexualities. More specifically, it reports on research examining t(w)een girls' discursive construction and negotiation of their femininities in the context of sexting. Using a qualitative method, the study attempts to contribute to the understanding of the multidimensionality of femininity. In order to do so, it brings femme theory into focus and contributes to its growth by analysing tween and teen girls' discursive positionings when narrating their sexting experiences. The results give evidence of the pervasiveness of femmephobia and draw attention to the fact that the use of specific linguistic strategies not only allow the participants in the study to occupy different femininities in their narratives, but also to regulate the in-group and out-group sexualities. Furthermore, the presence of coercive language provides a clearer understanding of the cultural devaluation of femininity.

In recent years, there has been an increasing interest in exploring the effect that social media has on the lives of adults in general and young people in particular (Livingstone, 2011). Extensive research has been devoted to ascertaining the types of actions teenagers engage in online (Ringrose & Eriksson Barajas, 2011) in a bid to shed light on the interpersonal dimensions that characterise social media (Brown, 2004; García-Gómez, 2017) and raise awareness of the potential impacts of the Internet on teenagers' development of gender roles and socialisation (Hyde, 2007). In so doing, young people's online sexual activities and their related risks have been an object of research (García-Gómez, 2018; Hasinoff, 2015; Lupton, 2016). These studies have highlighted young people's increasing consumption of sexually explicit material (Attwood and Smith, 2014) and have called attention to the outcomes of this practice: cyberbullying, sexual violence, sexting and sextortion (for an overview, see Katzer, Fetchenhauer, & Belschak, 2009; Ringrose, Harvey, Gill, & Livingstone, 2013; Ross, Drouin, & Coupe, 2019; among many others).

Given that young adolescents seem to be commonly involved in (un)willing sexting behaviour (Schloms-Madlener, 2013), scholars have discussed the legal considerations of sexting, the prevalence rates, the regularisation and criminalisation of the production, possession and sharing of sexually explicit material (for an overview, see Albury & Crawford, 2012; Karaian, 2012; Lee, Crofts, Salter, Milivojevic, & McGovern, 2013; among others). Furthermore, research specific to gender and social media has tried not only to assess the correctness of minors' online behaviours (Thurlow, 2014), but also to design appropriate social skills intervention plans that try to raise awareness of the risks children and teenagers take when they sext (Katzman, 2010).

Indebted to Gill's (2008, 2012) conceptual device that combines the ideas of 'compulsory' with 'sexual' and 'agency', feminist research on sexting practices has attempted to cast further light on compulsory female sexual agency – understood as a specific form of sexual empowerment (Ringrose, Harvery, Gill, & Livingstone, 2013). By exploring the heterosexualised norms of desirability negotiated online and the construction of girls' sexual morality, vulnerability and agency (Davidson, 2014), feminist scholars call attention to the presence of a 'new hegemonic discourse of feminine empowerment' (Gill, 2008, p. 67). In so doing, they have tried to challenge the traditional notions of free will and choice that humanist theories of agency take for granted.

In addition to this, feminist research, as Dobson (2015) argues, has concerned with exploring how social media facilitate the sexual objectification of girls and young women (Hasinoff, 2015; Naezer, 2018). This cutting-edge research suggests that 'discourse about sexualisation inadvertently pathologise conformity and exalt resistance to mass culture as the only healthy or genuine form of agency'. (Hasinoff, 2014, p. 10); that is, feminist scholars have attempted to shed further light on the complexity of agency by interrogating young girls' apparent conformity to sexualisation (Hasinoff, 2014). In particular, Hasinoff questions the commonly shared assumption that sexualisation is to blame for sexting. In doing so, she conceptualises sexting as media production and provides a new way of studying and thinking about sexting that seems to revolve around 'sexuality' and 'agency'.

By interrogating the over-simplistic view of (young) women being mere victims of the sexualisation of culture who are unable to make healthy decisions and choices about their own body, these feminist scholars propose the rethinking of assumptions behind sexualisation, empowerment and choice (Dobson & Ringrose, 2016; Hart, 2017). Although several attempts have been made to rethink these three key assumptions, young women's evaluative beliefs and motivations behind sexting have received scant attention (García-Gómez, 2017). In this paper, I argue that the exploration of t(w)een girls' own perception of femininity in their discourses of sexting opens up possibilities for gaining a deeper understanding of the complexity of young women's choice. In line with Hasinoff (2014), this article problematises the one-dimensional understanding of young women as passive victims of the sexualisation of culture. The aim is to contribute to the debate about the gendered discourses of youth sexualities by giving evidence of how the (d)evaluation of femininity sheds further light on the interrelationships existing between reproducing dominant gendered norms and showing individual agency.

Critical femininities: femme theory, femmephobia and the devaluation of femininity

Since the 1960s, there has been an ever-growing body of work on gender and language. Early studies on the area of language and gender revolved around two key paradigms: gender as cross-culture difference and gender as social power/dominance (Tannen, 1990; Zimmerman & West, 1975). Over the last decades, psychologists, sociologists and discourse analysts have investigated the ways gender affects discourse from varying perspectives and approaches (see, for instance, Eckert & McConnell-Ginet, 2003). As a result, there is a wealth of literature on female/male identity construction, gendered identities and expressions, normative gender roles and performances, and sexuality in both online and offline contexts (Butler, 1990; Ringrose et al., 2013; Hasinoff, 2015; Dobson, 2015; among many others).

In spite of the existing body of research on the (de)construction of femininity and masculinity (Coffey, 2019; Edwards, 2006; Gonick, Renold, Ringrose, & Weems, 2009), little attention has been paid to the emergent field of Critical Femininities in general and the devaluation of femininity and femmephobia in particular (Hoskin, 2017; Stardust, 2015). As Hoskin (2017) argues, femininity has been wrongly conceived as the source of oppression. In so doing, research has failed, on the one hand, to explore femininity within patriarchal discourse domination (Hoskin, 2019) and, on the other, to fully understand and learn about the multidimensional nature of femininity (Hoskin, 2017) and its impact on theorising social inequalities (Serano, 2007).

There is a growing body of literature that highlights the limitations of the gender binary and explores the tenets of gender identity beyond reductionist biological determinants (Carr, 2017; Ferguson, Carr, & Snitman, 2014). In this context, femme theory advocates against a binary conception of gender that revolves around white masculine cisgender heterosexual men (Shelton, 2018). In so doing, femme theory reconceptualises gender identity as a whole and deconstruct and demystify the complex ways in which hegemonic assumptions about gender, power and agency are produced (Hoskin, 2017). In this light, femme identity not only blurs the boundaries of gender normativity, but also it is understood, as Shelton (2018) argues, 'as inherently renegotiating power dynamics associated with multiple spheres of interpolated identities' (p. 24).

Femme scholars therefore purport to shed light into femme identity in general (Levitt, Gerrish, & Hiestand, 2003; Burke, 2009; among others) and the actual meanings of being femme in particular (Levitt et al., 2003; Dahl, 2017; among others). In other words, Hoskin (2013) has led cutting-edge research into how feminine devaluation has been overlooked. Furthermore, her studies have called attention to the institution of femmephobia – understood as the opposing force to femme identity – that gives evidence of how 'deviations from hegemonic norms of femininity function as a source of oppression' (Hoskin, 2017, p. 96). In this vein, Hoskin (2013) proposes the existence of four types of femmephobia: ascribed (i.e. covert devaluation present in language); perceived (i.e. open devaluation of perceived femininity); femme mystification (i.e. dehumanisation and objectification of those perceived feminine); and pious (i.e. humiliation of feminine enactments).

Hoskin's theories of femme fill in a significant gap in the literature by exploring the process of femme-identity development and the existence of femme identities that exist beyond butch-femme dichotomies. Furthermore, her research on feminine devaluation in queer communities, on the one hand, explores the processes through which queer femininities and femme identities exist within the larger LGBTQ community and, on the other hand, casts light on how femininities that cross gender and sexual orientations are devalued. Her theories of femme and femmephobia, therefore, make it possible to conceptualise the femme frame of reference as 'vulnerable to on-going evolution in the development of liberated and inclusive praxes for identity and identity-expression' (Shelton, 2018, p. 34).

In the light of this, the present paper starts from the premise that femininities are under-theorised and under-researched (Blair & Hoskin, 2015) and is built on Schipper's (2007) and Hoskin's (2019) rethinking of the possibilities for masculinity and femininity, and their role in gender hegemony. I build upon Schipper's (2007) conceptualisation of 'hegemonic femininity and multiple, hierarchical femininities *as central to male dominant gender relations*' (p. 85). Here I also use Hoskin's (2013; 2017) femme theory as a theoretical framework to explore the concept of essentialised femininity, feminine devaluation and femmephobia beyond the LGTBQ community. More specifically, this study contrasts cisgender white heterosexual tween and teen girls' perceptions of femininities when they navigate their sexual identities. In addition, it explores whether or not these perceptions align with 'proper womanhood' (Blair & Hoskin, 2015, p. 232) and restrict the expression of femininity to culturally authorised forms.

In so doing, this study attempts to shed further light on the internalised and externalised pervasiveness of femmephobia (Ibid.: 241) in these girls' perceptions of themselves and others who practise sexting. The primary focus of the current paper is to analyse the discourse characteristics and practices defined as 'proper womanhood' and feminine that, as Hoskin (2019) points out, 'are stigmatized across identities and regulated by femmephobia' (p. 3). More specifically, this study aims to explore the complexities of feminine (d) evaluation as it manifests across cisgender white heterosexual tween and teen girls' narratives about why they sext. In so doing, the present paper attempts to throw further light on the multidimensional nature of femininity. This, in turn, will make it possible to argue how tween and teen girls perceive occupying the feminine differently.

Method

Participants

The data I analyse are drawn from a larger study I have conducted as part of an anti-bullying programme in four secondary schools in the north of England. The programme targeted three main areas: teenage relationships, conflict resolution strategies and sex education (García-Gómez, 2017, 2018). As part of the programme, 81 female teenagers (aged between 14 and 17) and their 73 younger sisters (aged between 9 and 12) were invited to an information session about the project. Of the 76 teen and 69 tween girls who attended the information session, the parents of 68 and 61 of them respectively signed the consent form for the research to take place after their daughters had also agreed to take part in the study. Even though the catchment for the girls' schools is predominantly white lower-middle class and the population has low socio-economic status, all the participants classified themselves as white middle-class. These girls seem to relate, as Skeggs (1997) highlights, middleclass status to respectable femininity.

Given that the study is aimed at problematising the supposed sexualisation of tween and teen girls, the focus is on the 'schizoid pushes and pulls [that] operate as one of the new normative conditions' (Renold & Ringrose, 2011, p. 393) that these girls have to navigate. More specifically, I use a qualitative method, based on a rigorous pragma-discourse analysis of focus groups discussions among tween girls schoolmates on the one hand and teen girls school-mates on the other who comment on the social and personal consequences of having exchanged sexually explicit pictures of themselves with their close friends or their significant others as part of a consented game. Therefore, this study takes up the challenge by creating spaces for critical transformative dialogue among and for girls so that they can 'speak from positions outside the regulatory' (Jackson & Vares, 2015, p. 83). In so doing, I ground the study in the first-hand accounts of the way(s) tween and teen girls construct, negotiate and navigate their sexual gendered identities in the context of sexting.

Ethics

The intention to study female tweens' and teens' perceptions of consensual sexting posed an ethical question regarding the potential implications of analysing these narratives given the age of the participants. It is worth mentioning that 60% of the participants had taken part in the previous stages of the anti-bullying programme and their parents were fully aware of the prevalence of youth sexting. Given that their daughters were already using social networks to present images of themselves, parents seemed to understand this research as an opportunity to model healthy and responsible mobile phone use as well as an opportunity to raise awareness of the dangers to their daughters of sending and distributing pictures of their naked bodies.

In addition, the study ensures the anonymity and the privacy of the participants. For this purpose, I used their self-selected pseudonyms and offered no personal references. With regard to my analytical and ethical position, my focus is on the girls' narratives and the implications for social change. Even though these narratives are an opportunity for reflection and for identity work, I adopted a social constructionist orientation so the girls' narratives provided a context for them to engage in a relationship talk and tell me something about the cultural norms and, possibly, the community of practice norms that are attended to or challenged in this peer group of tween and teen girls who sext.

Guided discussion interviews

After having given a talk about teens' social media habits and having all the consent forms signed, small focus group discussions with four to six participants were held so as to discuss the effects of sexting in their interpersonal relationships. These guided discussions lasted between 25 minutes to 35 minutes and were conducted by one of their schoolteachers, a sociologist and a psychologist who tried to gather data about their specific social media habits and made sure everyone had the opportunity to intervene. All these discussions were cam recorded so that I could watch them as many times as needed while transcribing the interactions. The resulting conversations consisted of 13,745 utterances,[1] comprising eight discussions among the teen participants (7 hours and 21 minutes) and seven discussions among the tween participants (6 hours and nine minutes). Finally, all these utterances were classified according to their main discursive functions in the data. In general terms, all the utterances covered informative acts which aimed to (i) evaluate the t(w)een girls themselves positively in a direct/indirect manner; (ii) evaluate other girls; or (iii) evaluate boy positively or negatively in a direct/indirect manner. A more detailed analysis of the subclasses of informative acts identified will be provided as the analysis unfolds.

Exploring the multidimensionality and devaluation of femininity

Ascribed and perceived femmephobia

The inspection of the tween and teen girls' focus group discussions reveals how the participants in the study regulate their own and other girls' online sexual behaviour by enacting respectable essentialised femininity. More specifically, they create a positive sense of in-group membership by evaluating those who behave like they do positively and criticising those who deviate from the belief system. The inspection of the data reveals that these t(w)een girls' sexuality revolves around two prescribed supplementary discourses: the inappropriateness of sexual interest/desire (i.e. the age discourse) on the one hand and the conventional female sexual passivity and unresponsiveness (i.e. the gender of sexual discourse) on the other. In doing so, their sexual online behaviour seems to be circumscribed by specific containment strategies (i.e. femmephobia) that operate to maintain gender hierarchy and patriarchal relations. Discursively speaking, these containment strategies are built up by means of informative acts that may be classified into two main groups:

(1) **(In)direct positive evaluation of themselves**. These informative acts aim to evaluate these girls positively in a (in)direct manner which may comprise either a positive evaluation of their lack initiative (e.g. 'I'd never ask a boy for a date') or their lack of interest in sex ('e.g. My friends and I don't care about sex, we're girls!').

(2) **(In)direct negative evaluation of boys**. These informative acts negatively evaluate boys (e.g. 'Boys are all the same') and/or boys' sexual behaviour (e.g. 'Guys literally only want one thing').

Consider the following excerpts from the data where three 11–12 year-old tween girls and two 15 year-old teen girls reject their natural sexual awareness and exploit, as Egan (2013) highlights, a childish and innocent attitude:

Excerpt 1.

Joddy:	For me this is pretty fun when I'm bored because you kinda get to see what you can do … erm I mean I put on a cute outfit and take a pic showing off my erm curves you know I sometimes then I post it on Instagram
Anne:	My mum says I'm a pose maniac and I don't know erm I erm only girls our age can understand. Got pics I'd never ever show anyone you know we all have tricks to make our butt look smaller ((laughing))
Joddy:	Yeah my mum says I post everything on Instagram but it's not true
Maggie:	Boys are different they constantly send pics of their you know. Boys you don't even know
Anne:	Boys send them all the time and they ask you to send them pictures but I'm just eleven. Don't know what they're thinking of, they are not even theirs I don't know why they do this ((all laugh)) Boys will be boys
Joddy:	((laughing)) Yeah you know there are girls who like these pics as well and erm you know people call them names

Excerpt 2.

Mona:	I don't care what Sarah and Jordan said I've never, you know, I have never touched myself never ever!
Julia:	Guys are always bragging about their sexploits and drinking habits ((laughing))
Mona:	Yeah they speak about no other thing than that erm that they touch themselves and they want you to erm you know
Julia:	My cousin told me she has tried to touch herself every now and then but it does hurt
Mona:	My mom asks my brother why he spends so much time in the toilet and my dad usually jokes and says he's you know he goes to slap the salami
Julia:	Guys are useless ((laughing))

This excerpt illustrates how ascribed femmephobia is linguistically embedded. The discourse analysis of the excerpts, therefore, shows how the age discourse is intertwined with the gender of sexual desire discourse. By accepting boys' natural self-awareness (e.g. 'boys are different they constantly send pics of their you know', 'Guys are always bragging about their sexploits and drinking habits') and denying their sexual desire due to their youth (e.g. 'I'm just eleven', 'I have never touched myself never ever!'), these t(w)een girls endorse the enactment and achievement of essentialised femininity while comparing themselves with others who act differently (e.g. 'there are girls who like these pics as well and erm you know people call them names'). More importantly, the gendered normative dimension present in these narratives highlights how perceived femmephobia goes hand in hand with ascribed femmephobia insofar as these t(w)een girls' narratives prescribe a specific behaviour for girls and boys.

Pious femmephobia

The discourse analysis of both group discussions makes it possible to argue that ascribed and perceived femmephobias intertwine with pious femmephobia. More specifically, these girls' sexual online behaviour is delineated by specific containment strategies that are aimed at maintaining patriarchal norms of femininity as virtuous. Discursively speaking, these containment strategies are built up by means of informative acts that may be classified into two main groups:

(1) **(In)direct positive/negative evaluation of boys**. These informative acts range from negatively evaluating boys in general (e.g. 'All guys are wonkers') to evaluating their significant others positively (e.g. 'Mark is different. He loves me').
(2) **(In)direct negative evaluation of other girls**. These informative acts enforce social sanctions by evaluating sexually promiscuous females negatively (e.g. 'She does things, you know, she's a real slapper'). In so doing, these t(w)een girls cast themselves in a positive light.

These 12 year-old and 16 year-old girls' narratives (excerpts 3 and 4 respectively) perpetuate and enforce female morality (i.e. pious femmephobia) by evaluating in a negative manner those girls who act differently from their own belief system:

Excerpt 3.

Cheryl:	Some girls I know say these things to boys, Angela showed me the texts they were sending each other erm you know the 'I'm not wearing any underwear' kinda thing
Julia:	Angela and her friends get their knees dirty (laughing) but we're not like them, we're not sluts. Guys come after these girls like crazy because they want to date them or anything it's just sex they want. I'm just a girl and I'm not ready for a relationship
Alex:	They're just crazy! You can't send pictures of yourself because [you] know you're in love but who knows what he can do with them
Val:	They are just girls
Alex:	They think they're more popular because they do these things, but people speak behind their backs and call them names
Val:	They don't call them names, they just call them what they are

Excerpt 4.

Amanda:	Guys are obsessed, you know, they are curious about whether, you know, we have their urges
Prue:	Yeah they think we say we don't because we're lying but the things is masturbation is a private thing
Linda:	Me and my friends are quite open with each other about these things, because none of us see it as something to be ashamed of.
Amanda:	That's right. Guys want more sex than women, that's a fact erm we know that. Men, erm, we're not ashamed but I told Mark I'm not the kinda girl you've been waiting for
Prue:	The other day I heard Mark said to Anna 'do your knees a favour and get some kneepads' while laughing
Linda:	((laughing)) We all know Anna is a straight up trick.

As these two excerpts illustrate, it is common to find references to a slut discourse that allow these girls not only to embed themselves within a socially acceptable in-group (e.g. 'I'm not the kinda girl you've been waiting for'), but also they sustain patriarchal femininity by invoking the good/bad girl binary (e.g. 'They think they're more popular because they do these things') that, as Vares et al. (2011) rightly note, 'reinforce frameworks that place women's and girl's sexuality into narrow and repressive categories' (p. 148). Furthermore, the presence of coercive language shows how these girls seem to have assimilated expressions of ascribed femmephobia since they uphold masculine privileging (e.g. 'Guys want more sex than women, we know that') and devalue other femininities (e.g. 'Angela and her friends get their knees dirty (laughing) but we're not like them, we're not sluts'). Such devaluation of femininity revokes the element of choice by excluding and humiliating those other girls. This goes in line with Schippers' (2007) claim that showing sexual assertiveness is 'stigmatised and sanctioned when embodied by women.' (p. 95)

The discourse analysis of the data gives evidence of the fact that pious femmephobia can be seen as the result of enacting respectable patriarchal femininity. This, in turn, reinforces these t(w)een girls' gender- and sexual-based prejudices that revolve around the most common gender stereotypes that maintain femininity's subordinate status (Hoskin, 2017); that is, boys have a constant desire to have sex and sexually active girls are sluts (i.e. those who masturbate and/or have sex with boys). Such systematic devaluation of femininity underlines Hoskin's (2017) argument that 'femmephobia homogenises femininities and maintains the ideology of a monolithic femininity.' (p. 99)

Interestingly, both tween and teen girls justify this socially unacceptable behaviour (i.e. sexting) if they are in love. Consider the following excerpts where 11- and 12-year-old girls justify sending naked pictures if they are in a relationship (excerpt 5) and where two 16-year-old teen girls explain when and why they started sexting (excerpt 6):

Excerpt 5.

Pam:	I started dating Matthew few weeks ago. He's not my boyfriend but sort of we see other quite often and yeah I've sent him pics of my ((points to her breast)) don't know not proud or anything but
Andrea:	When you're a in relationship this is different you text him a lot and send silly stuff and he likes you and you like him and you send him things he likes you know what I mean
Pam:	I like him a lot and erm he wants to see me and I want to see him erm better me than watching porn
Andrea:	When you love someone, there is nothing wrong. It's like saying you like him and you trust him

Excerpt 6.

Danielle:	That's right. The first time my boyfriend asked me to take a pic of my bum, you know, erm I didn't want to do it, but it was like I was embarrassed but he insisted, well, he told me that all of his friends' girlfriends do it and well I [...]
Fabiola:	yeah, my story is pretty much the same. I started sending these pics when I started going out with my boyfriend. I haven't done it before but he insisted that it was ok and I kind of, I don't know. He asked me to send him some pics of mine and I felt embarrassed at the beginning, but I love him and I started taking pics erm I started sending pics in underwear, but he wanted more and you know I love him to bits and I knew he wasn't going to show my pics to anybody and I sent him some more [...] it's kinda weird, it makes me feel sexy [...]

These excerpts show how these t(w)een girls' sexuality is still constrained by expectations of conformity with notions of 'good girl femininity' (Jackson & Vares, 2015, p. 93). In particular, the discourse analysis of these excerpts casts further light on how pious femmephobia is composed of containment strategies that maintain patriarchal femininity as complementary and subordinated to masculinity (e.g. 'When you love someone, there is nothing wrong', 'you know I love him to bits and I knew he wasn't going to show my pics to anybody'). More specifically, their narratives show the tension between enacting respectable patriarchal femininity and justifying any active desiring agency (Griffin, 2004).

Although their narratives underline the sexual double standard since girls are supposed to justify that they are sexually active girls, this creates the space of 'new forms of knowledge and practice' (Gill, 2012, p. 737). Furthermore, pious femmephobia regulates these t(w)een girls' sexualites through coercive language acts insofar as they seem to understand that being is a relationship and subordinating their personal needs as one. As Lamb (2010) suggests, 'using active vs. passive, subject vs. object as ways of describing good vs bad sex, suggests to girls that there is only one correct position from which to have sex, the position that has traditionally been associated with men' (p. 299).

Femme mystification or fighting perceived femmephobia?

The discourse analysis of these girls' focus group discussions makes it possible to identify instances of femme mystification exclusively in the teen girls' focus groups. Although these teen girls' narratives seem to illustrate transgressing discourses that apparently push against their ascribed subordination (i.e. an attempt to fight against perceived femmephobia), close inspection of the data reveals how femme mystification regulates sexualities, while upholding and securing gender hegemony. The manifestation of this type of femmephobia operates, as (Hoskin, 2017) points out, 'by separating femininity from humanness – by erotising, exoticising, and objectifying' (p. 102–103). Discursively speaking, such manifestation is built up by means of informative acts that may be classified into three main groups:

(1) **(In)direct positive evaluation of themselves**. These informative acts range from evaluating the need to satisfy their sexual needs positively (e.g. 'I know how to pleasure myself') to justifying their sexting behaviour (e.g. 'All young people do it').

(2) **(In)direct positive/negative evaluation of boys**. These informative acts range from negatively evaluating boys in general (e.g. 'All guys are wonkers') to evaluating their significant others positively (e.g. 'Mark is different. He loves me').

(3) **(In)direct negative evaluation of other girls**. These informative acts comprise negative evaluations of queer women (e.g. 'She's a pillow princess') and queer sex practices (e.g. 'They u-haul too quick').

Consider the following excerpt from the data where these 15-year-old young women narrate they have sent pictures with sexual content to someone they were dating occasionally or somebody they had just met in a chat room:

Excerpt 6.

Anna:	((nodding)) I send pictures these kinda pictures quite often. I guess we all do so ((looking at the other girls)) It's not like such big deal, is it?
Carla:	Yeah, parents make a fuss about it but it's just, I don't know, it's just, it's like they don't understand
Anna:	They don't ((laughing)) We are not afraid of sex, it's not like when my parents thought it was a sin and they didn't have sex and now they are afraid of speaking about sex or making sex [...] I like my boobs and if I take a picture and I feel like, you know, erm polishing the pearl ((laughing)) I do it and I know how to satisfy myself, don't care if I'm chubby or if I don't have skinny tights I like the way I am
Carla:	My parents would give me a bollocking if they knew I took pictures of myself, but I enjoy doing it. I know they want to protect me, but I'm a grown woman. It's like I explore my body and I know how to pleasure myself, you know, there's nothing wrong erm I started, you know, being with boys when I was 12 and I know what I like and what I don't and if I like something I do it, why not?
Daniela:	yeah, it's like it makes me feel I'm pretty and I play with boys ((laughing)), you know, it's like you say 'You want to see my bum' and boys are all like 'whoo' and it's like you send them a picture and they would do anything ((laughing))
Anna:	Boys are so erm predictable, you know, you're chatting with somebody and he's saying things like he'd like you to work your hand along his shaft and then he sends a pic so you say something that you know will drive him crazy like I want you to bury your fingers inside of me ((laughing)) [...]

This excerpt illustrates the multidimensionality of femininity as these teen girls seem to associate sexting with being 'agents' and 'active' (Lamb, 2010). Although they self-present as sexually self-aware and sexually liberated, the discourse analysis reveals that their conceptualisation of femininity is still defined by its accommodation of male desires. That is to say, this agential embodiment does not seem to represent a direct affront to essentialised femininity insofar as their narratives, as Blair and Hoskin (2015) argue, support 'one facet of the systems of sex/gender/sexuality (i.e. female is feminine) can uphold another (i.e. feminine female is heterosexual)' (p. 240).

Although these narratives evoke the element of agency and choice, they fail to fight perceived femmephobia since they still underline the distinctive and complementary relationship existing between masculinity and femininity (Schippers, 2007). Furthermore, femme mystification can be seen in the self-objectification process present in these narratives where these teen girls perceive themselves as sexual objects of male desire (e.g. 'I play with boys [...] and it's like you send them a picture and they would do anything'). Apart from objectifying themselves, the discourse analysis of these teen girls' narratives makes it possible to identify examples of femmephobic regulatory language that regulate their own and other young women's sexualities; that is, these teen girls' prejudices seem to result in the dehumanisation and objectification of queer women. Consider the following excerpt where these 14-year-old young women justify why they sext:

Excerpt 7.

Magda: I have fun in my room when I'm alone you know but I'm not a fucking slut pussy tease ((laughing))

Jossiee: ((laughing)) we all have you know urgent needs sometimes

Ronna: Yeah, we are not like these erm how do you call them, Magda?

Magda: Carpet munchers ((laughing)) they u-haul too quick ((laughing)) you know they happily give their pussies to some slutty nympho. We know how to please ourselves

Ronna: You're talking about the pillow princess and her girlfriend. I know they do sext each other because they post it on facebook and instagram sometimes

Jossie: Do you remember when I had a quarrel with Mary 'cos I asked her who was the man in the relationship and oh girl I ruffled her feathers

Ronna: ((laughing) yeah when they showed me the kinda things they say to each other and they told me that was real sex I asked her how she knew she was a lesbian if she'd never had sex with a man. Then she said she was a gold star and I didn't know what she meant. Ginna told me she was proud 'cos she's never ever had a dick

Jossie: I could tell Mary was a lesbian miles away she's so so the type, but Ginna is so pretty.

Monna: I told her she just hasn't met the right man yet ((they all laugh))

During teen girls' focus group discussions, it was common to find instances where the participants justify their sexual behaviour by contrasting their female masturbation habits and the reasons for sexting and having casual sex with men with those of queer women. As the excerpt illustrates, these girls not only diminish the negative social evaluation of their sexual behaviour by criticising two queer young women in their group of friends (e.g. 'I could tell Mary was a lesbian miles away she's so so the type'), but also disqualify, as Hoskin and Hirschfeld (2018) highlight, those who transgress normal coordinates of gender and sexuality (e.g. 'I told her she just hasn't met the right man yet'). These young women tend to assume that a queer relationship is imitating a straight one (e.g. 'I asked her who was the man in the relationship'). Furthermore, their narratives mirror the processes of perceived femmephobia and femme mystification since they (i) exclude other sexual behaviours that fall into stereotypes (i.e. queer women become emotionally invested in a relationship very quickly (u-haul), a queer couple comprises a butch and a femme), and (ii) humiliate these queer women (e.g. 'pillow princess', 'eat cunts'). These narratives, in turn, are examples of homophobia.

Conclusion

This study has purported to bring femme theory into focus in order to examine the gendered discourses of youth sexualities. In so doing, the present study has attempted to contribute to its growth by analysing the (d)evaluating discursive strategies tween and teen girls deploy when narrating their sexting experiences. In line with Hoskin and Blair (2015) and Hoskin (2013); 2017; Hoskin & Hirschfeld (2018)), I have explored how the construction and negotiation of these t(w)een girls' sexual identities illustrate examples of femmephobia and the devaluation of femininity.

Contributing to and expanding on this body of work, my intention has been to intervene in the debates on sexualisation, sexual agency, and choice by illustrating these t(w)een girls' percep-tions, beliefs and implications of occupying different femininities in their narratives. Furthermore, the discursive exploration of the ways in which the participants perform an ideology while constructing and negotiating their (sexual) gendered femininity has made it possible to highlight the complexities and multidimensionality of femininities. The use of coercive femmephobic language has shown, in line with Hoskin (2017, 2019)), to act as a regulatory force that maintains normative femininity and relates femininity to a gender expression performed for masculine consumption.

By analysing these tween and teen girls' narratives, I have identified the systematic devaluation of femininity and highlighted the pervasiveness of femmephobia. The discourse analysis of these girls' narratives has made it possible to explore the multidimensionality and devaluation of femininity. More specifically, the analysis has given evidence of both ascribed and perceived femmephobia in these t(w)een girls' narratives where they place the emphasis on the 'good girl' femininity (Jackson & Vares, 2015, p. 93) and enact the cultural discourse of 'childhood innocence'. Furthermore, the analysis has also suggested that ascribed and perceived femmephobias can be claimed to intertwine with pious femmephobia insofar as these girls' sexual online behaviour seems to be delineated by specific containment strategies that maintain patriarchal norms of femininity as virtuous. Finally, the discourse analysis has identified examples of femme mystification exclusively in the teen girls' narratives that regulate these girls' and other girls' sexualities, while upholding and securing gender hegemony.

Further investigation is clearly needed to map these emerging arenas for the study of the devaluation of femininity. Natural directions for future research include a further interrogation of these t(w)een girls' sexual choices by exploring how they actually negotiate their sexual gendered identity. It would be worth exploring how they talk about the consequences of sexting in private interviews since this will cast light on the femmephobic regulatory language young women deploy to regulate their own and others' sexualities.

Note

1. The term utterance refers 'to complete communicative units, which may consist of single words, phrases, clauses and clause combinations spoken in context' (Carter & McCarthy, 2006, p.17).

Disclosure statement

No potential conflict of interest was reported by the author.

Funding

The present study was financially supported by a grant from the Ministerio de Economía y Competitividad. This article is part of the long-term research *"Persuasion in Promotional Discourse: Linguistic resources and communication strategies"*..

References

Albury, K., & Crawford, K. (2012). Sexting, consent and young peoples ethics: BeyondMegan's STORY. *Continuum: Journal of Media and Cultural Studies, 26*(3), 463–473.

Attwood, F. & Smith. C. (2014). Porn.Studies: An introduction. *Porn Studies, 1* (1–2), 1–6.

Blair, K. L., & Hoskin, R. A. (2015). Experiences of femme identity: Coming out, invisibility and femmephobia. *Psychology and Sexuality, 6*(3), 229–244.

Brown, B. B. (2004). Adolescents' relationships with peers. In R. M. Lerner & L. Steinberg (Eds.), *Handbook of adolescent psychology* (pp. 363–394). Hoboken, NJ: John Wiley.

Burke, J. C. (Ed). (2009). *Visible: A femmethology* (Vol. 1& 2). Ypsilanti, MI: Homofactus Press.

Butler, J. (1990). *Gender trouble. Feminism and the subversion of identity*. New York and London: Routledge.

Carr, G. V. (2017). Black Americans and transgender identity. In K. L. Nadal (Ed.), *The sage publication of psychology and gender* (pp. 458-457). Thousand Oaks, CA.

Carter, R., & McCarthy, M. (2006). *Cambridge grammar of English*. Cambridge: Cambridge University Press.

Coffey, J. (2019). Creating distance from body issues: Exploring new materialist feminist possibilities for renegotiating gendered embodiment. *Leisure Sciences, 41*(1–2), 72–90.

Dahl, U. (2017). Femmebodiments: Notes on queer feminine shapes of vulnerability. *Feminist Theory*, *18*(1), 35–53.

Davidson, J. (2014). *Sexting: Gender and teens*. Rotterdam: Sense Publishers.

Dobson, A. (2015). *Postfeminist digital cultures: Femininity, social media, and self-representation*. New York: Palgrave Macmillan.

Dobson, A., & Ringrose, J. (2016). Sext education: Pedagogies of sex, gender and shame in the schoolyard of tagged and exposed. *Sex Education: Sexuality, Society and Learning*, *16*(1), 8–21.

Eckert, P., & McConnell-Ginet, S. (2003). *Language and gender*. Cambridge: CUP.

Edwards, T. (2006). *Cultures of masculinity*. London: Routledge.

Egan, R. D. (2013). *Becoming sexual: A critical appraisal of the sexualization of girl*. Malden, MA: Polity.

Ferguson, A. D., Carr, G., & Snitman, A. (2014). Intersections of race-ethnicity, gender, and sexual minority communities. In M. L. Miville & A. D. Ferguson (Eds.), *Handbook of race-ethnicity and gender in psychology* (pp. 45–63). New York, NY, US: Springer Science and Business Media.

García-Gómez, A. (2017). Teen girls and sexual agency: Exploring the intrapersonal and intergroup dimensions of sexting. *Media, Culture and Society*, *39*(3), 391–407.

García-Gómez, A. (2018). From selfies to sexting: Tween girls, intimacy, and subjectivities. *Girlhood Studies*, *11*(1), 43–58.

Gill, R. (2008). Empowerment/sexism: Figuring female sexual agency in contemporary advertising. *Feminism & Psychology*, *18*(1), 35–60.

Gill, R. (2012). Media, empowerment and the 'Sexualisation of Culture' debates. *Sex Roles*, *66*(11), 736–745.

Gonick, M., Renold, E., Ringrose, J., & Weems, L. (2009). Rethinking agency and resistance: What comes after girl power? *Girlhood Studies, Special Issue: What Comes after Girl Power? 2*(2), guest editors, 1–9.

Griffin, C. (2004). Good girls bad girls: anglocentrism and diversity in the construction of contemporary girlhood. In A. Harris (Ed (Ed), *All about the girl: culture, power and identity* (pp. pp.29–43). New York: Routledge.

Hart, M. (2017). Being naked on the internet: Young people's selfies as intimate edgework. *Journal of Youth Studies*, *20*(3), 301–315.

Hasinoff, A. A. (2014). Blaming sexualization for sexting. *Girlhood Studies*, *7*(1), 102–120.

Hasinoff, A. A. (2015). *Sexting panic: Rethinking criminalization, privacy, and consent*. Champaign, IL: University of Illinois Press.

Hoskin, R. A. (2013). *Femme theory: Femininity's challenge to western feminist pedagogies*. (Master's thesis). QSpace at Queen's University, Kingston, Ontario, Canada.

Hoskin, R. A. (2017). Femme theory: Refocusing the intersectional lens. *Atlantis*, *38*(1), 95–109.

Hoskin, R. A. (2019). Femmephobia: The role of anti-femininity and gender policing in LGBTQ+ people's experiences of discrimination. In *Sex Roles*

Hoskin, R. A., & Hirschfeld, K. L. (2018). Beyond aesthetics: A femme manifesto. *Atlantis: Critical Studies in Gender, Culture & Social Justice*, *39*(1), 85–87.

Hyde, J. (2007). New directions in the study of gender similarities and differences. *Current Directions in Psychological Science*, *16*, 259–263.

Jackson, S., & Vares, T. (2015). `Too many bad role models for us girls': Girls, female pop celebrities and 'sexualization'. *Sexualities*, *18*(4), 480–494.

Karaian, L. (2012). Lolita speaks: 'Sexting', teenage girls and the law. *Crime Media Culture*, *8*(1), 57–73.

Katzer, C., Fetchenhauer, D., & Belschak, F. (2009). Cyberbullying: Who are the victims? A comparison of victimization in internet chat rooms and victimization at school. *Journal of Media Psychology*, *21*(1), 25–36.

Katzman, D. K. (2010). Sexting: Keeping teens safe and responsible in a technologically savvy world. *Paediatrics & Child Health*, *15*(1), 41–42.

Lamb, S. (2010). Feminist ideals for a healthy female adolescent sexuality: A critique. *Sex Roles*, *62*, 294–306. doi:10.1007/s11199-009-9698-1

Lee, M., Crofts, T., Salter, M., Milivojevic, S., & McGovern, A. (2013). Let's get sexting': Risk, power, sex and criminalisation in the Moral Domain. *International Journal for Crime and Justice*, *2*, 35–49.

Levitt, H. M., Gerrish, E. A., & Hiestand, K. R. (2003). The misunderstood gender: A model of modern femme identity. *Sex Roles*, *48*, 99–113.

Livingstone, S. (2011). Internet, children and youth. In M. Consalvo & C. Ess (Eds.), *Handbook of internet studies* (pp. 348–368). Oxford: Wiley-Blackwell.

Lupton, D. (2016). Digital risk society. In A. Burguess, A. Alemanno, & J. Zinn (Eds.), *The routledge handbook of risk studies* (pp. 301–309). London: Routledge.

Naezer, M. (2018). From risky bheaviour to sexy adventures: Reconceptualising young people's online sexual activities. *Culture, Health and Sexuality*, *20*(6), 715–729.

Renold, E., & Ringrose, J. (2011). Schizoid subjectivities? Retheorising teen-girls' sexual cultures in an era of 'sexualisation'. *Journal of Sociology*, *47*(4), 389–409.

Ringrose, J., & Eriksson Barajas, K. (2011). Gendered risks and opportunities? Exploting teen girls' digitized sexual identities in postfeminist media contexts. *International Journal of Media and Cultural Politics*, *7*(2), 121–138.

Ringrose, J., Harvey, L., Gill, R., & Livingstone, S. (2013). Teen girls, sexual double standards and 'sexting': Gendered value in digital image exchange. *Feminist Theory*, *14*(3), 305–323.

Ross, J. M., Drouin, M., & Coupe, A. (2019). Sexting coercion as a component of intimate partner polyvictimization. *Journal of Interpersonal Violence, 34*(11), 2269–2291.

Schippers, M. (2007). Recovering the feminine other: masculinity, femininity, and gender hegemony. *Theory and Society, 36*(1), 85-102. doi:10.1007/s11186-007-9022-4

Schloms-Madlener, K. C. (2013). *The prevalence and characteristics of sexting behaviours among adolescents and adults in Cape Town, South* Africa. *MA dissertation*. University of Cape Town. http://core.ac.uk/display/29057008

Serano, J. (2007). *Whipping girl: A transsexual woman on sexism and the scapegoating of femininity*. Emeryville, CA: Seal Press.

Shelton, P. (2018). Reconsidering femme identity: On centering transcounterculture and conceptualizing trans femm theory. *Journal of Black Sexuality and Relationship, 5*(1), 21–41.

Skeggs, B. (1997). *Formations of class and gender: Becoming respectable*. London: SAGE Publications Ltd.

Stardust, Z. (2015). Critical femininities, fluid sexualities and queer temporalities. In M. Laing, K. Pilcher, & N. Smith (Eds.), *Queer sex work* (pp. 67–78). New York: Routledge.

Tannen, D. (1990). *You just don't understand. Women and men in conversation*. New York: William and Morrow Company.

Thurlow, C. (2014). Disciplining youth: Language ideologies and new technologies. In A. Jaworski & A. Coupland (Eds.), *The Discourse Reader* (3rd ed., pp. 481–496). London: Routledge.

Vares, T., Jackson, S., & Gill, R. (2011). Preteen girls read 'tween' popular culture: diversity, complexity and contradiction. *International Journal Of Media & Cultural Politics, 7*(2), 139–154. doi:10.1386/macp.7.2.139_1

Zimmerman, D., & West, C. (1975). Sex roles, interruptions and silences in conversation. In B. Thorne & N. Henley (Eds.), *Language and sex: Difference and dominance* (pp. 105–122). Rowley: Newbury House.

Index

Note: Page numbers followed by "n" denote endnotes.

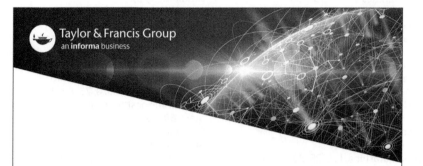